To Annie,
   My beloved
      "black Mama"

/ love you more
   than words can
express.

            Chryota

NORMAL FAMILY

NORMAL FAMILY

ON TRUTH, LOVE, AND HOW I MET MY 35 SIBLINGS

CHRYSTA BILTON

Little, Brown and Company

New York Boston London

Little, Brown and Company
Hachette Book Group
1290 Avenue of the Americas, New York, NY 10104
littlebrown.com

First Edition: July 2022

Little, Brown and Company is a division of Hachette Book Group, Inc. The Little, Brown name and logo are trademarks of Hachette Book Group, Inc.

The publisher is not responsible for websites (or their content) that are not owned by the publisher.

The Hachette Speakers Bureau provides a wide range of authors for speaking events. To find out more, go to hachettespeakersbureau.com or call (866) 376-6591.

ISBN 9780316536547
LCCN 2021948099

Printing 1, 2022

LSC-C

Printed in the United States of America

For my family

And here is a doctrine at which you will laugh. It seems to me, Govinda, that love is the most important thing in the world.

—Hermann Hesse, *Siddhartha*

AUTHOR'S NOTE

To write this book, I relied upon personal journals and called upon my own memory of these events. I also drew on thousands of my mother's photos and home videos, and in-depth conversations with my mother, father, sister, and others who appear in the book. I cross-referenced their memories with my own and the memories of others whenever possible and researched facts where I could.

I have changed the names of several people, and in some cases also modified identifying details to preserve their anonymity. I occasionally omitted people and events, but only when that omission had no impact on the truth or the substance of the story.

PROLOGUE

There's a knock on the front door.

"It's for you, Chrysta!" my husband yells from the kitchen without having to look. It has been this way all morning: one perfect stranger after another, standing on my porch, luggage by their side, arms outstretched to hug me, their older sister.

I walk down the stairs and open the front door to greet another sibling. The first had been surprisingly warm, kind, and likable. The second, too. *What will the next be like?* I wonder. *Will they be like him?* I open the door, smiling as brightly as I can. After an awkward hug, I introduce myself.

"I'm Chrysta," I say, trying my hardest to put this stranger at ease.

"I'm Grace," the woman standing in front of me replies. My eyes scan hers as I laugh uncomfortably at the uncanny physical similarities between us.

"The other siblings are in the back," I say, helping Grace with her bag as I usher her inside.

As she walks through the front door, a bit shy, I am struck by a familiar, loud braying sound. It is my own laugh, complete with the guttural gasps for air. As I wander back to find out which of them is making that sound—*my sound!*—I see the dozen siblings who have already arrived standing in a circle, arranging their toes in a lineup for a photo because, according to another sibling, we all share the same feet. I slip off my sandals and add my right foot to the circle, and sure enough, my big toe has found its doppelganger—a dozen of them.

I am learning that most of us share physical traits—the same dimple on our left cheek, the same prominent eyebrows, the same muscular forearms. There are some distinct personality quirks as well, like the constant spaced-out gaze that makes friends feel like we don't care what they have to say, when really we do—we just can't help being lost in the clouds. Or always having the battery of whatever device we're using linger at 1 percent.

Then, again, I hear that roaring, echoing laugh.

Then, again, another knock.

"It's for you, Chrysta!"

But this time, as I run back into the living room and open the front door, I recognize the person waiting on the other side.

"I still can't believe you invited them here," Kaitlyn, the one sibling I grew up with, here in Los Angeles, whispers to me with a scowl as she looks past me and toward our brothers and sisters. She is less than enthusiastic that I agreed to host this "reunion."

"Couldn't you have chosen a neutral spot at least—somewhere that's not your personal space where you live with your children?" she asks.

"Kait, they are all very sweet," I say, hoping to ease her concerns. "Just go outside and meet them."

"These are strangers, Chrysta," she says, hardly concealing her panic behind a dissociative gaze. "Just because we share biology with them doesn't make them our family." Then, as she looks past the hallway and out toward my backyard, where she can see one sibling now playing with my toddler, Kaitlyn leans in and wonders aloud, "How do you know someone won't steal something?"

I look at her irritated expression and can't help but laugh at the ridiculousness of the situation we now find ourselves in.

"Kait," I say, trying to hold a straight face. "If the worst thing that comes from this weekend is that one of our siblings, who we have never met, steals something from my house, I will consider it a rousing success."

Kaitlyn is not amused.

"I told my therapist about this," she says as she looks at the luggage, reminiscent of the baggage claim area of a small-town airport. "And she agreed: this is very strange."

She pauses for a moment; clearly she'd just heard our laugh, too.

"What are they like? Do they look like us?"

"A lot like us."

"Where's Mom?" she asks, still lingering with one foot out the door.

This reunion is my mother's worst nightmare. We have known about the siblings—that there are anywhere between three dozen and a few hundred—for more than a decade, since the shocking day the story appeared on the front page of the *New York Times*. Since then, Mom's coping strategy has been to pretend the whole thing never happened rather than face the reality that she was partially responsible for it.

My decision to meet and host the siblings is a dose of reality so vivid it threatens to completely upend all the illusions Mom has ever harbored about our family. And she wasn't happy when I told her I was doing it.

I take a deep breath as I look out toward the street and see my mother's navy-blue Prius pull around the corner and park, the rear jutting out at an angle and several feet from the curb. I watch with the same combination of love and anxiety my mother often inspires in people as she reluctantly makes her way out of her car; her face is red from crying. She opens the rear door to grab her sidekick, a pudgy Pekingese beagle with tiny legs and as much separation anxiety when it comes to my mother as my mother has when it comes to Kaitlyn and me.

Mom is dressed in her usual several shades of orange, head to toe, to match her orange apartment and orange dog, Gracie. Wearing orange is one of the many lingering traditions she still carries from a life she spent as a pioneer in many of the new age religions—and a few cults—to come out of Los Angeles in the sixties, seventies, and eighties.

"Hi, Mom," I say, smiling warmly, hoping I can defuse some of the intensity of her inner world by simply refusing to acknowledge it.

She approaches, and as I open the door a bit more, she bursts into sobs.

"I pulled over and cried for an hour before coming here," she explains.

I stand, quiet and resolute.

Her eyes dart back and forth, waiting for my reaction, perhaps hoping she can bully me into canceling my plans. I invite her in, a demonstration to signify that there is nothing she can do to stop me.

"This is a bad idea, Chrysta," she warns, abruptly ending her display and turning irate as she walks right past me and into the house. "A really bad idea."

PART ONE

MANHUNT

When I was three years old, my mother started a tradition she called the Golden Memory Box. At the end of every December, with the Christmas tree still sparkling in the corner of our living room and me off playing with whatever exciting new toys Santa had brought me—and there were always a lot of toys, regardless of whether the money spent on them should have been used to pay the rent—Mom would turn on Nat King Cole and ceremoniously waltz around the house collecting treasures from the past twelve months. She would carefully stack my most precious drawings, paintings, rocks, and seashells from our walks and the hundreds of photos she'd taken of my every step in a large box. Then, with a ballpoint pen and her giant, round, larger-than-life handwriting, she would label it CHRYSTA'S GOLDEN MEMORY BOX, along with the year and a few elaborately drawn hearts and stars. When my little sister Kaitlyn arrived a year and a half later, a second box was added to the tradition, though the boxes became much more disorganized, and eventually years were skipped and the tradition slowly died.

Sometimes, on a random Saturday, my mother would suggest that we "take a trip down memory lane" and slide a chance year's box out from under her bed. On one such afternoon, a few months after learning about our extended biological family, I sat cross-legged on the floor as we dug through one labeled CHRYSTA 1993. Unlike other tours into the past, this time I noticed something about my childhood that didn't

3

add up. I pulled out dozens of photos of me and my father—pictures of him hugging me at my ninth birthday party, others of me sitting on his lap while he strummed a song on his old acoustic guitar, yet more of him chasing Kaitlyn and me around the house as the "tickle monster"—and I realized I had no recollection of his being around then. Not a single memory was attached to a single photograph. I felt like a stranger looking at my life. I thought to myself, *Look, he must have been there.* But I could not recall him visiting even once in 1993.

I kept rummaging through the box and came upon a framed eight-by-ten photograph, professionally shot, of two little foxes snuggling in the snow. For months in 1993, I'd been obsessed with this particular animal, and upon seeing the image I was immediately taken back to the delight I'd felt when I'd unwrapped this gift. I turned the frame over, and on the back, in Sharpie in my mother's giant round handwriting, was a note: TO CHRYSTA BEAR, LOVE MOMMY AND But it stopped there. While I did not remember the moments captured in the photographs with my father, I did recollect every minute detail of the woman whose name was now hidden in Wite-Out, erased haphazardly by my mother. (I call it haphazard because if you really looked, you could still see her name.)

Sitting on the floor now, staring down at, on the one hand, photos of Dad during times I hardly remember him being around and, on the other hand, the deliberate removal of the name of someone whose presence still felt meaningful to me all these years later, I realized these boxes weren't memory boxes at all, but a heavily curated version of my life, the way my mother hoped I would remember it. There were no empty bags of cocaine in the boxes, or eviction notices from landlords, or photos of the father who had lost most of his teeth while living in a broken-down motor home on Pico. There was no trail of the broken hearts our mother left behind as she bounced from one girlfriend to the next to survive and provide for us. No photos of our childhood cats and dogs who we'd loved and who were later sent to live "on a farm" when we had to move into yet another friend's home while Mom got back on her feet. And while many more handsome and put-together photographs of our father did exist, it was because, as I'd later learn, my mother had paid him to be there. A dozen times a year, Mom would clean Dad up, give him a shower, maybe send him to a dentist, and then have him appear on the stage of our lives. He would do a little guitar solo, and Mom would snap several rolls of film in the hope that any trace of our more painful memories would be replaced with these picturesque ones. The going rate for our father's Academy Award—winning performance: a crisp twenty-dollar bill.

Staring at Sable's name, hidden under white paint, suddenly released in me a sweep of unprocessed grief I never realized I had, followed by questions about what had really happened to her, and if she ever missed me. I realized then that if I wanted to know the whole, possibly painful truth about my life, I wouldn't find it in my mother's retelling. So I began digging for the details she had left out. To my good fortune, every once in a while—perhaps due to sheer exhaustion at keeping track of so many "fibs," her tender word for bending the truth—Mom would get into a short-lived mood of openness, and the truth would spill out of her like an over-poured martini. I'd seize on these moments like a defiant child, pouncing on the crack in the sidewalk you are supposed to skip over, and ask as many pointed questions as I could because I knew that in a few minutes the conversation would be over, and any details that brought my mother pain would later be vehemently denied.

"Tell me again how you met Dad," I would ask my mother. It was a query I'd asked five thousand times, and each time, a new fact would be gifted to me, entirely by accident and despite her best intentions.

The story of how I came into this world didn't begin in a bedroom, or bar, or on a beach with two lovers holding hands, gazing into each other's eyes under a pink sky as they professed their mutual adoration. It began in a much more unlikely place: a hair salon called Michaeljohn's on the corner of Camden and Brighton Way in Beverly Hills.

It was 1983, a few ovulation cycles before I would be conceived, and my mother, Debra, was in her early thirties. The Summer of Love, which she could have been the poster child for, had faded over the past decade and a half and been replaced by skyscrapers, Wall Street, and the beginnings of the Cold War, special thanks to then president Ronald Reagan, who Debra, a die-hard liberal, found "adorable" despite his political leanings.

While the world was on edge from a geopolitical standpoint, she found it as exciting a time to be alive as ever. Michael Jackson's *Thriller* was pushing through the top of the album charts, a sign of sociological progress made more poignant for her because she had just fallen madly in love with a talented singer and actress named Ann Weldon—Annie for short—who was Black and twenty years her senior. On a whim, Debra had decided she would start a new career as Annie's music manager (even though she had absolutely no idea what the job entailed and no experience in the music industry). She was enjoying a torrid affair with Annie while booking her gigs, which included opening for Jane Fonda at Paramount Studios in Hollywood and for Dizzy Gillespie at nightclubs throughout Paris.

In addition to being happily in love and enjoying the challenge of turning a straight woman bisexual (a favorite sport of my mother's), she had a new lease on life special thanks to a program called Alcoholics Anonymous, which she'd discovered in the process of getting her little sister, Diane, off heroin. For almost a year before finding AA, Debra had done everything to get Diane clean. She'd bang on her sister's bedroom door, begging and pleading for her to come out.

"Shhh!!! I'm studying to be a director!" Diane would shout while she put a needle in her arm and nodded out to reruns of *I Love Lucy.*

One afternoon Debra called the Beverly Hills Police Department for help but they said they'd come only if Diane was a "danger to herself or someone else"—heroin addiction not qualifying. So Debra planted a gun on Diane and called 911.

"She's got a gun and just threatened to kill me!" she screamed to the operator.

From jail, Diane—furious with her sister for framing her—was given a choice between spending a month in jail or checking into a six-month recovery program. She chose the latter and began the process of withdrawal at a treatment center in Pasadena called Impact.

While Diane was in rehab, Debra wrote her a letter, interrupting midsentence as if they were having a conversation to write, "Hold on, I have to go make some carrot juice." Debra then went into the kitchen and did a line of cocaine. In that moment, which Debra would later recall as "a powerful moment of clarity," she realized that she was also an addict and had been in denial. Watching the miraculous transformation that took place in Diane's life after rehab, Debra began attending AA meetings—determined to get sober herself after spending most of her teens and twenties getting high on every drug, religion, and sexual experiment to come out of the 1960s and '70s.

My mother had always been a hedonist, yearning to overdose on everything, especially life. When the Beatles meditated in the Maharishi's Ashram in India, Debra was there. When Bhagwan Rajneesh, later known as Osho, needed a visa to continue operating his new age cult in Oregon, Debra was the person they summoned to tap her political connections. When Warren Beatty lived in the penthouse suite at the Beverly Wilshire during the McGovern presidential campaign and the filming of *Shampoo*, Debra rented a suite next door—where she wrote her college thesis on communism for UCLA in between seducing women with Warren. She'd counted Jeff Bridges as her first serious boyfriend and Eva Gabor among her many high-profile closeted girlfriends. Men loved Debra, women loved Debra, and Debra loved a good adventure.

Debra was striking. She had thick blond hair, high cheekbones, and a strong, attractive face, which was softened by a childlike innocence and the mischief emanating from her deep brown eyes. She had a feminine presentation that was often confusing to men, who chased her around with little luck. Her bright red lips always matched her long, perfectly painted red fingernails. She wore an antique eighteen-karat-gold coral ring on her right pinky finger that made her look like an Egyptian goddess and that she loved because it reminded her of the ocean. She also had enormous breasts that usually roamed free under a delicate blouse because she hated to be constricted. Beyond her looks, though, it was Debra's contagious enthusiasm for life and her unshatterable confidence that were intoxicating to everyone who met her. When they no longer excited her, they were usually just left with a broken heart while her curious dark brown eyes darted off to look for whatever shiny new thing might be waiting around the corner. Now that she was sober and done partying, the adventure she'd set her heart on was motherhood. What she wanted more than anything was a child.

The obstacle was that Debra was a lesbian. And in the early 1980s, she did not know a single gay person who had started a family. It was rare for even a single straight woman to start a family on her own—at least on purpose. The American dream still clung fiercely to the idea that the one and only healthy way to raise a child was within the nucleus of the nuclear family: father, mother, 2.5 children. It was revolutionary enough that Debra, having come of age in Beverly Hills in the 1950s in a high-society family—the prized granddaughter of a former governor of California, Culbert Levy Olson, and the daughter of a prominent judge in Los Angeles—now lived her life *somewhat* openly gay in the sense that she'd admitted to herself, and to a select group of trusted friends, that she preferred women.

There were zero playbooks for Debra to operate from. There were no openly gay icons or role models. No sperm banks handing out pamphlets outlining alternative routes to parenthood for gay couples. No *Modern Family, Ellen,* or *Will & Grace* television shows. As a rule, Hollywood had few story lines that dealt directly with homosexuality; gay and lesbian characters in film and print, what few there were, often died or met some other unhappy ending. The AIDS epidemic, which had been labeled the "gay plague" by a popular televangelist named Jerry Falwell, was in full swing. The atmosphere for lesbians and gay men in the early '80s, even in liberal Los Angeles, wasn't just uncomfortable; it was hostile.

Debra would think of having a child, then turn on the television or the radio and get a stomachache as she listened to the opinions of popular figures such as the singer and anti-gay-rights activist Anita Bryant, and Falwell saying things like "Please remember, homosexuals do not reproduce! They recruit! And, many of them are after my children and your children."

Debra worried that having a baby as a lesbian and single mother would make life incredibly hard for a child. She was also older than most of the mothers she knew and aware that she didn't have a lot of time before her biological clock ran out, especially if she wanted more than one child. So, when the big, pressing urge to have children first hit her four years before that fateful day at the hair salon, she did what any logical person would have done in her situation: she decided to go straight. It was not ideal, but it was doable—she hoped.

She'd met a perfect gentleman for the job: Sol West "the Third," the handsome heir to an oil fortune. Sol was from San Antonio and on the hunt to buy an estate in Los Angeles. Debra, who at the time was building a successful career in real estate, had become Sol's broker. The two would sit in the back seat of his black limousine and go from open house to open house through the rolling hills of Bel Air as Debra enthralled him with slivers of her life story: about the night she slept on the Sphinx in Egypt or the time she introduced Tina Turner to Buddhism. Her stories had a mythic quality—and you wanted to believe them—but sometimes they were so insane it took a real leap of faith to trust the narrator. Still, Sol's rugged, wild, Republican heart skipped a beat as he walked from room to room, following this crazy blond Democrat from Beverly Hills. He was so captivated by her that he sent her two dozen red roses after their first date, and then bought the third property she showed him, on the spot, before even going up the driveway.

After escrow closed, Debra handed Sol the keys to his new kingdom and he reciprocated, inviting her to live with him. She had her own wing of the property, filled with designer clothes, fur coats, and an unlimited expense account. She even attended weekly therapy sessions to try to "straighten out." Though the straightness never did take hold, Debra grew to love Sol in her own way. Like her, he had grown up in a deeply dysfunctional family. (After his older brother died of a heroin overdose, Sol's sister-in-law, also an addict, stipulated in her will, which was made public after her own eventual overdose, that Sol could inherit his brother's fortune only if she were buried dressed in her favorite baby-blue nightgown in her favorite blue Ferrari 330 America. Sol fought the order in court but ultimately lost. It was the most famous burial in San Antonio history.)

More important than being in love with Sol was Debra's sense that being with him would make her parents proud, even if they were dead. Sol's wealth and good manners—not to mention his gender—were everything her father would have wanted for her. She also felt that Sol would make a caring dad. And so, a few months after moving in, Debra convinced Sol to begin trying to get her pregnant. For two years they tried. Every month, when she was ovulating, Debra and Sol would make love, and then Debra would get on the bed in a yoga position with her feet up on the wall, to make sure the pregnancy took, as Sol lay next to her, watching the financial news on TV. A few weeks later, she would look down in disbelief at a negative pregnancy test. Eventually, she and Sol visited a fertility specialist named Dr. Cappy Rothman, who ran a new fertility clinic called the California Cryobank in Century City.

Debra found out during their meeting that, to her great surprise, Sol was the one with the fertility problem. Cappy explained that Sol had a low sperm count caused by a varicocele under his testicles, likely a result of having spent so much time in those late-seventies-era 115-degree hot tubs.

"It's a common problem," Cappy explained to the couple. "Luckily, a very simple surgery will fix it."

In the months that followed, Sol refused to set a date for the operation. Debra pushed, which led Sol to confess the truth: he hadn't had a very happy childhood, and he wasn't sure he wanted kids.

Debra was furious. For two years, she and Sol had been trying to get pregnant. She wondered now if some part of him had known all along that he couldn't give her children. She felt betrayed.

"Either you set a date for the surgery, Sol," she said, "or I'm leaving you."

"You'll never leave me, Debra," he replied smugly. "You're going to be the wealthiest woman in Los Angeles. You'd be an idiot to walk away from all this."

Sol proposed marriage to Debra soon after this exchange, during what was meant to be a romantic horseback ride at his family's San Antonio oil ranch. She fell off the horse she'd been riding bareback and broke her knee, which my mother took as a sign from the universe that their relationship wasn't meant to be.

After several months of soul-searching, with the financial anxiety of Debra's childhood never far from consciousness, she eventually moved out, but not before accepting Sol's $50,000 to jump-start her career as her secret girlfriend Annie's "music manager." (Debra happily spent the entire sum on what she would later refer to as her "honeymoon" with Annie, her "client," who would become the first of my many second mothers.)

Having given up on finding the right father, Debra reached the point where she was comfortable just finding the right sperm. But it couldn't be just any sperm. A one-night stand at Pips or the Daisy wouldn't produce the little Buddha that Debra yearned for. She needed someone gorgeous. Talented. Someone who looked the part with brilliance and a pedigree.

Debra asked her friend the actor and notorious playboy Warren Beatty if he'd have any interest in helping her have a child.

Over the years, Warren and Debra had become close friends and sometimes lovers, bonding over their shared appreciation of women.

"I'd never met anyone who loved women as much as I do until I met Debra!" Warren would boast to friends whenever introducing her. Warren politely declined Debra's request.

She briefly moved on to what she felt was a brilliant idea: to use Annie's brother's sperm.

"C'mon," she'd said to Annie. "Then it'll really be like it's our baby—with both of our genes."

Annie had a family history that Debra found fascinating. Her maternal line traced back to a love affair between a plantation owner's son and an enslaved woman in the Midwest. The plantation owner's son (Annie's great-great-grandfather) had fought to have the enslaved woman (her great-great-grandmother) and their children freed, then asked to be buried next to his love when he died. Annie's father's side, meanwhile, descended from Black Choctaw Indians. Annie used to laugh and say to Debra, "Honey, I'm the best of all worlds. I've got Black, white, and red blood running through my veins."

Annie was a gorgeous, impressive woman with a radiant smile and a deep, powerful voice. She'd been raised on a farm in Oklahoma in the late 1930s. Her father, a liberal minister and farm owner, had shielded his six children from racism so fiercely that Annie didn't know it existed until she moved to California as a teenager and began singing in nightclubs—where she was told to use a different entrance from the white patrons'. In the '50s and '60s, she made a name for herself performing in gay and lesbian bars like the 524 Club in San Francisco. The gay owners happily let Annie use the front entrance, and to that underground community, Annie became a star. She opened for Dinah Washington and became the first Black actress to be cast in leading roles with the American Conservatory Theater in San Francisco—before moving to Hollywood to play Mary in *Shampoo*. My mother had gone to see Annie perform at a women's rights rally, falling madly in love as she'd watched Annie strut across the stage in a long beige gown, full orchestra behind her, singing "I Am Woman."

Annie agreed to have a baby with Debra. And her brother even agreed; he was flattered. But his wife was having none of it. "No way!" she'd yelled at Debra once she'd caught wind of the plan, her eyes as inflamed as if she'd just learned that Debra was having an affair with her husband.

Debra was learning that it was not as easy as she'd hoped to get friends to father a child.

Soon Debra stumbled across an alternative solution while reading an article in the *Los Angeles Times* about an organization called the Repository for Germinal Choice, which was giving away the sperm of Nobel laureates with the grand intention of "advancing the human race" through their genetic generosity.

The "genius bank," as Debra called it, consisted of a middle-aged man with a briefcase who came into her living room like a traveling salesman, but rather than peddling Bibles or Encyclopedia Britannicas, he was shilling "one-page profiles of men carrying 'genius sperm.'" While there were no photos of these brilliant men ("to protect their identities"), it seemed like the best option Debra had. There was just one problem: the genius bank, like almost all sperm banks at that time, had an explicit "no gays or single women" policy, two categories that it had deemed categorically unfit to raise the next generation.

Debra managed to distract the owner of the Repository from his many prejudices by titillating him with all the genetic potential waiting to be tapped if they were to mix Nobel Prize sperm with the eggs of a California governor's granddaughter. A week later, she sat in her kitchen next to the man with the briefcase and flipped through a dozen anonymous donor profiles, finally choosing the sperm of a "mathematics prodigy" at Stanford University.

The following week, a giant silver cocoon arrived on her doorstep. She carefully carried the metal vessel inside and opened it on her kitchen counter. Steam from the dry ice that filled the tank poured up into her face and then cleared to reveal three vials of genius sperm, with an applicator built in. Debra was ovulating, so with the help of her sister, Diane, she lay down on her dining room table and they attempted to impregnate her. Unfortunately, Diane had no idea what she was doing, and the first vial went all over the dining table.

The second try went where it was supposed to, and all Debra had to do now was wait.

When she didn't get pregnant after the first attempt, Debra wondered if this was another sign from the universe. So, before trying the third and final vial of sperm, she hired a private investigator. A week later, she opened an envelope, pulled out a photo, and there, staring back at her, was the baldest, most unattractive professor Debra had ever seen. She stared down at the photo and envisioned giving birth to an awkward little boy with a prematurely receding hairline, and she quickly returned the silver metal tank from whence it came. Nobel Prize or not, Debra decided that she needed to know the father of her children. And he had to be good-looking.

Not knowing where to turn and ready to give up, Debra meditated. With her eyes closed, lying on her bed under a skylight in her and Annie's shared bedroom, she recalled a moment two years earlier when she was sitting at her guru's feet in a castle he owned in New Jersey. It was 1982 and a rare honor to get a visit with Bhagwan Rajneesh, who had taken a vow of isolation and silence while his commune in Oregon was making a daily spectacle on every news channel across the United States. Sheela, Bhagwan's "secretary" and second-in-command, had arranged the meeting, unaware that Debra was having an affair with her nemesis on the compound, a woman named Françoise Ruddy, who now went by Ma Prem Hasya. Debra was led into Bhagwan's private retreat in the mountains at four in the morning and then instructed to sit cross-legged on the floor among a muster of multicolored peacocks. Bhagwan sat above her on his jewel-encrusted throne, dressed in his long white flowing robes, his signature long gray beard equally commanding.

"What is it you would like to know, Debra?" he asked in a gentle, kind voice.

Debra bowed her head and then asked the question burning in her heart: "Bhagwan, more than anything, I want to become a mother. Please tell me: will I have children?"

The guru closed his eyes and sat there quietly. Debra waited, on edge. She knew that Bhagwan had instructed his followers not to have children, as he needed his women to be his "warriors" and felt that children would distract them from his larger mission to "build a new society." He opened his eyes, smiled a warm beam of pure joy, and reached down to slowly touch various parts of Debra's body. First, he put his hand on her head—the crown chakra. Then he moved on to her throat chakra, then to her heart chakra, and then—appropriately, given the question at hand—to her "sacral" chakra.

He smiled, looking into Debra's eyes as his hand rested there for a moment, and then gave her his answer. "Yes, Debra, I see it very clearly. You will have two little Buddhas."

Remembering this interaction two years later, childless, staring up at the skylight in the ceiling above her bed, Debra wondered if perhaps the guru had just been a con man as so many had believed.

"God, higher power—whoever, or whatever, you are," she said aloud, "if you do exist, and I am meant to have children, please send me a sign."

But no sign came. At least not that evening.

The next day, Debra, now uncharacteristically forlorn over her assumed fate, walked into a hair appointment at the Michaeljohn Salon in Beverly Hills, put on a robe, and sat in a chair. Her stylist started to untangle Debra's thick blond hair.

"Any luck with the manhunt?" the stylist asked.

Debra shook her head no.

The little bell on the salon's front door rang. As it did, Debra glanced over her shoulder.

Standing at six feet tall, the stranger in the doorway was the most physically beautiful man Debra had ever laid eyes on. He had intense, ocean-blue eyes, a sun-kissed olive complexion, and a thick head of sandy-brown hair that he kept brushing away from his face. He was dressed in a crisp white button-down, neatly tailored tweed slacks that showed off his muscular, lean physique, and gently worn-in brown leather loafers. The sunlight from the giant glass doors behind him streamed in, framing his body so he almost glowed; he looked like a god who had just descended from heaven straight into Michaeljohn's.

Debra couldn't help but stare at this handsome man as he sat in the chair next to her. She carefully observed his ears, his profile, his large, capable-looking hands, and she knew, with absolute certainty, from that second, that she had found him. The One. Not the man she would fall in love with and marry and live happily ever after with, but the man she would convince to jerk off into a cup so she could go home, pull out a turkey baster, and impregnate herself.

"I'm Debra," she said, a big sparkle in her eyes as she reached over to shake his hand. "Who are you?"

The answer to that question carried more weight than Jeffrey Harrison could ever have imagined. During the course of his haircut, Debra found out that he was twenty-five years old and single, and had just moved to Los Angeles from Hana, Maui, where his wealthy mother and stepfather had retired after raising Jeffrey on the East Coast. He was modeling and working as a waiter while trying to find a gig playing guitar, as he was a songwriter and a musician. Debra's eyes widened. Aesthetic beauty *and* artistic talent! Immediately, her nightmare of a balding scientist was replaced with a dream of a violinist. She learned that Jeffrey had rejected his parents' offer to pay for college in favor of studying Transcendental Meditation in Italy and surfing the beaches of Hawaii. His father had gone to Yale and Harvard and his mother to Wellesley. His uncle was the chairman of the Federal Reserve Bank of New York.

"Oh," he added, almost as an afterthought. "My great-uncle was Supreme Court justice Oliver Wendell Holmes Jr."

Debra's heart palpitated.

"You know, I know everyone in the music business," she said, turning up her notorious Debra charm. "I'll help you any way I can. You should give me your phone number."

If Jeffrey's gift in life was his looks, Debra's was her ability to talk people into things. Over lunch the following week, Jeffrey found himself agreeing to give a woman he barely knew a cup of his sperm to fulfill her lifelong dream of having a child.

In return, she'd give him $2,000.

"There's just one other thing," she said as she laid a deposit of $1,000 on the table.

"Sure. What's that?" he asked.

"Jeffrey, I want you to swear on your soul, or to God, or whoever you pray to, that you will never do this for anyone else but me."

Jeffrey tried not to laugh. He had a job. He wasn't trying to make a living by going up to women on the street and offering to sell them his sperm. It seemed like a strange request, but he looked at Debra with a very serious expression and shrugged his shoulders.

"Sure. No problem."

"If you want to have your own kids one day, fine. But no one else like *this*. Do you understand? This is very important to me."

"I swear," he said, "that I will never do this for anyone else."

PERFECT SPERM

Millions of tiny glass-like beads slid back and forth, their tails propelling them frantically in every direction, in search of something solid to grip on to.

"He's a good one!" Cappy Rothman, the head of the California Cryobank fertility clinic, said to Debra as he looked up from his microscope with a grin. "He has plenty of sperm!"

Debra let out a huge sigh of relief. For the past week, she had lain awake every night with the almost debilitating fear that Jeffrey, like Sol, would be infertile.

"Normal sperm count is between twenty million and a hundred and fifty million sperm per milliliter," Cappy continued. "This guy has well over two hundred million sperm per milliliter. That's like half a teaspoon." Then, with a smile, he asked Debra, "Do you want to see it?"

"Of course I want to see it!" Debra said, quickly taking Cappy's seat in front of the microscope. She stared in awe at two hundred million tiny sperm swimming around the glass dish, each one the seed of a living being.

She lifted her head from the eyepiece and exhaled a deep guttural breath filled with hope. Everything about this decision felt right. When she'd sat in this exact chair with Sol two years earlier, nothing had felt right. The genius bank had certainly not felt right. Warren hadn't even felt right. It felt like all along, the universe had been guiding her to this moment, and Jeffrey's extraordinary sperm count was just one more confirmation that he was the man meant to be the father of her children.

"Do you want to see something else fascinating?" Cappy said, eyebrows raised. "You're ovulating, right?"

Debra thought she was and became excited by whatever Cappy had up his sleeve. He instructed Debra to go to the bathroom and get a small sample of her own cervical mucus. When she returned, he carefully switched Jeffrey's sample with hers under the microscope.

"Right before you ovulate," Cappy explained, "a fernlike pattern appears in the cervical mucus. It's called ferning. For the entire rest of the month, the fern just disappears, and there is no discernible pattern."

Cappy closed one eye and peered into the device, rotating its dials like a mad scientist until the image was in focus. "Look—there it is!"

Debra took Cappy's place once again and then let out a gasp at the pattern she saw in the prism of the lens. Her mind drifted to the awe she had felt as a child, looking at the spirals inside seashells, or staring at the stars in the sky while she sat nuzzled in her father's arms. She felt that life was all too organized, too brilliant, to be just coincidence, that there must be some higher purpose or form of existence out there, some bigger plan we didn't have insight into. She wondered what the plan for her was. And for the first time since she had started this long journey to become a mother, she felt sure that whatever it was, it involved Jeffrey.

Jeffrey, meanwhile, was having a much less mystical experience as he sat next door in a small, sterile room, arm stretched out as a Russian woman took his blood to make sure he had no STDs and was HIV-free.

He tried his best not to look as the large needle went into his arm, so he looked away, and when he did, he saw something strange through the cracked-open doorway: a line of college-age men walking back and forth.

"Who are they?" Jeffrey asked the nurse, curious.

"Oh, they're the regular donors," the nurse said matter-of-factly.

"Do they get paid for that?" he asked, stupefied, suddenly forgetting all about the needle in his arm.

"Of course," she said.

Jeffrey sat quietly for a moment, taking it in. From the minute he had been ushered into a tiny alcove to retrieve his "sample," *Playboy, Penthouse,* and *Hustler* magazines laid out on a small table, until now, when he was being poked and prodded to have his blood analyzed, he'd felt like he had taken mushrooms and was on some kind of psychedelic trip where he had suddenly morphed into a prized horse being tested for breeding. It was wild enough that a stranger had come up to him in a hair salon offering to pay him for a little jar of semen so she could have a baby with it; that there was an entire business—which, by the looks of the lineup of men, was doing quite well—built around this concept just floored him. Now he understood why Debra had made him swear that he would never do this for anyone else.

Just as he was about to ask for more details, Debra entered the room.

"How's it going over here?" she asked with a big smile on her face. Jeffrey quickly snapped out of his stupor and pretended not to have seen the men through the doorway.

In the coming weeks, Jeffrey got to know the staff at the California Cryobank quite well.

He'd cleared the fertility hurdle with flying colors, and his first batch of blood work had come back HIV-negative, but he still needed to go in several more times. Debra had arranged for Jeffrey to make ten separate frozen donations. She was planning on using his fresh sperm, since she had a superstition that fresh sperm was of higher quality, but the frozen samples were her backup plan in case Jeffrey got cold feet. So, in typical Debra fashion, she arranged to take Jeffrey to the Cryobank each time he donated, paying him in $200 installments and using the drive over as an excuse to get to know the future biological father of her child. Jeffrey was learning quickly how Debra operated:

she always thought ten steps ahead and usually didn't involve other people in her planning process, even if they were meant to play the starring role in said plan.

Ten donations later, once fifty vials—or ampules, as they were called—had been stored safely in a cryo chamber, it was time to get to baby making.

Debra had many friends who'd been through horrible custody battles with children. She wanted to ensure that this baby was 100 percent hers. To do that, she'd been told by a lawyer that it was important to be inseminated at a doctor's office; otherwise Jeffrey could theoretically claim the baby as his. Debra also really wanted her samples fresh.

She switched her new lunch spot to a fancy restaurant on Robertson Boulevard called the Ivy, which had just opened and where Jeffrey worked as a waiter, shuffling soft-shell crab and chardonnay among the celebrities and Hollywood agent types. She confirmed when she was ovulating with her doctor and then drove over, walked in past the restaurant's white picket fence, and requested a seat in Jeffrey's section. She slipped a warm coffee mug out from under her silk blouse and placed it on the table in front of her, next to her purse and keys.

"Hello, ma'am," Jeffrey said as he approached the table, sneaking the cup into his waiter apron. "What can I get you today?"

"How about an iced tea and a pastry?" Debra replied with a mischievous grin.

Jeffrey placed Debra's order and then ran to the bathroom to retrieve a sample. A few minutes later, he returned with Debra's cup; it was sitting next to her iced tea and a croissant on a tray in his right hand.

"Here's your beverage, ma'am," he said as he placed the tea and croissant on the table in front of her. "And here's your cute little baby," he whispered.

Debra placed the cup back under her shirt to keep it warm, like a hen sitting on an egg. She gulped her iced tea and then reached into her purse, dropping two hundred-dollar bills on the table before driving her white Jaguar XJ12 a few blocks west to her gynecologist's office, where the doctor used a small syringe to inseminate her.

Debra's genius plan was not working. Every month, she'd find Jeffrey wherever he happened to be when she was ovulating—once they met at a gas station parking lot—but after three months of trying, she wasn't pregnant.

Debra started to wonder if the problem might be the drive from Jeffrey to the doctor's office. Perhaps his sperm got damaged on the way, she thought, or perhaps her new baby's soul just didn't like the idea of being brought forth in a gas station.

"Look, Jeffrey," she said one afternoon when she'd offered to drive him to work so he could skip the bus that day. "This clearly isn't working the way we are doing it. Why don't we just do it the old-fashioned way?"

She smiled flirtatiously and Jeffrey became visibly uncomfortable. Already he was starting to feel that, like most women who encountered him, Debra was falling in love with him. (She wasn't.) If he slept with her, what would stop her from later claiming he was the actual father and demanding financial help with the baby?

"No, no, no. Definitely not!" Jeffrey said, shaking his head. Then he took a second look at Debra, to see if he should reconsider. No, he would not be sleeping with her and then be on the hook for this child, he decided. Yet he saw how desperately Debra wanted this baby, and he wanted to help, not just for the money anymore. He'd started to see Debra as a friend; he was impressed by her wheeler-dealer, confident persona, and he shared her spiritual outlook on life. He felt that he was doing a good thing by helping this woman fulfill her lifelong dream of having a baby, and hoped that the universe would repay him with good karma.

As the sun set over a mildly chilly December evening in Los Angeles, Debra went to the nearby Canyon Country Store in Laurel Canyon and purchased a plastic turkey baster. She headed to pick up Jeffrey in Benedict Canyon, where he was staying with a friend, and then drove back up Laurel, onto the cul-de-sac where she was living with Annie. She parked in the driveway. Silently, both nervous, she and Jeffrey got out of the car and walked through the front door of the modest contemporary home. (Annie was, thankfully, off filming for her new recurring role in a TV series executive-produced by Jane Fonda called *9 to 5,* so the house was empty.)

While Jeffrey sipped on a beer in the kitchen, Debra lit some candles in the bedroom and placed an empty water glass on the counter. Once Jeffrey felt adequately buzzed—he couldn't have gone through with this insane plan unless he had something to take the edge off—he grabbed the glass, went into the bathroom, and closed the door.

A few minutes later, he emerged, the glass in hand containing his sperm. Debra was lying on her bed and motioned for Jeffrey to come lie next to her, which he did, uncomfortably, as close to the edge of the bed and away from Debra as he could get without falling off.

Debra grabbed the turkey baster and the cup and inseminated herself, then they both closed their eyes and chanted three Hindu oms.

A few moments later, Debra opened her eyes.

"Do you feel that, Jeffrey?" she asked. "The baby's here. I know it."

"It is?" he asked, looking around the room, unsure where, exactly, the baby was.

THE BIRTH CERTIFICATE

I was three weeks late, and there was no sign that I'd come out any-time soon. My aunt Diane, younger than my mom by five years, was terrified—not because of any potential health risks, but because, as the days wore on, it was becoming increasingly likely that I was going to be born a Scorpio (which Diane's ex-girlfriend had been) rather than a Libra (which Diane believed was the best sign because that was her sign), and so something had to be done. Rather than leave this all to fate, Aunt Diane had decided to take matters into her own hands by dragging my mother on a hike to the top of Franklin Canyon, behind the Beverly Hills Hotel, in hopes of inducing her labor. Diane had only thirty-six hours before the stars changed to Scorpio.

"I can't go any further!" my mother complained as she held on to her pregnant belly with one hand and her bright orange Christian Dior parasol, which she was using to try to block out the rays of the crisp October sun, with the other.

"Just keep walking," Diane instructed between breaths, half pushing her sister along the trail, half dragging her own self up.

Debra and Diane were a strange breed of sister. They were all they had left of their family and they loved each other deeply, but there was constant jockeying for control.

Twenty minutes into their hike, the plan worked. Suddenly, halfway up the hill, Debra felt the most intense pain of her life.

"It's happening, Diane! I just had a contraction!" The two smiled with excitement until Debra felt the pain course through her body once more and screamed, "Oh my God! We have to get to the hospital—*now!*"

Diane clearly hadn't thought this through. Getting her sister up the hill while not in labor was a hell of a lot easier than getting her down while Debra was experiencing the intense undulations that now overwhelmed every part of her body every few minutes. For anyone else in the canyons that day, it must have sounded like an animal had been caught in a trap. Debra screamed the entire way down the hill and into her Jaguar, and the two sisters raced off to Cedars-Sinai, the waves of horrific pain increasing with every speed bump and L.A. traffic light.

"Drugs! I need drugs!" Debra yelled as a nurse wheeled her into the birthing room. Drugs, though, were not part of the plan.

"They're on the way!" Diane assured Debra, seemingly enjoying watching her sister in extreme pain. "The nurse said just a few minutes!"

In truth, Diane had not ordered any meds from the nurse and was committed to sticking with Debra's original plan, which involved just breathing and walking around the hospital room doing squats.

Debra had spent half of her pregnancy practicing this moment in her weekly Lamaze classes. She was haunted by all the horrors she and Diane had experienced growing up, starting in the birthing room, and determined not to repeat them for another generation. Back in 1949, when their mother, Bicki, was nine months pregnant with Debra, Bicki fell out of the car on the way to get ice cream (there were no seat belts in cars back then), causing her to go into early labor. Debra was born breech with a broken collarbone and then placed in an incubator for two days before she was ever held by her mother. It was a jarring way to enter the world, and Debra often wondered how much this experience colored the rest of her life.

When Diane was born, their father, John, was so hopeful he would finally get a boy that when he saw her for the first time—a girl with a giant red birthmark all over her face—he found his new daughter so ugly that he was said to have vomited all over the hospital floor. Diane's "strawberry" disappeared after a few months, but it was clear that her father never loved her the way he loved Debra.

To make matters worse for both sisters, Bicki had been put under the drugged spell of twilight sleep, a common procedure in the 1940s and '50s; it had left her awake enough to feel pain but asleep enough not to have the faintest memory of having given birth to her children. It goes without saying that Bicki did not go on to breastfeed. She was not a cozy-fuzzy mother.

Perhaps to heal their own early wounds as much as to give me a different life, my mother and Aunt Diane had been determined that Debra stay awake—that she feel, and experience, and remember every second of giving birth to me. Then the excruciating reality of labor came up against the dreamy fantasy of a natural childbirth, and for Debra all bets were off.

For twenty-six long, miserable hours, Diane continued to assure Debra that the epidural was on its way, but it never came. (Diane did try to appease my mother with a boom box blasting Marvin Gaye and Al Green.)

As morning turned to afternoon on a chilly, golden October day, the birthing room slowly filled up with a large group of women dressed in early-eighties-era high-waisted blue jeans; ironed, tucked-in button-down shirts; chunky jewelry; and oversized blazers. This was in stark contrast to what was going on in the neighboring rooms, where more "normal-looking" couples—yuppie husbands and doting housewives—were delivering children.

When it finally came time for active labor and as Debra's pain became more unbearable than anything she'd ever experienced in her life, she had a full-fledged panic attack. She was suddenly unsure if she was equipped to become a mother after all.

"Wait, no, I'm not ready! Put her back in!" she screamed.

"Sorry, Debra, it's happening," the doctor said. "Now push!"

Debra's sweat-drenched hand squeezed Diane's as she pushed…and screamed…until…finally…there I came…into her arms. All ten pounds of me. My mother looked down at my face, trying to get a glimpse of my smushed eyes through rolls of baby fat. I wasn't the cutest baby, but to my mother I was the most beautiful child she had ever seen—half her, and half Jeffrey. She kissed my head and held me close as I instinctively found my way to her breast, and she was overcome by a rush of dopamine and love and awe that far surpassed any drug she'd ever taken.

"We did it, Deb," Diane said as she bent down to kiss my head. "She's a Libra. A few more hours and she'd have been a Scorpio."

My mother looked down at me, held my little finger, and whispered, "My little treasure. This is the beginning of a great love affair."

The following morning, as Diane and Annie returned and more friends started arriving with flowers and baby presents, a nurse entered the room and handed Debra a birth certificate to fill in. Debra took the pen with a smile and, in her giant, larger-than-life handwriting, carefully spelled out my name: Chrysta Carolyn Holmes Olson. There was never any question that I would get my mother's last name. She felt pride knowing that her father's line of governors and judges and suffragettes would be carried on for another generation. Chrysta had been Jeffrey's idea. He had seen the name signed in the corner of a painting in an art gallery and called Debra from a pay phone to suggest it. Debra ran the numbers with a numerologist, as one does, and after replacing the *i* with a *y* on the woman's suggestion, it was settled. Carolyn, my first middle name, was an ode to Debra's mother's side of the family, after her favorite aunt, an artistic woman who, according to family lore, had stood up from her deathbed, walked over to the piano, and played one verse of "Moon River" before passing away. Holmes, my second middle name, was taken from the man Debra believed to be Jeffrey's great-uncle, Supreme Court justice Oliver Wendell Holmes Jr.

Debra moved down the document to sign her name above the line that requested the mother's signature. Then she realized she had a problem, as she was unsure what to do above the line that asked for the father's signature. For what seemed like an eternity, her pen just hovered there.

The nurse stood over Debra, peering up at the clock across the room, getting visibly impatient as my mother gripped the pen in her hand.

"You know, the father can't make it today," Debra finally said nervously as she looked at the nurse. "He's at work. I will just sign the line for him."

The nurse's hand came down to stop her. "I'm sorry, but the father has to be physically present."

Diane was sitting nearby, watching.

My mother looked back at that word: "father." It was such a short, simple word. A wave of intense emotions pulsed through her. She thought about her own father, the look of pride and amusement on his face whenever she'd show up at his courtroom, a blond, wild teenager interrupting an important case as she waved a speeding ticket in the air with a grin, wanting his help getting her out of it, and then she thought about how much she missed him. Her heart broke at the thought that John would never meet this beautiful baby lying next to her, and that I, in turn, would never get to know him, the man who had meant more to her than anyone.

The excitement of my birth momentarily gave way to sadder memories: the cold fact that except for Diane, every single person in her family was dead—all of them from the dark curse of addiction, which just made it worse, because there was always the lingering feeling that she could have done something to save them. Then an even more horrible thought occurred to Debra. The single most important relationship in her life had been the one she shared with her father. She looked down at me, this beautiful child asleep in her arms, and couldn't breathe at the idea that she might be harming me by depriving me of a father figure. That this child's father would be just an empty blank line—a black hole where a glowing star was meant to be.

"Can you please hand me a phone?" Debra said to the nurse, who was still standing there impatiently.

"Debra, what are you doing?" Diane asked, lunging to get to the telephone as quickly as she could as soon as she saw that her sister had that familiar look of I've-got-a-plan-and-it's-probably-not-a-good-idea-but-just-try-to-stop-me written all over her face.

"I'm calling Jeffrey to come sign the birth certificate," Debra said, grabbing the phone from the nurse before Diane could get to it.

"Honey, I don't think that's a good idea," Diane said, now attempting to grab the phone from her sister.

But it was too late. Debra held the receiver tightly in her hands, shoving Diane off, and she started dialing.

"Jeff, I need you to come to the hospital to sign Chrysta's birth certificate."

"I don't have a car," Jeffrey said—he was likely stoned, or sleeping, or both—as he registered that it was Debra on the phone and what she was asking. "I don't even know how to get over there."

"I'll get you a taxi," Debra said, defiant. "Jeff, you can't just be completely anonymous." He paused for a moment, and Debra could tell he was planning his way out. "Please come. I'm begging you. Just to sign the birth certificate—that's it. You don't have to do anything after that—I promise. You don't have to see her ever again. She's going to need this—psychologically. Otherwise you will just be this big blank space in her life. Please. I'll pay you for it."

Jeffrey showed up at the hospital a few hours later and was so far out of his element that he himself looked like he needed a stretcher. He was wearing sunglasses, which he refused to remove, and a tattered boater hat, which did not hide his face as much as he would have liked it to. Debra's gang of women had returned by then, bringing food and drink and merriment. It was probably the first time in his life that Jeffrey had been in a room full of women who could care less about his good looks.

Awkwardly, Jeffrey followed Debra's instructions to hold out his arms as she placed me into them.

"She looks like you, doesn't she?" Debra asked, eyes twinkling at the sight of my father holding me.

He gave me a few uncomfortable pats on the back and then returned me to my mother's arms as quickly as he could, as if this were a game of hot potato. As Debra watched Jeffrey hold me, however briefly and uneasily, she was flooded with a sudden, intense connection with him that she herself did not understand.

Jeffrey, on the other hand, just cringed. He looked around at all the eyes on him, at all these lesbians intently watching for his reaction. He imagined they all anticipated that he would take one look at the child and say "Oh my God, this is my baby!" with an adoring gaze, which was the exact opposite of how he felt. All he could think about in that very moment was, *What's the fastest way out the door?*

In truth, the other women were judging not Jeffrey but Debra. As she looked at Jeffrey, they looked at her, none of them capable of understanding why Debra had brought this man here. Chief among them was Aunt Diane, who identified as a radical feminist and fought the patriarchy and all forms of male dominion and oppression. She hated men and didn't understand why her sister was so hung up on the role of a father in this child's life. She looked at Jeffrey, this oddball in his stupid hat and sunglasses, and just shook her head in disapproval.

Debra reached over and handed Jeffrey the birth certificate and a pen. Jeffrey glanced down to where the blank line was. He didn't want to do this; he felt he was being pressured into more than he'd signed up for. But some part of him also felt for me, and so, with the flick of his wrist, Jeffrey signed his name, then handed the paper back to Debra and left the hospital as quickly as he had come in.

Later that afternoon, Debra, Annie, and Aunt Diane brought me home to my new house on Weepaw Way in Laurel Canyon, and for a moment, everything was wonderful. Debra would stay awake all night for weeks in happy disbelief, cupping my tiny hand in hers as I nuzzled her breast. She'd slip out of bed in the morning, when she got too tired to hold me any longer and needed to sleep, and plop me with a laugh into the big strong arms of Annie, who was, to her great shock, starting to love the idea of being my second mother. Annie had begun referring to herself as my Black mama. She would throw me over her shoulder while she was on a conference call, pat me on the back with a tight squeeze, and announce, "You may not have come out of my womb, child, but you sure as hell came outta my heart!"

Debra smiled to herself at the thought of two women raising a baby together. Who would have ever thought it? Not just two women, but a mixed-race lesbian couple, raising a child together. She felt pride in it, like she was the pioneer in some future beautiful story about what a family could be, coloring outside the lines of what society and her parents had told her life should be. She almost forgot about Jeffrey entirely.

A few weeks into this daydream, on a gold-and-yellow-peppered November afternoon, my mother decided to take me to her secret spot in Franklin Canyon, where Diane had taken her the morning before I was born, to experience my first afternoon in nature. She got me dressed, and carefully placed me on her lap to breastfeed as she kept my body balanced behind the steering wheel, an incredibly dangerous maneuver that she performed to prevent me from crying hysterically. On the route, Debra realized that she'd forgotten to bring diapers and pulled into the Canyon Country Store. Holding me, now quiet, in her arms, she paused for a moment at the newsstand and contemplated the women's magazines, one of which had a cover story about single women becoming parents. Debra smiled. It didn't matter to her in that moment that her situation was a bit different from the ones in the magazine since the story featured heterosexual women, none of whom had conceived with a turkey baster. She just claimed the part of the headline that suited her own narrative. *That's me!* she thought. *A modern woman!*

When she got to the canyon, my mother found a clearing in the dappled shade of a giant silver sycamore, then took off her shirt and undressed me down to nothing so she could breastfeed me in the "healing energy" of the crisp November sun, whose rays shone directly onto our bare skin through the leaves above. As I lay there, she studied my tiny body, and her thoughts drifted back to Jeffrey. Trying to parse my features as if sorting loose change, she wondered which traits I'd inherited from my father and which had come from her.

She plopped a kiss on my pink cheek, gently rolled me off our blanket, and set me on a big, beautiful bed of leaves and brush. She closed her eyes and said a prayer of gratitude for her life, feeling more optimistic for the future than she'd ever felt. Life was grand. "Thank you, Universe," she whispered.

My mother could never have predicted just then that, like the bed of poison oak on which she had accidentally just laid me, in a few weeks, she would be "let go" from her snazzy new mortgage broker job when it became clear that Debra's priorities were with her new child and not with selling mortgages. In no time, the phone would ring back home on Weepaw Way, where Annie would be told by her agent that her TV show would not be renewed for another season, and she, too, would be out of a job. At that same newsstand that Debra had left just minutes earlier, hiding in plain sight among the *Harper's Bazaar* and *Vogue* magazines, was a giant photograph of my father, bare-chested and in a cowboy hat, with his jeans suggestively unzipped. Unbeknownst to her, the same month I was born, her perfect, "blue-blooded" Jeffrey, the father of her baby, was the centerfold of *Playgirl* magazine, appearing on the inside in a several-page, full-color, completely nude spread as "Mr. November 1984."

MR. NOVEMBER 1984

It was early afternoon and Jeffrey stood outside a large stucco house, newly built in the flats of Beverly Hills, wearing a police uniform. He adjusted the badge, then the holster around his waist, took a deep breath, and knocked loudly on the front door of the home.

"It's the police!" he shouted. "Open up!"

When no one answered, he knocked again, this time harder. After a moment and still no answer, he turned the knob, found the door was unlocked, and burst in, finding several women sitting in the middle of a modern pastel-pink living room; they were dressed in costume jewelry and oversized sweaters with polka dots and were sipping expensive champagne. Their eyes moved from one another to Jeffrey, jaws dropped at the sight of this gorgeous, tan, six-foot man dressed in a police costume, and their chatter went dead.

He had the room.

"Three women were seen entering this building," he explained in a serious, domineering tone as he scanned the room until his eyes met those of a beautiful brunette wearing a cheap plastic crown. "They were seen assaulting a man—and they stole all of his bodily fluids!"

The women burst into laughter, but Jeffrey didn't break character. He walked right up to the woman with the crown.

"You—up against the wall. I'm going to frisk you." He pointed to her two friends. "You and you also. Now!"

The three women stood up and quickly placed their bodies against the wall, facing it, as Jeffrey had instructed them.

He walked over to where they stood and patted his hands down their bodies, one by one, starting with the shoulders, then gently across the hips, down to the feet. Finally, he landed on the last woman, the brunette with the crown. After her body check, he flipped her around to face him, his face inches from hers. His hand hovered over the giant rock on her left hand, which he momentarily took stock of.

"Miss, I'm going to have to interrogate you," he whispered.

"No, please don't! No!" she pleaded as Jeffrey walked her to a chair in the center of the room. He instructed her to sit, then reached down and pressed the red Play button on a large black boom box. The thud of synthesizers filled the room as Jeffrey started to remove his shirt to the beat of the Eurythmics' "Sweet Dreams (Are Made of This)."

Ten minutes later, he walked out of the house, rebuckled his belt, and stuffed eighty dollars and two women's phone numbers into his back pocket. This was the sixth strip-o-gram job Jeffrey had done over the past few weeks, and he felt he was getting the hang of it. Today's gig—in the early afternoon, at this big house, with these rich, attractive women—was certainly an improvement over yesterday's birthday party inside a public bank, where the air-conditioning was freezing and the audience consisted of random people he watched entering and exiting the building throughout the entire performance.

"What guy wouldn't want to be in my shoes, stripping naked for a room full of beautiful, drunk women?" he asked his friends at the time.

Jeffrey walked half a block to where his car was parked at a meter, the windows down so his dog, Ziggy, had enough cool air to breathe. Hearing Jeffrey approach, Ziggy jumped up with excitement, wagging his tail and climbing on the door to greet him. Jeffrey smiled, opened the door, and the massive 120-pound Alaskan malamute jumped into his arms.

Jeffrey had not set out to adopt a dog. He was determined to fly solo, always breaking up with girls as soon as the pressure to get more serious inevitably came up; likewise, he didn't love the idea of attaching himself to a job, a pet, a plant, a house, or anything else, for that matter. His mantra was "Freedom above all else." Then Ziggy had shown up a few weeks earlier, needing to be rescued from a bad situation at the house next door, and like an angel, he'd turned all of Jeffrey's concrete emotional walls to Silly Putty with a single, slobbery kiss.

Jeffrey reached into the car to grab a plastic water bottle and the metal dog bowl he now drove around with everywhere, since Ziggy went everywhere with him. As he was pouring the water into the bowl, suddenly, seemingly out of nowhere, a man drove by screaming loudly at Jeffrey, like he'd just recognized a celebrity.

Jeffrey looked up, confused, as the man put his car in reverse and backed up until he was parked right in front of Jeffrey and Ziggy, staring at the two of them with his jaw dropped.

"Oh my God!" the man called out his window. "Are you Jeffrey Harrison?"

"Yes, that's me," Jeffrey replied, confused, suspicious. "Why?"

"A blond lesbian was just on TV talking about how you don't need a man anymore to have a child!" he yelled, eyes wide. "She said she paid you for your sperm and she showed your picture on TV!"

"What?" Jeffrey said, shocked. "Are you kidding me?"

The man drove off as Jeffrey stood there, feeling around in his pockets for his keys, his shock turning to anger as he imagined a close-up of his face on every TV set in America. He was supposed to be anonymous, and now his name and picture were being blasted all over national television?

Just a day earlier, Jeffrey had gone over to Debra's house with Ziggy and agreed to play with the baby for thirty minutes for a "donation." Whatever Debra felt she needed to do for this baby, Jeffrey had rationalized, was fine. But even he had his limits. For example, there was the first time Jeffrey had walked into my nursery, when Debra had referred to him repeatedly as "Daddy." She'd bent over the crib, whispering in gentle coos to the small, sleepy thing, "Daddy is here!," and then, as if she'd wanted to make absolutely sure the child had heard it, like she was training a parrot to say one word and one word only, she'd say it again: "Look who it is, Chrysta—it's Daddy! Daddy is here!" "Look, Chrysta—it's Daddy!" Daddy! Daddy! Daddy!

"No, it is not 'Daddy'!" Jeffrey had said, flustered. Being "Daddy" wasn't part of the deal. But there was no use arguing with Debra. She didn't hear or seem to comprehend anyone else's point of view. She had zero boundaries and seemed to think she could just bulldoze people into doing whatever she wanted. When she made him place his signature on the birth certificate, and each time she made him swear he'd never donate to anyone else, Jeffrey had tried to be understanding. But this—this! Going on TV and talking about him as if he were just a vending machine for sperm, with his picture being blasted to the nation without his permission? This was not part of the deal.

As he sat in the car in his stripper police uniform, Jeffrey's mind exploded into paranoia and resentment. He decided, right then and there, that he was no longer going to keep up his side of the deal. Debra couldn't control him. She wasn't his wife! He didn't owe her a thing. It wasn't any of her business whether he slept all day or stripped down naked in front of a group of people to make a living—both things she had recently expressed her displeasure about. She was trying to weasel her way into getting him a more "grown-up" job. How dare she make him swear!

I'm done, Jeffrey said to himself as he started the engine and began driving toward Century City, where the Cryobank office was located. He parked, walked inside the building, entered the elevator, and pressed the button for the ninth floor as the door closed before him.

PART TWO

A MAN IN THE FAMILY

Standing in the middle of thousands of completely naked women in Yosemite National Park, holding my mother's hand, I barely hit her knees as I looked out at a dark forest filled with long-and-wild-haired, bare-breasted women, sunlight flickering through the trees.

It's among my earliest memories; I was three years old. As I took in my surroundings, I had no consciousness that I was a separate entity from my mother. She and I and the thousands of females floating by in every direction were like some ancient Amazonian civilization, at one with the surrounding mountains, pine trees, and dry summer air. There wasn't a man for miles.

"Where are we, Mama?" I asked.

"Amid the birthing of the feminist revolution, Chrysta," she said matter-of-factly, ushering me toward a circle of naked women as I tried to pronounce "feminist" and "revolution."

"Annie!" I shouted as I ran up to a woman with the same strong, golden brown legs as Annie's. The woman looked down and smiled at me and I was overcome with disappointment and shame at having just embraced a stranger, thinking she was Annie.

"I miss Annie," I said to my mother, a sentiment I was then expressing often. "When will we see Annie?" I asked.

"She's on vacation," my mother said. "You will see her soon!"

In truth, Annie was not on vacation.

By the time I was three, my mother and I had lived in five different houses, with as many different women; some had stayed for weeks, others for months, and one (Annie) for a couple of years. I don't remember a lot about those houses except a vague sketch of a room or a random piece of furniture. As for the women themselves, the only one who had any lasting impact was Annie.

It's hard to pinpoint what, exactly, set off the downfall of my mother and Annie's relationship. It had something to do with money problems, something to do with a flirtation Annie had started with a male newscaster, and something to do with an affair of my mother's. The relationship finally ended when my mother returned home one morning to find several voodoo dolls spread across her and Annie's shared bedroom, needles placed in their hearts.

"Annie has lost it!" my mother mumbled to herself.

"Chrysta Bear," Mom said gently later that evening, "I need you to go pack your favorite toys, because we are going on an adventure!"

I happily did as I was told, excited for whatever adventure was in store. I objected only once I realized Annie would not be joining us.

When my questions about Annie became more frequent, my mother got down on her knees, held my palms in hers, and explained gently that "the secret of life" was to be "comfortable with the unknown," and that one day I would realize that "the only thing that never changes is change itself."

My mother always talked this way to justify whatever decision she was making as an opportunity for spiritual growth. At the time of our feminist adventure in the woods, we'd been living away from Annie for almost a year, moving between a few different places with different girlfriends of my mother's until she finally secured another mortgage broker job for herself, at which time we settled into a 1920s Spanish Colonial condo at the corner of 6th Street and Crescent Heights. The apartment was all white: white stucco walls, white wool carpeting, a white runner up the stairs so I wouldn't hurt myself if I fell as I ran up and down the many, many steps. The place was two stories, with two bedrooms upstairs for Mom and me, and another bedroom downstairs, which sat empty and became a place for me to play while my mother took real estate conference calls on the floor above.

There was a small kitchenette on the upper level of the apartment with white tile countertops, and the master bedroom had a large stucco balcony where my mother often sat with me in her arms, looking out at West Hollywood and downtown, still breastfeeding me at three years old.

It was in that apartment on 6th Street that my mother pushed my long blond hair out of my face one afternoon, turned my small head toward hers, and gave me the bit of Debra wisdom that I would try to grapple with for years to come.

"I need to tell you something important, Beanie Face," she said in a whisper to intimate that whatever she was about to say required my attention. "We choose our parents before we are born. You were just a little soul flying up in the sky, and you looked down at all the mommies you could have been born to, and you chose to come through me because your soul needs to learn something it can only get through our relationship—and my soul needs to learn something through you. Do you understand? We are great teachers for each other."

I sat looking at my mother's warm brown eyes, trying to understand. I felt lucky to have snatched up my mother before someone else got to her. I thought my mother was the most spectacular person in the world.

My mind drifted to my father, who I hadn't seen in several months.

"Did I pick my daddy, too?" I asked.

My mother got visibly uncomfortable at the question. Feigning a smile, she explained, "Yes, you picked your father, too." Then she tried to change the conversation. "Should we go for a walk?"

"Where is my daddy?" I asked.

"Oh." She paused. "He's traveling."

"Where is he traveling?" I asked.

"Oh, somewhere far away," she said.

"When will he come back?" I asked.

"Jesus, Chrysta!" she finally burst out, obviously irritated as she pushed me off her lap. "Can you drop it? My God. You're so intense!"

"But where is he traveling?" I asked, unsure why she was upset by such a simple question.

She stood up and stormed out of the room.

Our conversations went in circles like this, a few times a day. Each time, the story changed. Sometimes Daddy was "traveling." Other times I was told that he was "working." Other times my mother simply didn't answer, as if she hadn't heard the question. Often when I peppered her with too many questions about "Daddy," my mother would lose her patience, then feel bad about her outburst, and she'd pick up the phone, say something I couldn't hear or understand, and my father would appear, like magic, at the front door a few hours later with his giant dog, Ziggy, by his side.

My father's infrequent visits followed a predictable pattern. I'd see him walking up our driveway. He'd sometimes bring me freshly picked pink flowers tied into necklaces or fairy wreaths that he'd put around my neck. After a quick argument with my mother over whether Ziggy could come inside with his dirty paws and fleas, my father would win, and then he'd walk straight into the kitchen with Ziggy, to the fridge, where he'd rummage for something to eat, usually yogurt poured onto a piece of toasted whole-grain bread spread with a bit of berry jam. Then he'd plop me on Ziggy's back as if the dog were a pony and help me gallop around the house and down the stairs. I'd laugh hysterically as my father transformed into the tickle monster, which was what he'd named himself, and for the next adrenaline-filled thirty minutes, he'd toss me in the air or throw me across the room onto my mother's bed while she followed behind us screaming, "Jeffrey, be careful!"

Sometimes my father would bring his guitar and make up a song about dogs and kittens and silly animal adventures. His voice was soft and gentle, and his entire being filled with magic whenever he picked up the instrument. During this period, my mother got along well with

Jeffrey when she wasn't fighting with him over his roughhousing or how he needed to get a haircut or wash his clothes. They'd chat about politics—my father always had some wild conspiracy theory that only he would believe—or he would seek my mother's advice about a woman he was pursuing or needed to end things with. Above all, my mother would watch me smiling from ear to ear as I followed him around like a puppy, and she'd feel that she had done the right thing by having him over.

My father never lived with us, but I just assumed that was the way families were. You had a full-time mommy, and sometimes you lived with an additional female "friend" of Mommy's, who might disappear at any moment, never to be seen again, and "Daddy" came around every few weeks when he was missed too much.

Then the tickle monster disappeared. My constant harassing cries of "Where's Daddy?" had stopped resulting in his showing up. As I sat in that empty apartment downstairs, I felt sad that there was nothing I could say or do to make him appear at the front door.

My sensitivity was perhaps compounded by two factors: my mother was now working much of the time to try to keep us afloat financially, and I had just started attending preschool up the street at a local Jewish private school, where I was encountering "normal" families for the first time.

We weren't Jewish, but my mother felt it was important to give me a spiritual foundation, not really caring what the specific flavor was. While it had occurred to my mother that I might feel different because I was the only non-Jewish child there, she had not realized just how much I would start noticing the differences in our family makeup.

On the first day of preschool, when my mother accompanied me to class, I watched with curiosity as mothers *and* fathers came together to drop off their children. Then I started to pick up a few ideas on the playground that confused me.

"Are you and Daddy married?" I asked my mother one afternoon. She became visibly uncomfortable at the question.

"No, your daddy and I are good friends."

"Why doesn't Daddy live with us?" I asked another day.

"Not all daddies live with their mommies," she told me.

"What is a lesbian?" I asked on yet another afternoon, as we were driving home.

My mother almost rear-ended a car as she turned and stared at me, unsure how to answer. While my mother at times was very open with her sexual orientation—even appearing on TV to declare herself a trailblazer—she was fully in the closet in certain environments, like at my school and at work among her real estate associates and clients. She had, until that moment, assumed that no one at drop-off had guessed her sexuality; clearly someone had. She didn't answer my question.

"Am I a lesbian?" I asked.

"We don't really know yet," she said matter-of-factly.

"What's a lesbian?" I asked again, hoping to get an answer. The question, from my perspective, was as innocent as "What's a giraffe?," but it bothered my mother.

"Chrysta, can we talk about something else?"

"Where's Daddy?" I tried. Which resulted in another outburst.

My mother had carried the secret hope, hardly articulated to herself, that she could turn Jeffrey into a pseudo father so I would have a healthy connection to one male figure and so it appeared that we bore some resemblance to the *Father Knows Best* family, even if it was pieced together with some unconventional glue. But as the years went by, she'd had to contend with the idea that even if she had been able to rope Jeffrey into playing the role of Dad, perhaps he wasn't a desirable candidate in the first place.

This realization had started a few months after I was born, when Jeffrey crashed and totaled the car Debra had bought for him less than a week after she'd gifted it to him. Then Debra found a cop costume among Jeffrey's things, and he told her, with a chuckle, that he was now making extra cash as a "comedic strip-o-gram"—not to mention as a Chippendales dancer. Debra was embarrassed by these new details and shocked that Jeffrey showed no sign of embarrassment himself.

There was, on top of this, the constant smell of pot on Jeffrey, which came up against my mother's goal to raise me in a "sober" home.

Debra wrote off these things as Jeffrey just being an eccentric hippie who refused to live by the norms of a capitalist society.

The real alarm bells started ringing only after a series of late-night phone calls that began at around the time I turned two. Jeffrey would call my mother at around 4 a.m., stoned, to tell her in a euphoric rant that Mother Mary had come to him on the beach in a religious vision to explain that he was "the Messiah."

My mother had written off the first calls as a couple of bad trips. She'd done enough drugs in her day to know that a person's mind could concoct some lively imagery while stoned. (The first time she took LSD, when she was fifteen, she'd driven through Coldwater Canyon in her '57 white T-Bird with white tuck-and-roll seats, convinced she was a fish in the sea and that all the other cars were other fish.) The part Mom couldn't write off was that, after one of these calls, Jeffrey came over, sober as could be, and was still convinced that the Blessed Virgin had come to him and informed him of his purpose.

Debra had taken Jeffrey to two different therapists to try to figure out what was wrong and hopefully come up with a cure. (Jeffrey had only agreed to this because Debra paid him to go with her.) The sessions had concluded with little insight. There was no getting Jeffrey to open up about anything. Debra suspected that Jeffrey had been deeply hurt over his parents' divorce, but he refused to discuss anything meaningful about his past with Debra or her therapists. After he explained that he'd seen Mother Mary on the beach, the therapists had privately suggested to Debra that perhaps it was a good idea for her to start looking around for a new male figure for her daughter.

After one therapist met with Jeffrey for two hours, Debra asked him, after Jeffrey had left, if there was anything that could be done to help him, so he could be a good father.

"Well, if you believe in miracles," the therapist had said to her.

After a few more late-night phone calls, my mother resolved to remove Jeffrey from the picture entirely, hoping I wouldn't notice.

To patch the daddy hole in my heart, she decided to replace Jeffrey with what she hoped would be a better alternative, inviting a young, clean-cut real estate broker named Dennis to move into our downstairs bedroom.

"Chrysta, meet Dennis," my mother had said one afternoon. "He's going to be joining our family!"

I bought into her enthusiasm fully and loved Dennis from that moment on.

Unlike Jeffrey, Dennis didn't drink or do any drugs, he went to bed early, and he was gentle in a way my father never was, so my mother never had to keep her eye on him to make sure I didn't break a limb. Dennis was also comfortable with hugs, whereas my father had often plopped his dog, Ziggy, between us when I got too close. Dennis was also gay, and thus he had the support of all Debra's close friends, as well as Aunt Diane, who had never liked Jeffrey and had been pushing my mother to cut ties with him since my birth. Dennis was a part of their "tribe"; Mom's friends felt he understood the significance of what they were up against. Jeffrey, as a ravishingly good-looking straight man, did not.

My mother couldn't have cared less what her friends thought; all she cared about was that I adored Dennis, and so did she. For almost a year, Dennis lived downstairs, and life was wonderful. While my mother was on conference calls or out finding new business to bring into the mortgage brokerage, I would run down to Dennis's bedroom, and he'd turn on Barbra Streisand, and the two of us would dance around the house, dressed as ballerinas, hysterically laughing. One Christmas, my mother, Dennis, and I spent the afternoon decorating the Christmas tree, and then we went to the Taper theater in downtown L.A. to see *The Nutcracker*.

No difference here! my mother thought to herself as she glanced around at all the sweet, nuclear families in the theater and then looked over at me in my little green velvet dress, holding her hand and Dennis's as I watched "Dance of the Sugar Plum Fairy." She smiled, feeling as though she'd found the perfect Jeffrey replacement.

Then one afternoon, a year into the Dennis chapter of our lives, I came home to find his bedroom empty, cleared of all his things. All that was left was an unmade bed and the empty dresser that had predated his arrival.

"Where's Dennis?" I asked.

"Dennis has gone on vacation!" my mother exclaimed. "Don't worry. He will be back soon!"

Once again, I bought into my mother's enthusiasm. I was curious about where Dennis had gone but excited when my mother told me that whenever he came back, he would certainly be bringing me lots of gifts. (Later I'd learn that Dennis, once he got comfortable, had started having boyfriends visit the house, the frequency of which had bothered my mother enough that she'd asked him to leave.)

As with Annie, I was sad when I occasionally noticed that Dennis had not returned from his trip, but my questions about him eventually faded. Soon I had moved on to a new obsession: I wanted a sibling!

"Mommy," I'd started to say with all the theatrics of my four-year-old self, "I love you more than all the cars and stars in the universe, but…"

"But?"

"Can't I please—*please!*—have a little brother or sister?"

"One day," she'd say back to me.

"Tomorrow?" I'd follow up.

"Probably not tomorrow," she'd say, laughing.

"Then when?"

"Jesus, Chrysta!" she'd blurt out once again. "You are so obsessive!"

It's true. I had learned early on that my mother had a hard time saying no to me, that if I just pressed for what I wanted long enough, I'd usually get it.

One sunny November morning in 1988, I asked again, for what was likely the millionth time, and for whatever reason, my mother turned to me with sudden enthusiasm and belted out, "Why the hell not? Chrysta, let's do it!"

The idea of a single gay mother having one child was one thing. But two? Debra's friends thought she'd gone mad.

"You'll be two million dollars in by the time you have put two children through college," one of her more rational friends said when she'd initially broached the subject of having a second kid.

"The universe will provide!" Debra assured her friend.

If she was going to have a second child, my mother wanted me to have a full biological sibling. Sure, Jeffrey was eccentric, she thought, but he was also kind, and spiritual, and gorgeous.

Maybe I wrote him off too quickly, she thought now, wondering if he'd been okay these past six months without her to check in on him.

My mother walked into her bedroom, got out her phone book, and called the last number she had for Jeffrey. She hadn't seen or heard from him in several months, and the man who answered the phone (a friend of Jeffrey's whose couch he had been crashing on) told her he hadn't seen Jeff in several months either.

"Where is he?" Debra asked.

"No idea."

"Did he leave a phone number?"

"Nah."

"Is he okay?"

"I truly don't know."

"Do you know anything?" she barked at him.

At this point, the man remembered an address that Jeffrey had once given him for a commune in Venice Beach called the YESSSSSSS Center, run by a guy named Darhada. "Maybe he's there?" the couch friend said.

Debra scribbled the address down and, after leaving me in the care of our new nanny, Alba, she drove into the heart of Venice.

Jesus, Debra said to herself as she pushed open the gate to the graffiti-covered house. She could smell incense and pot coming through the open stained glass windows.

At the time, there were no multimillion-dollar Frank Gehry homes for sale along the canals, or artisanal coffee shops offering short cortados and homemade croissants. Instead, the part of the city that had once been home to one of the world's greatest amusement piers was now simply known as the Slum by the Sea. Needles were sprinkled along the canals, and the streets were lined with open sewers, homeless encampments, and gang members hiding from the police. (The Venice Shoreline Crips were, at that time, involved in a fierce clash with the Latino Venice 13 over who owned which crack cocaine sales territories.)

My mother was as much out of her element here—exiting her white Mercedes in her blouse, pearls, and bright white silk pantsuit with shoulder pads—as she was as a lesbian single mother in her late thirties driving into the parking lot of my Jewish preschool.

A clearly stoned guy with long hair and dirty clothes answered her knock.

"Do you happen to know Jeffrey Harrison?" she asked.

"Yeah, he's sleeping in the back," the guy said, pointing.

Debra was used to Jeffrey keeping strange hours, so it didn't strike her as unusual that he was still sleeping at two o'clock in the afternoon. She was just excited that she'd found him, and relieved that he was alive.

She walked inside, passing several people getting high, others sleeping on old brown couches stained with God knows what.

"Jeffrey?" she called out as she wandered past several rooms covered in dingy carpeting before she came upon an open door to the backyard, where she spotted what could barely be called a structure—more like a stucco cave meant for firewood and black widow spiders—with a pair of large male feet sticking out. She recognized Jeffrey's toes immediately; they were the exact same toes as mine, which she'd kissed and washed and put shoes on every day for the past four years.

She walked outside and bent down to peek into the tiny outhouse. The shed had a single window, at the top of which was haphazardly nailed a bright pink Indian scarf that blocked the blazing afternoon sun. She crouched down, leaning into the doorway of his tiny shed, and saw Jeffrey's famished-looking, unbathed body, dirt etched into the arches of his feet. He was on a mattress, wrapped in an old, itchy wool blanket. She started to feel a very heavy weight press down on her.

Who is this person? Debra asked herself. Certainly he was not the same beautiful young pedigreed surfer she had met at the hair salon years prior. Anger overwhelmed her. She wanted to wake Jeffrey up and slap him across the face for not being who she needed him to be.

She took a heavy breath and spotted a small, makeshift altar where an old postcard of Mother Mary, its edges frayed, sat—the image of the woman who so often spoke to Jeffrey in his dreams. Next to the postcard was a tattered copy of *Autobiography of a Yogi* and a wilting pink flower—the same kind of flower Jeffrey used to show up with and give me. Suddenly, Debra's anger vanished.

"Jeffrey, wake up," Debra said in a loving voice, nudging his foot. "Come on. It's time to get you out of here and take you home." Debra was now under the delusion that Jeffrey's proper "home" was wherever she and her child were, and it didn't occur to her that Jeffrey might not see it that way.

Later that evening, Christmas came early when I woke up and found my father moving into the downstairs bedroom with his big scruffy dog, Ziggy.

Euphoria doesn't come close to how I felt. Justice is better.

In an instant, I'd gone from being part of a family of two, with an occasional visitor, to living full-time with my mommy and daddy, just like everyone else at school, with the promise of a sibling any day. I even had a dog!

A SIBLING FOR CHRYSTA

One night a few weeks after my father moved in, after I'd kissed him good night and then kissed Ziggy, too, my mother took me into her arms and tickled my back while I dozed off into some sweet dream. My father was rubbing my mother's feet (again, for twenty dollars) and she whispered to him, "Jeff, let's do it again."

Debra didn't need to explain what the "it" was; Jeffrey looked over at me sleeping and understood immediately. Ever since Debra came for him in Venice, he'd suspected that she had something up her sleeve. He'd seen Debra inching closer to him, day by day, with those big wide eyes. She'd bring him a new shirt that she'd bought at some fancy department store, or a new set of dress pants. A friend would "randomly" arrive at the apartment who just so happened to be a hairdresser and offer to chop Jeffrey's scraggly shoulder-length hair into a nice short cut, as if this visit was just coincidence. As if all of this wasn't a part of Debra's plan to extricate the hippie from Jeffrey, leaving only the parts of him that she found acceptable and "proper."

"Oh my God!" Jeffrey now said as he processed my mother's request, shaking his head. "If we do it twice, Debra, it will be like we have a *real* family."

"Yes!" she exclaimed. "Exactly!"

Debra looked at Jeffrey, who was still by her feet. Seeing the hesitation on his face, she thought about the best way to frame the offer.

"Like a real family, Jeff. But a new, exciting, modern family that doesn't play by all the old rules."

Debra was doing what she always did: playing the director, producer, and leading lady of her own production, assigning roles as she saw fit. Jeffrey wasn't falling for it. He was already participating on a level far beyond what he had initially signed up for.

"And most importantly," she added, looking over at me sleeping soundly, "this precious child, Chrysta, will have a sibling."

Our little production of *Debra's Happy Family* wasn't without perks for Jeffrey. He lived rent-free in a nice apartment, had complete access to a refrigerator filled with fresh food, and even had some pocket money to buy pot with. He also had the vaguely gratifying experience of being adored by a sweet child who was half him, after all. Jeffrey could dip in for a quick sing-along with me and then walk away as soon as the fun ended and the parenting began.

Debra watched Jeffrey's awkward body language as he carefully slid a sheet over her foot before continuing with her massage, scratching his head and mumbling to himself.

"I'll pay you eight thousand dollars, Jeff," she said, plucking the number right out of thin air. Business was good this month and she could afford it. She loved the number eight, which she said represented infinity in numerology and was a good number for bringing in abundance.

"Fine," he submitted. "On one condition," he added after a moment of reflection.

"What?"

"I am not getting a nine-to-five job," he said sternly. "I'm not cutting my hair short. I'm a hippie from Hawaii and you are not going to change me. Got it?"

Debra paused, considering this and likely annoyed that Jeffrey had any terms to propose at all.

"Fine," she agreed, reluctantly.

"And one more thing," he said.

"What?" she asked, growing impatient.

"You may never talk to my parents."

Debra sat motionless. A few weeks earlier, she had gently broached the idea of calling Jeffrey's parents to get to know them over the telephone, and he now knew enough about how Debra operated to know that whatever her plan was, it was much larger than a simple telephone call.

"I'll be the kids' father," Jeffrey continued, seeing Debra growing uncomfortable. "But my parents are not going to be their grandparents—got it? If you ever reach out to my parents because you want grandparents for the children, that will be it. I'll be done, Debra."

"Fine," my mother said after a very long, irritated pause.

"I want you to swear to it."

"I swear."

With my little sister, it took only one try. Debra lit a candle while Jeffrey went into the downstairs bathroom.

"Ohhhmmm," he heard Debra chanting from above as he tried to concentrate on the empty glass in front of him.

Ten minutes later, he came out, glass in hand, feeling anxious. He took a few hits from a joint in his pocket to settle his nerves, then walked up the white carpeted steps to join Debra on her thousand-thread-count, floral-printed duvet, a brand-new plastic turkey baster sitting on the table next to her. Jeffrey watched as Debra lay on her back, eyes closed, attempting to shift into a state of "receptivity" as she awaited the arrival of the next little soul in her womb.

In future tellings and retellings, my mother would insist that she could sense a new little being, Kaitlyn, come into the room right away. Maybe she did actually sense it, or maybe she framed the story this way later to instill a sense of magic in my sister and me, and to imbue her own character with divine power.

My mother opened her eyes and turned to look at Jeffrey lying next to her, shocked by what she saw: his eyes were closed and he was crying! Big, powerful, flowing tears were trickling down his cheeks.

"Are you okay, Jeff?" she whispered.

Jeffrey didn't respond.

"Jeff, are you okay?" she asked him again, her voice sharper, more concerned.

He opened his eyes and turned to look at her.

"I asked Babaji to personally come to watch over this little soul's life," he said, taking in a shaky breath through his tears. "I read that if you pray to the point of tears, then the Lord himself will appear. So I thought about the factory farming industry in the United States that ruthlessly kills millions of chickens every day, and I started crying deep, powerful tears."

Debra sat up, staring at Jeffrey for several moments without blinking as she mulled over the idea that he had tried to conceive a child with her while visualizing millions of chickens being slaughtered.

My mother, too deep in with Jeffrey now to go back, started doing something new: she just ignored when he said things like this, and chose to see only the parts of him that she preferred that he have.

"It's horrible," he said. "Those poor chickens."

"Ohhhmmm," Debra chanted.

"Those poor, poor chickens," he sobbed.

"Ohhhhhhhmmmmmmmmm."

PYRAMID FEVER

My mother bought into her first pyramid scheme a few years before I was born; it took place during the stagflation of 1980, a painful recession and inflation in one. The once booming housing market had collapsed, and Debra, like many of her friends in real estate, was in a serious cash crunch. She had heard about "pyramids" over the years from enthusiastic friends but had simply laughed them off as Tupperware parties or scams.

Her ears had perked up when one of these friends called her up to say there was a new pyramid on the other side of town, in Calabasas, where you could, supposedly, "turn five hundred dollars into twenty thousand in just a few days."

"Twenty thousand?" Debra had repeated back with curious excitement. "How?"

"Yep," the friend promised. "You just need five hundred to buy in."

Debra knew it was against the law to even attend a pyramid meeting, but a part of her felt she was above the law because her father had been a judge and her grandfather the governor. No matter how much trouble she'd gotten into growing up, she could always wiggle her way out of whatever bind she was in by dropping a few names (an eternal pastime of hers). She sped across the 405 freeway and rolled up to a charming house with a white picket fence. She went inside and looked on in amusement at a sandy-blond-haired man dressed in crisp khakis and a fitted polo shirt as he drew circles with people's names inside them on a giant whiteboard. Debra dropped her $500 (which she had borrowed from a friend) on the table and announced that she was in!

"All you have to do is bring two people in under you," the man in the polo shirt said as he scribbled a new circle at the bottom of the whiteboard and wrote "Debra" inside it. "Then those two people bring in two more people, and all of a sudden, you are at the top of the pyramid and you get twenty thousand dollars in cash."

"Sounds good to me!" Debra said, not entirely sure how it all worked.

She got her two people but then quickly realized it wasn't that easy. It soon became apparent that she'd have to help her two people get *their* four people, or she'd be out $500, because so many people were already in on the pyramids that finding fresh blood was not as easy as Mr. Polo Shirt had made it out to be.

Within a few days, Debra had managed to help her people, and their people, bring in a huge assortment of other people from all over town who were, miraculously, not already in on the pyramid. A week later, on a weeknight when traffic would usually have subsided, there were so many pyramid schemes popping up across Los Angeles that there was bumper-to-bumper traffic on every major freeway and side street and in every canyon in town. In Benedict Canyon, Debra stared in amazement through her car window as men and women were just stopped on the road, sitting in front of their cars, counting out hundred-dollar bills. (*Time* magazine would later call this moment the "great California pyramid scheme mania of 1980." People were renting warehouses to host new pyramids, there were runs on banks for fifty- and hundred-dollar bills from people trying to get in on games, and Frank Sinatra, Debra's former neighbor, was even rumored to have started a pyramid at a private club called Pips with a $100,000 buy-in and a $1 million jackpot.)

The trick with pyramid schemes, Debra had been told, was to get in early and out as soon as you can, before there was no one left in Los Angeles to recruit. So, on the night Debra was set to "cash out," she stood in front of the giant whiteboard, gleaming as she looked up at her name now written in a circle at the top. She asked the pyramid's accountant, an older woman with a green plastic visor and a Tiparillo cigar hanging out of her mouth, for her $20,000, which she watched counted out in crisp hundred-dollar bills.

"Nineteen thousand six hundred…Nineteen thousand seven hundred…Twenty thousand dollars." Just after Debra stretched out her hand to take her cash, stuffed it into a large duffel bag, and turned to leave, the front door burst open and a group of LAPD cops raided the house.

"Freeze!"

"Down on the ground!"

"No one move!"

Debra watched in shock as the cops took every dollar out of her satchel, including the $500 she had borrowed to get into the game in the first place. Her father, Judge Olson, was no longer around to get her out of this debacle. And it turned out that without him, she was not above the law, though I'm not sure if this is a lesson my mother would ever quite learn.

She vowed never to do anything that insane for money again. By 1981, a few years before I was born, she'd made good on that promise to herself and was holding down a "normal" nine-to-five job, working for a bank called Unity Savings, essentially running the loan department. After a couple of years, when the married-with-kids bank officer whom she reported to made inappropriate advances, she was forced to quit. That's when she got into another doomed get-rich-quick scheme. So began the cycle: a real job followed by a fake job, culminating with no job.

When she was very pregnant with me, my mother took a different bank job, at Topa Savings and Loan on Santa Monica Boulevard, where this time her boss was an alcoholic, which brought its own challenges. In the morning, he'd quote her one very low interest rate for her mostly gay developer clients, and then, after Debra had written up the contracts for these jumbo loans, the executive would call her later that evening, after several martinis, to announce that the interest rate had gone up. Her clients were, understandably, enraged. Debra couldn't stand working under these conditions, but given that she was now expecting me, she felt she had little choice but to deal with her new boss's drunken power plays. She was going to play it straight, she'd promised herself, to secure the family.

A month before I was born, my mother walked into work at 9 a.m. and found her boss, the alcoholic, standing with his secretary in Debra's office.

"We are letting you go," he said under the stench of alcohol on his breath. "We think you'd be better suited for a different kind of job."

"Why?" Debra demanded, furious.

"Well," he responded, "we've discussed it, and we think you are really much better suited to be an artist painting sunsets in Hawaii than someone working for a bank."

Debra stood there, dumbfounded. She had worked hard at this job, all through her pregnancy, and she'd brought in an incredible amount of business, even while struggling with severe morning sickness. On several occasions her boss had expressed his disapproval of her having a child without a husband, and she now felt that this was a ploy to steal her Rolodex of clients and remove her from the job before she had her baby and was deemed by society to be less fit for the position.

"Well, if we are all being honest," she finally said, trying to hold it together (now on the brink of giving birth), "whoever says they would rather be sitting here in this miserable shithole of gray filing cabinets and gray walls than on some beach in Hawaii is a fucking liar."

She managed to find a loophole in her health insurance that got her paid enough to live on for my first year of life, but she could stretch those $5,000 monthly checks for only so long. Her heart broke at the idea of placing me in the care of a nanny while she went back to a corporate job. If she was just clever and resourceful, she felt sure she could find a way to both make money and be able to spend all her time with me. Thus came pyramid scheme number two.

Each time a new one began, my mother told everyone the same thing. "We're going to make millions!" she'd bellow. It wasn't that she was saying this to persuade people to buy in. She genuinely believed it—that there was a pot of gold waiting around the corner, and the next deal, the next pyramid scheme, would be the map she needed to find it.

At around the time I was eighteen months old, my mother got a call from Robert Adler, who everyone referred to as Bobby. Bobby, who she had met years earlier when she was fully submerged in her cocaine addiction, was a ladies' man, known for his crazy entrepreneurial schemes. Debra was a great marketer—she could sell you the socks you were wearing, at a markup, because of her contagious enthusiasm—and Bobby wanted to see if she'd be interested in helping him start a new multilevel vitamin company, United Sciences of America.

"Is this a pyramid scheme, Bobby?" she'd asked him one evening, breastfeeding me with one hand and holding the phone with the other.

"No. No. It's different," he'd said. "It's vitamins! We've got every scientist in the world working on this thing. These vitamins can cure cancer. AIDS, even! This is going to be people helping people who don't want to sell out to corporate America."

My mother was past due on the rent and knew she needed to make something happen quickly.

"Okay, I'm in," she said. "What do I have to do?"

Within a few months, in the autumn of 1985, Bobby moved his United Sciences meetings to Debra's living room, where she quickly became his top salesperson, bringing thousands of people into the United Sciences dream.

"This is people helping people," she'd say enthusiastically into the telephone as she ran through her Rolodex.

United Sciences was, within six months, on fire. Checks for $2,000 started to land in my mother's mailbox. Then $5,000. Then $10,000. A month later, she got one for $20,000. United Sciences was exploding into a nationwide phenomenon. Debra was the top salesperson, helping Bobby sign up ten thousand new people every month. Debra loved that she could stay home all day with me, just sitting on her telephone for a few hours, making calls from her bed, and then leave the house and take me for a leisurely walk outdoors. To celebrate all her newfound good fortune, she put a down payment on a sweet little two-bedroom house for the two of us and purchased a car for Jeffrey. She had the money to pay him regularly for his foot massages and for coming over to play Daddy. She'd started doling out money to every struggling friend she'd made over the past decade. She was proud of this new venture. "We're sharing health and wealth! What could be better?" she'd exclaim with a smile.

As she was unpacking the moving boxes at our new house, high on life and grateful for this financial miracle, her phone rang.

"Debra speaking."

"Turn on NBC," the voice on the other line said in a frantic tone. "Now!"

Debra ran to her television, grabbed the remote, and turned the TV to channel 4, where the news anchor, Connie Chung, was in the middle of a massive exposé on United Sciences of America, breaking the news that the company was under investigation by the FBI.

Debra quickly ran to her bedside table, pulled out several uncashed checks from United Sciences, and raced to the bank as fast as she could to deposit them. None of them cleared. Thankfully, she was able to pass herself off as less involved than she actually was and was not among those indicted.

Once again, Debra promised herself there would be no more pyramid or multilevel marketing schemes. She was going to get a normal, boring job, and be a normal working parent, just like everyone else. She sold the house she'd just purchased at a loss and went on the hunt for another real estate job.

Once again, my mother found herself in a precarious situation. Her new boss was a woman named Martha, who ran a mortgage brokerage and whose business practices were allegedly so deceitful that she went everywhere with a bodyguard, in case a former client might want to see her harmed. Martha came into the office in a great mood on some days and a foul one on others, raging at Debra whenever she was stressed that a deal might fall through.

During one particularly wild tantrum of Martha's, my mother became so overwhelmed that she almost gave birth to my sister five months early.

She was rushed to the hospital and told she was going into labor, at which time she got an idea "from the universe."

"I am not having a premature baby!" she screamed as the contractions intensified. "Give me morphine! It will chill me out, and it will chill the baby out! Give it to me now!"

There was no arguing with my mother, and against his better judgment, her doctor administered a small dose of morphine into my mother's veins. It was the first drug to hit her system in almost ten years. Miraculously, she did not go into labor that day.

My mother stared out the window, the morphine gently drifting through her veins, and took a deep, relaxed breath, her first deep breath in months, and was put on strict bed rest.

It occurred to her that she needed to find a way out of her pyramid schemes, and insane bosses, and the stressful confines of the nine-to-five world. But how could she do that, and still provide an abundant life for herself and her two little children and their eccentric father?

Perhaps, she thought, the answer to her problems wasn't in another normal job or another get-rich-quick scheme. Perhaps she was looking in the wrong place altogether. She decided to call on the universe for another miracle.

TWO MOMMIES

I asked for a sibling. I got four. And a second mother. And a mansion. Also a dozen white doves, a potbellied pig, an Egyptian iguana, a Dalmatian, and the shock of my life.

This new turn of events, one that would introduce me to a new side of my mother I had yet to meet, began on a breezy spring morning in March of 1989. It was a few days after my little sister, Kaitlyn, had come into the world, and life, at least from my four-year-old, three-foot-tall vantage point, was marvelous. My mother had been working from home for several glorious months (doing mortgage deals), on strict bed rest after almost going into labor with Kaitlyn.

Since that scare, my mother had made all her deals from bed, which meant I could waltz into her bedroom at any time and have an audience for one of my princess pageants.

My father had moved out, but this time he landed on his feet, moving in with a new girlfriend named Heather, an Asian American woman in her midtwenties who was set to inherit millions from an incredibly rich uncle. My father and Heather had met—where else?—at the California Cryobank, where she worked. Jeffrey kept this small detail about Heather's employment a secret from my mother, since it would have generated some questions he was not prepared to answer.

Over the past five years, my father had been donating to the California Cryobank two to three times per week, a fact that he'd carefully kept from my mother somehow, even when he was living with us. While my mother never had any idea that my father was doing this, it was harder for him to keep his secret from the various women he'd dated during this period. Girlfriends were never thrilled when they found out Jeffrey made his living this way, and his donating often became a point of contention. He'd promise he would stop, but women could always tell when he was lying because he would suddenly lose interest in sex. Perhaps because she had met my father through the sperm bank, Heather was the first woman who didn't seem to mind.

My father had first caught sight of Heather at the Cryobank when she was wandering around the back office after he'd arrived for a donation. She had silky black hair, large black eyes, and a petite frame, plus a crooked front tooth that added some character to her otherwise traditionally beautiful features. Jeffrey had smiled when he caught Heather checking him out, grabbed a pen from the front desk, and scribbled a note asking for her phone number. Soon after, he moved in with Heather, into a giant estate at the top of Mulholland that belonged to her rich uncle. The pair kept various parts of this story a secret from everyone around them: from Heather's uncle, who would not have been thrilled to discover that a man had moved in downstairs; from the California Cryobank, which had an explicit "no dating donors" policy; and especially from my mother, who would have gotten hysterical if she'd learned who Heather's employer was.

Under normal circumstances, my mother would have prodded Jeffrey with a million questions about this new girlfriend, but given that he had started to show up at our apartment clean-shaven, in washed clothing, and looking more and more like the man she had first met, she dropped her interrogations and was simply grateful to this new woman.

Jeffrey seemed to be cleaning up his act in ways that went beyond his appearance. He'd started to come over to see me of his own accord, without asking to be paid for the visits, and he'd even taken me out on a father-daughter date, on his suggestion, which came as a delightful shock to my mother. I got myself dressed in my favorite flowery dress, and my mother anxiously waved goodbye as my father drove me to Heather's uncle's estate. The house was so large, with so many floors, that I got lost for what felt like hours, then finally found my father, to my great relief, playing a grand piano in the ballroom.

When my mother returned from the hospital with me and baby Kaitlyn in tow, she found Jeffrey sitting outside our apartment, playing his guitar as he waited for us to arrive. He stood up, held Kaitlyn in his arms for the first time, and smiled comfortably.

"Oh my God, she looks exactly like I did when I was a baby," he said in astonishment, giving her a little kiss. (He was right: Kaitlyn was the spitting image of young Jeffrey, with her big blue eyes and what Debra always described as a "dolphin-like" face, though I'm not quite sure what that means.)

For the first few days of Kaitlyn's life, I was living in a floaty dream. The house was filled with all my favorite people: Annie, now just a friend, had come back into the fold; Aunt Diane; my god-mother, Damian; my father; and my new baby sister, who I got to hold whenever I wanted and dress up like my own little doll.

My mother, on the other hand, was a mess. She'd been juggling me, her job, and the sleep deprivation that accompanies having a newborn, a four-year-old, and a pile of bills. Every time she felt the physical symptoms of a panic attack set in—increased heart rate, difficulty breathing—she would set a panic attack in motion at the thought of having a panic attack. She was desperate to create a calm, gentle environment for baby Kaitlyn, but the overwhelming pressures of her life felt insurmountable.

Then she got a phone call from out of the blue.

The woman on the other end of the line, a successful realtor named Fay, had recently left her husband and three children on the advice of a therapist after admitting she thought she might be gay. (This 1980s licensed medical professional felt it would be "too damaging" for the kids to have a lesbian mother.) She had gotten Debra's phone number from a mutual friend who thought she and Debra would hit it off now that Fay was out of the closet and ready to date. Debra invited Fay over later that afternoon, and as Fay sat on the edge of Debra's bed, watching her breastfeed Kaitlyn, she fell in love with my mother. While Mom often had this effect on people, it was further intensified by Fay's recent coming out and her tendency toward romanticism.

"You must be Chrysta," she said warmly as I waltzed around my mother's bedroom. "I'm Fay."

Fay was attractive and put-together, with short blond hair, expensive but casual clothing, and warm, smiling eyes. She looked like she could have been on the cover of the fashion magazines at the grocery store—a late-eighties-era embodiment of the capable, attractive working woman.

Something about Fay—maybe the confident way she walked around with baby Kaitlyn over her shoulder, or the attunement she offered me, or the sparkle that glistened in her eyes whenever I caught her staring at my mother—told me that this woman, whoever she was, was going to be more significant than the past half dozen.

"Chrysta," my mother said a few weeks later, coming into my room with Fay behind her. "You remember Fay, don't you?"

"Well, Chrysta," Fay said with tears in her eyes, bending down to hold out her arms to me. "Now you can call me Mommy Fay."

I sat processing the words, catching my mother's glance with a question mark.

"Most kids only have one mommy," my mother explained, taking my hand in hers. "But now you are going to be the luckiest little girl in the world, because you'll get to have two mommies!"

I smiled, not really understanding the implications of the statement but buying into my mother's enthusiasm.

I am the luckiest girl in the world, I told myself.

In a matter of days, I went from meeting Fay as she sat at the edge of my mother's bed to calling her Mommy Fay and sitting between her and my mother, Kaitlyn on my mother's lap, as Fay drove a huge truck with all our stuff piled inside to a $4 million estate in a gated city on the remote edge of Los Angeles. I would later come to learn that the house was one of a set of luxury spec homes in a brand-new private city of L.A. called Hidden Hills, which was being developed by a friend of my mother's. In typical Debra fashion, my mother had convinced the developer to let us all live in the house rent-free for one year while she and Fay showed it to buyers. The pitch was that Fay would sell all the empty houses on the block within a year, Debra would handle all the mortgage loans with Martha, and together, my two moms would make enough on the dual commissions to buy the house we were moving into—all cash.

It wasn't that Fay needed the money. She was already doing well from her life as a top real estate agent, and as part of her proposition to Debra about being her girlfriend, Fay had told my mother she could quit working altogether.

"Just imagine it, Deb," Fay had said that first day on the bed in her calm, confident, decisive voice. "You can sit by the pool all day breast-feeding Kaitlyn, and be a full-time mommy to Chrysta, and I'll go out and work and support us."

It had been music to my mother's ears.

My mother often had this effect on women. Once she'd come to terms with her sexuality (with the help of drugs) in her twenties, she'd started to think of herself as a kind of female Don Juan, able to "turn" straight women gay. My mother's sister, Aunt Diane, had been jealous of her for this, always afraid that if a woman she was dating met her older sister, she would secretly prefer Debra. With Fay, whatever it was that was so captivating about my mother had knocked the wind out of her. And Aunt Diane was thrilled at the idea of Fay and my mother getting together, perhaps because that would take Debra out of the dating pool.

Ordinarily, Fay wouldn't have been my mother's type at all. Physically, Debra had always liked her opposite: dark-skinned women, usually of Jewish, Middle Eastern, or African descent. Emotionally, she'd always been drawn to what she called "dangerous women"—women who had difficult, interesting backgrounds. Fay was whiter than milk toast, with her short blond hair, gentle manners, and devout Catholic background. Years earlier, Debra would never have considered dating Fay—not because she wasn't physically attractive (she was), or because she wasn't a catch (she was), but simply because she wouldn't have struck Debra as all that *interesting*. Fay simply wouldn't have been dangerous enough for Debra. However, Debra was looking at the world a bit differently now. Maybe interesting wasn't all it was cracked up to be.

When I first set foot inside our new ten-thousand-square-foot Country French estate, with six bedrooms and more bathrooms than we could possibly use, I was greeted by a foyer larger than the entire footprint of our previous apartment. The house had corridors that belonged in a hotel. There was a giant, roaring fireplace in almost every room (my mother's favorite feature) and a grand staircase in the center, at the top of which I could look down over an imposing marble landing. I immediately turned the landing into a theater, putting on elaborate musicals that everyone could (or should I say was forced to) watch. There was a yard the size of a ranch surrounded by rolling meadows that stretched in every direction and were encircled with a never-ending white picket fence. The house sat on a wide, newly poured cul-de-sac, where there was plenty of room for me to learn to ride a bike with no cars zipping by. Best of all, given that every other home on the street was still being developed—years later, these homes would sell for double-digit millions and house celebrities like Justin Bieber, Kim Kardashian, and Jessica Simpson—there was no one around to judge our sweet little lesbian family.

Back in 1990, there were no smartphones filled with apps that allowed anyone to find a new home, and no websites where people could compare house prices; you couldn't find a house without a real estate agent, and an agent's ability to find the perfect home to satisfy a client's tastes was a highly sought-after skill. Fay, who always found herself excelling at whatever she tried, was one of the best.

She was so good, in fact, that with her Rolodex of wealthy clients, who were making a fortune off Reagan's tax cuts for the rich, she was flipping houses on an almost weekly basis. Money was flowing so abundantly that my mother regularly found $30,000 checks just sitting in random drawers, uncashed and entirely forgotten about.

Given all the cash sloshing around and all the extra time that had suddenly been freed up for her, my mother decided to build the zoo she'd always dreamed of on our new property, starting with Pharaoh, a rare Egyptian iguana with a spiral tail that Debra and Jeffrey happily brought back from the pet store like two giggly five-year-olds. Then came Isis, an Abyssinian cat that cost $1,200. Then Denmark, my Dalmatian puppy, named after our ancestral land, which my mother always had a deep reverence for. Then several finches that were turquoise, gold, red, and white—the "rarest and most expensive of color combinations." My mother decided to breed them. Suddenly there were tiny boxes filled with thousands of dollars' worth of bird eggs spread out in one of the (many) empty bedrooms in our house. Soon there was also a massive saltwater fish tank installed in our kitchen, larger than me by far.

Fay was handy around the house, fixing things Debra would not have attempted to figure out herself. Fay was also, unlike my mother, an incredible cook. I went from breakfasts composed of colorful cereal concoctions to large sit-down meals at our new kitchen island. Sometimes Fay even invited me to cook with her; we often made chocolate pudding, and she let me sneak the tops (the best part) off everyone else's servings and eat them.

My father, too, loved this new lush environment and was around more than ever, sleeping over with Heather and Ziggy in one of our many guest bedrooms. He and my mother were getting along great, and for a moment, even Aunt Diane had stopped begging her sister to get rid of Jeffrey. Everyone could see that he was getting his act together. To Mom's great shock, he even asked her if he should marry Heather. Never in a million years did Debra think Jeffrey would overcome his fear of commitment and settle down.

"Do it, Jeffrey!" she exclaimed in joy. "Propose to her! Do it!"

My mother was happier than ever, which made me happier than ever. I'd started to love Mommy Fay like she really was my second mother. Kaitlyn, who'd been held and fed and rocked to sleep by Fay from practically her first days of life, truly couldn't tell the difference. Fay was, in every way, Kaitlyn's other mother.

After a few months of living with Fay in this new life, bigger and brighter than the last, my mother still wasn't able to shake the guilt that Fay had abandoned her children to live as an "out" lesbian.

"Children need their mother, Fay," my mother said to her one afternoon, deciding to frame it as an ultimatum. "I can't be with you in good conscience if you're okay just leaving them."

Fay agreed with Debra, even though it was simpler and easier to just start fresh with a brand-new family. It wasn't that Fay didn't love her children—she did, and she thought about them daily with a broken heart—but integrating her old life, filled with so many lies, was more difficult and painful than simply compartmentalizing it. She worried that being gay would harm her kids. But she was also happy now, and in love, and she wondered if she and Debra could create a new kind of family, together, with all the kids in one house. So they decided to bring the kids home to Fay, starting with a few visits at our new home, and then some sleepovers, with the goal of eventually having them with us half the time.

Fay had three children: Emily, who was six, just a few months older than me; Robby, who was eight; and Chris, who was fifteen.

Emily was my size and blond and had bulging red eyes that told me from the first hate-filled glance that our relationship was going to be fraught. On our first playdate, she'd been nice to me in front of Fay and my mother, and then, as soon as no one was looking, she'd shut me in my bedroom, tied me to a chair, and threw Cheerios at my head violently, one at a time, aiming with such precision and hatred, like I was a human dartboard, that I truly thought she was going to kill me.

"I can do whatever I want to you because I'm three months older than you, so that gives me power," she told me maniacally as she held a Cheerio in her hand, closed one eye, and took aim. "If you tell your mom about this, next time it will be something worse than Cheerios," she added.

Robby, the middle child, was pudgy, shy, introverted, and much less obvious about his mixed-up feelings. Robby showed his ambivalence by placing a paper bag over his head before agreeing to speak to my mother.

Chris, the oldest, a handsome teenager who played the guitar, was the only one who seemed to be okay with his newly broken and then put-back-together-again home. Chris was taken by my mother, fascinated by her stories of world travels and religious explorations, and mind-blown that she had partied with so many famous people, like the time she smoked hashish with Leonard Cohen in the mountains of Idra, Greece. Or the time she learned a Buddhist chant that could get you whatever you wanted, and chanted to meet Mick Jagger, and then proceeded to spend a platonic week with him at the Bel-Air hotel. She'd been in the room when he recorded the song "Goin' Home," made out with Anita Pallenberg in a limousine, and allegedly gave Mick the inspiration for the lyric—possibly the most famous lyric in all rock and roll history—"You can't always get what you want, but you get what you need," which she said with a smile after he asked her to bed.

While everyone adjusted in their own ways, each of my new siblings, Chris included, agreed: I was a spoiled brat who got whatever she wanted from her mother, not to mention an exorbitant amount of attention from Mommy Fay—who was as eager to please my mother as my mother was to please me.

The anger of my new siblings, while misplaced, was understandable. They had gone from seeing their mother every morning to seeing her only a few times in the course of almost a year and speaking to her over the phone on Christmas. Then suddenly here they were: visitors in their mother's new family.

The situation at their nearby Catholic school didn't help either. When word spread that Emily and Chris and Robby were having sleepovers with two lesbian mothers like some sort of "gay Brady Bunch," a group of parents and teachers got together to try to have Fay's children thrown out. There were meetings among parents, dirty looks wherever we went, and concerned letters written and slipped into mailboxes. Playdates and sleepovers were canceled, as if letting kids come over to our place was akin to sending children home with known pedophiles. Right when things were about to turn toward pitchforks and torches, Sister Frances, the head nun, allowed the kids to stay in school on the condition that Fay and my mother never set foot on campus.

Perhaps the worst aftereffect of this new family formation was the reaction within Fay's own family. One day she went to get the mail and opened an envelope containing a handwritten letter from her Catholic mother. In blue ink, her mother had written, "Here's your sister with her kids, in our family line, and here's you"—she'd made an arrow pointing outside a drawn image of their family tree. The message was clear: Fay was no longer a member of their family because she'd made this "decision" to be a lesbian, and it was wrong. The kids could see their grandmother or their aunt only with their father. Fay was not welcome.

In this environment, it probably wouldn't have made a difference how I acted toward my new siblings. In their minds, I was the interloper with a mother who had always been gay, who had broken up their once perfect family.

In the whirlwind of Fay's kids' problems and the challenges that come when two families attempt to "blend" together, there was one tiny, concerning detail about Mommy Fay that my mother had overlooked: Fay loved to drink wine.

Now, as I turned five, my mother was almost ten years sober. I'd never known her drunk or on drugs; no matter how difficult things had been, I'd had the stability of her being conscious and sober for my entire early childhood.

THE PARTY HOUSE

It's unclear what finally made my mother drink. It could have been the parties at our house, which grew bigger by the day. It might have had something to do with our new home being so far away from her sober friends and regular AA meetings that she'd largely stopped going. It might have been all the spending. It could have had something to do with the temptation of a woman named Peggy, since alcohol and romance often went together for my mother. Or maybe she just felt the need to mess it all up because she wasn't comfortable with things going well. Or maybe things had been going so well that she felt invincible and that she deserved a little fun.

My mother and Mommy Fay had started entertaining on the weekends, and our house had quickly become the hub for a growing contingent of affluent lesbians in L.A. in the late 1980s, many of whom were still in the closet and married to men. On the weekends, our back-yard often filled with as many as fifty women who swam in our gigantic pool, complete with waterfall, and ate lobster and crab served with heaps of caviar at the driftwood-and-glass dining table my mother had bought for a fortune because "it makes me feel close to the ocean!"

Throughout this period, my mother generally kept me by her side, putting me on her back and pretending we were dolphins diving in and out of the ocean while we swam, and bringing me breakfast in bed with a rose in the mornings.

I'd gotten used to the situation with Fay's children, who, to my relief, still spent some evenings at their father's house. As much as I hated Emily and she hated me, I'd grown to like Robby and Chris, and the routine with them had started to feel more permanent, like they were my brothers and sister. Mom got a little antsy when Fay began referring to her as her "wife," even though it would be twenty years before gay marriage would even be possible in California. Just the idea of being tied to one person for a lifetime made my mother break out in hives. Still, to the great shock of all those who knew her, she seemed to be settling into monogamy with Fay.

I'd absorbed my mother's enthusiasm for our new family by osmosis and started bragging to anyone who would listen at my new preschool—a Waldorf school in Northridge called Highland Hall, where the teachers told me gnomes and fairies lived in the forest that was the school grounds, and I believed them—that I was "more special" than everyone else, because while most kids have only one mommy, I had two. My mother probably could have thought through this language a bit more carefully, given how obnoxious I sounded repeating it, but if any of the other kids or parents at this new school were judging us, as the kids and parents had judged Fay's children at their Catholic school, I was oblivious to it.

Things started to go wrong a few months after Kaitlyn's first birthday, when my mother returned in crutches from a weekend trip with Mommy Fay to Santa Fe. My mother explained that she'd been walking up to a toy store—in a new pair of boots meant to protect her from the snow—when she'd slipped on some ice and cracked her patella in two places on the curb. What she left out of her story was what had happened the night before the accident, when she'd gotten the idea to pop a bottle of chardonnay. It would have been my mother's ten-years-sober birthday in a few weeks, and she'd celebrated by getting drunk. The next morning she'd had the accident, which she took as a sign from the universe that she'd made a big mistake. She promised herself she would never take a sip of alcohol again.

Soon after the New Mexico trip, over the course of a single week, Fay had a multimillion-dollar property in escrow fall out because of rapidly climbing interest rates, and my mother had a different multimillion-dollar mortgage contract with a large bank in New York also fall apart. It seemed all our recent good fortune was a last hurrah before a housing crash, partially set off by Iraq's invasion of Kuwait, and with it ballooning oil prices, and partially due to rapidly rising interest rates, a credit crunch, and a sharp drop in consumer demand. Not only had my mother spent every dime we had on new furniture, a white BMW, pets, and private school, but in anticipation of the new deals that were set to close in the following weeks, she'd already spent half of what she expected to take in, using credit cards to plan a two-week vacation to Maui for the whole family. Here we were in this big playhouse with no income, tens of thousands of dollars in debt, no prospective clients, and Mom on crutches.

Unsure of what to do, my mother decided not to do anything at all. Instead, she sat in front of the green Italian marble fireplace in her bedroom, her broken knee propped on a pillow, and ordered twelve bottles of the finest wines available from the local liquor store, which were promptly delivered to our doorstep.

That's when the parties really started.

The green fireplace in my mother's bedroom was now always roaring, even when it was ninety degrees out. And the more wine she drank, the less she left her bed. The rest of the party made its way to the bedroom, where my mother and Mommy Fay now held court in their pajamas. They called themselves "the lesbian John and Yoko," which amused my mother endlessly. It seemed that the only time the reality of the situation—mounting credit card bills, the lack of client prospects, my school tuition, which was now several months overdue—registered was when she was sober, so naturally, my mother resolved to be sober less and less often. Fay got progressively nervous, wondering aloud what they were going to do, to which my mother responded that Fay needed to "trust in the universe," and that a solution would present itself.

Most days, I could walk into any room in the house and find it filled with stylish women. My mother would explain that so-and-so was a Swedish "heiress," or such and such person was Portuguese royalty, married to a famous jazz musician. Mom had slept with many of these women and loved to share their interesting and colorful backgrounds with me. Few if any stood out to me except for a redhead named Peggy Caserta, who my mother said was a "legend"—famous for having been Janis Joplin's lover and for "launching the Grateful Dead in her garage" in San Francisco in the sixties. Peggy commanded the room with her wild stories, which she told with dramatic gestures and long pauses. Peggy and I would play croquet together for hours in our giant backyard, and she'd by turns thrill me and make me furious because she refused, unlike everyone else, to let me win.

As the economy collapsed and my mother's debt increased, inside our little bubble, we were living like anything was possible. Each day, more women showed up. The doorbell would ring when cases of champagne and merlot were delivered, each bottle costing hundreds of dollars, which we no longer had, and which my mother just continued to put on new credit cards and checks that started to bounce.

I had free rein to do whatever I wanted, prancing happily through the house amid a twenty-four-hour party. My father would come over and put me, Kaitlyn, and Ziggy in a red wagon and race us around the house, gliding across the floors until one of us inevitably spilled out onto the marble. If I ever wanted to find my live-in nanny, Alba, I'd just go around opening closet doors until I found her asleep with her one-year-old curled up next to her. Throughout all this, my step-brother Robby continued walking around with a paper bag over his head, perhaps, in retrospect, because he felt uncomfortable with my mother's new habit of traipsing through the house completely nude with her new reptile, Egypt, on her shoulder.

Sometimes things were just downright weird. One day my mother hung up the phone with some business prospect she'd been chatting with, rose out of bed, threw a robe over her flannel pajamas like she meant business, and announced to everyone that she had "a plan!"

The "plan" revealed itself to be another multilevel marketing scheme. Mom had pawned the last remaining jewelry she still had from her parents to fund an infomercial for water filters, the multilevel's signature product, and then had a team of plumbers come by to install giant plastic water filter heads on every faucet in our house while a team of electricians put telephones in every room, some closets and bathrooms included, because Mom insisted that wherever she was standing, she needed to be able to answer the calls from all the millions of prospective customers who she was sure would dial the 800 number advertised on the infomercials. This wasn't just another get-rich-quick, we're-going-to-be-millionaires ploy. This was my mother's one and only idea to save us from ruin. It would be different from all the other failed pyramids and multilevels, she assured her more skeptical friends, because—rather than holding meetings at our house and calling everyone in her phone book to sign them up under her—she'd had the brilliant idea to use the television to reach the masses! She felt like a genius. My father, too, was giddy with excitement. Mom had put him in a position directly under her in the water filter company, which meant both were sure that after the infomercials ran, they'd be swimming in cash.

After the infomercials ran, for reasons beyond my mother's control, the multilevel didn't pan out, at which point she realized that she would not be able to buy back all her precious family heirlooms, and that we would not be millionaires anytime soon. To make matters worse, she didn't feel in love with Fay any longer.

"Money problems just make everything look ugly," she'd later reflect. She hoped the spark would return if they could turn things around financially. She felt she could not break up with Fay, that it would not only devastate her but confuse all the kids, especially Kaitlyn, who was attached to Mommy Fay at the hip since birth.

Debra was out of ideas. The housing crisis was now in full swing, and it had left the multimillion-dollar houses unsellable. The developer who had lent us our home wanted the gay Brady Bunch out. My mother and Mommy Fay were not just tens of thousands but several hundreds of thousands of dollars in debt.

Then one evening, while my stepsiblings were with their father, Mom showed up after having been gone all day trying to find a new job and announced that she, Mommy Fay, Kaitlyn, and I were all going out for a much-needed family dinner. She took my hand in hers with a strong grasp that I had started to miss, and we got into the car and went to the Bistro Garden in Beverly Hills so I could order my favorite dessert, chocolate soufflé. As Kaitlyn, her face covered in red sauce from her spaghetti, made silly expressions across from me at the table, I watched as my mother's mood started to change from loving to belligerent. I stared at the half-filled glass of red wine she was holding, which she spilled as she spoke. She poured another glass, filling my stomach with knots. Something about my mother was different, but I couldn't make sense of it.

On the drive home from dinner, in our brand-new BMW, I looked out the window at the streetlights and storefronts that jutted out and receded as my mother swerved across lanes, her left foot propped on the dashboard, as it always was. She and Mommy Fay laughed as the car took another swing into the lane next to us, and I looked over at Kaitlyn in her car seat, sound asleep.

We got home safely that night, but I couldn't sleep. Something terrible was happening to my mother that I couldn't understand. I wanted to fix it, but I didn't know how.

A few days later, I woke up, walked into my mother's room, and saw movers.

"Where are we going?" I asked my mother, wondering if, maybe, she had sorted out all our problems with a new venture, and we were moving to an even bigger house.

"We're going on a new adventure!" she proclaimed. "We're moving to a darling house with lots of trees and I'm going to get you a beautiful new birdhouse with twenty white doves, and we can have your seventh birthday party there and you're going to love it. Oh—and the best part of all! You will be sharing a bedroom with Emily."

When we pulled up in the moving van to that "darling house with lots of trees," I was sure it was haunted. At the end of a cul-de-sac in Woodland Hills, the house was big and dark, with ivy covering all the windows. I soon learned that this house belonged to Fay and was where she had lived with her ex-husband and their children before she came to live with us.

The kids simply called it "the Divorce House."

THE DIVORCE HOUSE

I sat on a wooden ledge inside a giant metal birdcage, closing my eyes tight as I tilted my head toward the sky—to where my mother had told me God lived—and prayed.

"Dear God," I whispered. "Please get rid of this family."

I had, for the past hour, been focusing my attention so intently on this prayer, to the exclusion of all else, that I was completely unaware of the fact that my hair, my flamenco dress, and my bare legs were all now covered in bird droppings from the dozen white doves sitting on several large branches above me.

Even deeply in debt and after filing for bankruptcy, my mother had continued to try to give me the world, this time by building a life-size "dove sanctuary" for me to play in with twelve doves. To me, it had sounded like a wonderful idea. Doves! A cage I could stand in!

Now, a year in, I would've gladly traded the birds for the return of the mother I loved. I made every attempt to let my mother know how I felt, but for now, my pleas, whether to God or my mother, got me nowhere. It was 1992, I was seven, and home life was filled with chaos. While Fay struggled to sell a single house, she and my mother fought constantly; when Mom wasn't drinking in bed at home or nursing a hangover, she was often just missing from the house entirely. Fay, who was a heavy-but-functional drinker, and still deeply in love with my mother even as she felt my mother pulling away, did her best to try to keep the family together, packing our lunches and making family meals. But Fay was gone a lot, too, showing houses and hoping for a sale to get us out of our financial mess.

Things hadn't all been bad since we'd moved into the Divorce House. There had been a brief few months when my mother had returned to her optimistic self after she landed a role as third-party presidential candidate Ross Perot's "civil rights coordinator." Perot was a Texas billionaire running on an Independent ticket against the incumbent, George H. W. Bush, and the Democratic nominee, Bill Clinton.

"Perot is fighting for the real people, for me and you, baby," Mom had explained to me with excitement at the idea of following in her grandfather's footsteps by getting into politics. "He's not a corrupt politician like the others."

When Perot angered my mother by saying, during a television interview, that he would likely bar homosexuals from his cabinet, she called her friends the women's rights attorney Gloria Allred and the wealthy feminist activist Peg Yorkin, and they all flew to Dallas, where Perot agreed to meet with them.

"Ross, you just lost all of Hollywood and the progressive Democrats by saying you would never have an openly gay person in your cabinet," my mother informed him.

"Well, Debra," he said with his sweet, Texas accent, "I just don't know any gay people."

"Well, Ross," she retorted, "*I* am a gay person."

She reached into her purse and pulled out a photo album full of pictures of Fay, Fay's children, and me and Kaitlyn, and put it in front of him.

"All right, well, I guess I can change my comment and say I will appoint people based on their merit," he said, at which point Gloria slipped a piece of paper in front of him saying just that, and made him sign it.

After their meeting, the *New York Times* called for a quote from Mom on Perot's reversal, and she felt like a gay rights hero when a late-night talk-show host referred to her as "Ross Perot's lesbian." The publicity had brought some scary ramifications, including anonymous death threats at my school. Mom kept Kaitlyn and me home, by her side, as she devoted herself around the clock to campaigning and fund-raising for Perot. Suddenly, all of us children were wearing oversized Ross Perot T-shirts to bed, and Mom and Mommy Fay were briefly getting along as they daydreamed about moving the whole family to Washington, DC.

When Perot dropped out of the race, and it became clear that Mom wasn't headed to the White House, she was thrown into a deep depression. Her weight had dramatically risen from all the financial stress, and she told Fay that what she needed was to spend a week alone at the Ashram, an expensive, new age wellness center in the Santa Monica Mountains above Malibu, where she hoped that by taking long hikes in the mountains with celebrities like Raquel Welch, Jane Fonda, Shirley MacLaine, and Governor Jerry Brown, and by meditating under crystals in a giant geodesic dome, she might be able to get her weight down and her drinking under control and that, in turn, she might be able to get our family back on track. Instead, she'd met a cute Italian yoga instructor at the Ashram named Marine who she promised herself she would just be friends with.

While all this was going on, I'd been left with the choice between spending a summer alone with my doves or hanging out with my step-sister, Emily, along with her three best friends who lived next door, a trio of girls, each a year older than the next, who collectively went by their last name, the Williamses.

I hated being at the Williamses' house. Their grandmother, a short-tempered, angry woman, was always in the kitchen in a plastic apron cooking fish, the smell permeating every room. The Williams parents were always in their bedroom with the door closed, screaming at each other, and the kids always had the television's audio on full blast, perhaps hoping to drown out the noise of their parents' yelling. The sounds and smells were a form of sensory torture for me.

Emily and her friends loathed having to include me in their plans, and they got a sick pleasure out of forcing me to watch reruns of *Are You Afraid of the Dark?* My mother had always been fiercely protective when it came to shielding me from anything she deemed too dark. This show was the scariest thing I had ever seen at that point and I didn't conceal it well. One of the girls would catch me holding my fists tight against my chest, my eyes squinting. She would then point this out to the others, who would erupt into laughter as they taunted me for being such a baby.

Witnessing the frightening images in the show coupled with the bullying was too much for me to take. My anxiety from both living inside my mother's alcoholic web and her crumbling relationship with Mommy Fay began to manifest in the form of panic attacks over a mounting pile of imagined fears. I believed that there were sharks in the deep end of our swimming pool and ghosts living in our toilets, and that Bloody Mary lurked behind the mirrors in our home. I couldn't swim in the pool, or go to the bathroom, or be left alone in a room with a mirror without hyperventilating. I also started to develop some obsessive-compulsive habits, switching the lights on and off in my bedroom five times when I entered or left, believing that some vague, terrible event would befall me if I didn't get the ratio right. Then I'd hop and skip my way to bed and back with an even number of hops and skips, landing on alternate feet because not doing this perfectly might, likewise, lead to immediate doom.

These new behaviors were only exacerbated after an incident that took place on the local McDonald's playground.

Our nanny, Alba, had taken Emily, Kaitlyn, and me to run around on one of the play structures that had become commonplace behind fast-food restaurants in the early nineties. As I climbed up hurriedly from one giant yellow tube to another, I noticed a cute boy playing near me. I wanted to make a good impression, so I ran up and introduced myself with my favorite opening line.

"Most people have only one mommy," I told him boldly, hands on my hips as I prepared to deliver the punch line. "But I'm special, because I have two."

I turned to run down the duct into the rainbow-colored ball pit below and ran straight into Emily; evidently, she had heard me. Her pink freckled face was lit up from the yellow plastic dome, eyes filled with rage and hatred.

"Don't ever tell anyone that we have two moms," she whispered, trembling and shaking me as she said it. "Do you hear me? It's embarrassing that our moms are lesbians!"

I felt that my mother was the greatest person on the planet, and had always assumed everyone else saw her that way. I was proud to be her daughter.

That night, I waited in bed for my mother to give me a kiss good-night, and contemplated telling her what Emily had said. I looked up at her as she walked in, dressed in the same pajamas she'd been wearing for days, and when she lay down next to me, I saw a tired look in her eyes, and that she had a glass of wine in her hand.

"Are you and Daddy married?" I asked her.

"No, sweetheart," she said, clearly flabbergasted, not realizing how much I needed her in that moment. "Your daddy and I did things a little differently than most people. We're just friends."

I decided not to tell my mother what Emily had said. I would play it safe, heed Emily's advice, and never again let anyone know about my having two moms. Hiding that my family was different would become a full-time obsession.

With my mother inaccessible to me, I was elated when my father showed up on my eighth birthday and told me he had a present for me.

"I am going to teach you a magic technique," he said, greeting me as he approached my birdcage, where I'd been sitting. "You can use this whenever you feel a scary thought or a sad feeling in your body, and like magic, it will disappear, and you will feel happy," he told me.

"Really?" I replied, thrilled at the idea.

"Really," he said. "Doesn't that sound good?"

I nodded with enthusiasm, and then watched as my father piled a piece of fruit, several pink flowers, and a postcard with an illustration of a woman with blue skin and ten arms on a small blanket between us, which he explained was our offering to the goddess Shakti. Ziggy sat next to us, nuzzling his nose in my lap and distracting me with his slobbery kisses.

"Now Chrysta," my father said, very serious. "I am about to tell you your secret word. You are the only person in the whole world who will have this secret word, and it is very important that you keep it a secret or it will lose all of its power. Do you understand?"

I nodded enthusiastically.

My father leaned in and whispered in my ear, "Ing."

"Ing?" I said, making sure I'd heard it correctly. It hardly seemed like a word at all—more like a half word that went at the end of other words, like sew*ing,* lov*ing,* hurt*ing.*

"Don't say it out loud!" my father shouted as he looked around to make sure no one else could hear, even though we were alone. He closed his eyes to re-center himself before reminding me with emphasis, "It's *your* secret word."

"I'm sorry," I apologized, sensing he was upset. He took a deep breath and gathered himself once more. "Now on the count of three," he said, "I want you to close your eyes and say your secret word over and over to yourself, but only in your head," and then in a stern voice he emphasized, *"Not out loud,"* and then, calm again, he asked, "Are you ready?"

I nodded, then closed my eyes and tried my best to think about that one word and nothing else, but my mind kept drifting.

After what felt like an hour to my small child's brain but was probably closer to five minutes, my father told me to open my eyes.

"Now don't you feel better?" he asked me.

I did. I was enjoying spending special time with my father, who had been completely focused on me for these five minutes. But later, as I ruminated over it, instead of easing my anxiety, my father's afternoon with me just made it worse. During our conversation, he'd explained the concept of reincarnation, and after I told him that I sometimes struggled to breathe (which my mother thought might be asthma), he suggested it could be something to do with a past life; perhaps I'd previously been hung in the Salem witch trials, for example, so I had that negative energy around my throat.

That night, inside our house, as I tried to wrap my head around having been hung in the late 1600s, my mother presented me with her own special birthday present: a potbellied pig named Polkadot, who she'd had flown in from a breeder in the Midwest.

"The pig is the most intelligent animal on the planet, above a dolphin and a dog," she told me with a big smile. Polkadot was the size of a puppy and came with diapers and a baby bottle, which I fed him with enthusiastically before he gave a few gentle snorts and fell asleep curled up with my mother, Kaitlyn, and me in Mom's bed.

A few days later, as I cuddled with Polkadot, my mother embarked on a business trip to Iowa with my father to visit a man named John Hagelin, who ran the Maharishi University there, and who was the head of the Transcendental Meditation movement in the United States. Hagelin was powerful and wealthy, and this trip was meant to be an informal job interview between Hagelin and my mother, as he wanted help developing a political arm for his movement and my mother had made a name for herself as a strategist in third-party politics after the Perot campaign. My father had jumped at the opportunity to join her, since he idolized Hagelin. Mom figured maybe she could get Jeffrey a job, too.

It was unclear to my mother how my father was making money to pay his bills, outside of her occasional "donations," but his lifestyle was meager and didn't require much, so she assumed that he was just working as a masseur. Still, she had started to worry about him again. He had not taken her advice to ask Heather to marry him, and his reluctance to commit was creating problems in that relationship; when Heather came over, which was less often, she and my father were often arguing. When Heather didn't come over, Dad would sometimes disappear into a spare bedroom to "meditate" for several hours, until my mother finally went looking for him. She'd walk in and find Jeffrey taking a massive hit from a bong as he sat in the lotus position with his eyes closed.

"The weed helps me go much deeper with the meditation," he told her.

My mother hoped that a job with the TM guru might refocus my father and help him settle down. Instead, it had the opposite effect.

Dad always had a difficult time traveling. He had a fear not just of airplanes, but also of freeways. Just getting him to come over to our house was a struggle of wills. But he was invigorated at the chance to spend time with John in Iowa, so he decided to get over his fears.

When they returned from their trip, my father discovered to his horror that his beloved Ziggy was dead. My father was no longer living with Heather, and was actually in between homes, so before leaving for the trip with my mother, he had decided to leave Ziggy on an empty boat that belonged to a friend, next to a nice patch of grass where the dog could roam. He'd left out plenty of food and water, and Heather had agreed to come check on Ziggy once a day. But apparently, an angry neighbor had become irritated with Ziggy's barking and decided to call animal control. My dad drove to get Ziggy back as soon as he got the call, but it was too late. They'd put Ziggy to sleep, they explained, because he was "dehydrated."

My father lost his mind.

"Why the fuck didn't you just give him some water?!" he howled, out of his mind with grief. He cried hysterically for days, blaming animal control, then blaming Heather for not picking Ziggy up when the first call came in, and then blaming my mother for taking him to Iowa.

My mother decided to host a funeral for Ziggy in our backyard with the entire family present. I stood next to Emily, Robby, Chris, and little

Kaitlyn, watching, confused, as Mom came outside with a large white sheet with which my father carefully wrapped Ziggy's giant, lifeless body. My father, with Fay's help, gently lifted Ziggy into the ground. As Fay started to pour dirt on top of Ziggy, my father couldn't take it anymore, and he jumped into the pit, crying hysterically as he hugged Ziggy's dead body. He refused to let anyone cover the grave, at which point my mother, feeling this was too horrific for the children, started screaming at him to get out of the pit.

I desperately wanted to help make my father feel better, so I walked around collecting whatever treasures I could find in the yard—little rose stems, and leaves, and acorns. I went to my room and placed them in a little box I cherished, then came back out and found my father crumpled on the ground next to the grave.

"Jeffrey, Chrysta's trying to get your attention," my mother said as I placed the box beside my father on the ground, hoping it might cheer him up.

"Leave me the fuck alone!" he shouted at my mother, his eyes swollen and red from crying, hardly noticing I was there. "This is all your fucking fault!"

"What are you talking about?" she barked back, now defensive. "I gave you my best thousand-thread-count sheet to put Ziggy in!"

"You never let Ziggy inside when he wanted to come in when he was alive! He had a bad life because of you!" my father yelled.

"Jeffrey, that's insane!"

He stood up and walked toward his car to leave. The gift I'd given him was on the ground.

To get away from the chaos surrounding Ziggy's death, my mother decided it was time for a family trip. We were going to Lake Arrowhead to celebrate Christmas: Mommy Fay, me, my four siblings, and Mom, along with her "yoga instructor," Marine, who, my mother had explained to Mommy Fay, would help with the kids.

"Can I bring Polkadot?" I asked.

"Polkadot is going to live on a farm tomorrow," my mother told me with a smile to cover the guilt she felt over having just decided to return Polkadot to the breeder. Mom wanted more than anything to make me happy, and what more exciting gift could she have given her eight-year-old child than an adorable baby pig? But she had realized why most people did not own pigs as pets, no matter how smart they were, after Polkadot kept us up all night with his snorting and scratching to get into the bedroom with us. From then on, there was always some farm where Mom claimed that the animals she didn't want to keep went, as if it was a better situation for them, and therefore actually a positive development. The question of why we got the animals in the first place always loomed but wasn't discussed.

Once we got to Arrowhead, my mother spent the next two days distracted as she drank and flirted with Marine, then suddenly announced that she and Marine had to rush home on important business. Poor lovesick Fay, in denial about what was really going on, was left to clean up our rental house in Arrowhead and pack up the car.

Rather than go inside with the other siblings, I sat outside and played alone in the snow, building a family of snow people, then getting anxious, because their heads were lopsided, and their faces weren't perfect. I tried to focus on my magic word, but then remembered the Salem witch trials and just felt like I was being strangled.

After Lake Arrowhead, a huge fight erupted after a game of hide-and-seek, when Robby, Emily, and I found a bottle of wine, some cash, and a breakup letter my mother had written to Fay—which in hindsight my mother would say she had decided not to give Fay—in one of our hiding spots. Robby showed the letter to Fay, who, in tears, dragged a mattress from one of the spare bedrooms into the living room. A few days later, my mother got a disturbing phone call from the telephone company while she was out at a business meeting.

"Hello, is this Debra Olson?"

"Yes, this is she," she said.

"Ma'am, do you have a three-year-old blond child and a Dalmatian?"

"Yes," she said, now concerned.

"Well, ma'am," the man from the phone company said, "one of our telephone operators was up on a pole and just saw your daughter running naked with the Dalmatian through an empty field."

My mother realized that her drinking was out of control, that she had been so distracted by the drama around her affair with Marine that she hadn't properly screened our new nanny, who had fallen asleep while I played by myself in the dove house and Kaitlyn and Denmark let themselves out into the street and into an empty field. Debra realized, as she sped home to retrieve her beloved Kaitlyn, that she wasn't giving either of us what we needed. She knew she had to leave Fay—I was not thriving in this family unit, and neither was she. Still, she was filled with guilt about what separating from Fay would do to Kaitlyn. She tried several times, unsuccessfully, to quit drinking on her own, then decided to go to an AA meeting, her first in several years.

A few weeks later, as I sat in my birdcage, cupping one of my doves, playing in some faraway land in my head, my mother came to find me.

She was, to my great shock, in a happy mood and present and sober.

"Chrysta," she said. "Do you want to go on an adventure?"

"What kind of adventure?" I asked.

"A special outing, with just me, you, and Kaitlyn. How does that sound?"

It sounded wonderful.

As we walked toward her car, I wondered what the day had in store.

"Are we going to the park?" I asked.

"No, honey."

"Are we getting ice cream?"

"No, Beanie, you will see!"

"Are we going to visit Daddy?"

"No," she said, pausing, perhaps thinking about my father. But whatever she was thinking she didn't share with me.

"You'll see. Just get in the car," she said, holding Kaitlyn in her arms and buckling her in.

STABLE SABLE

We pulled up to a large white house that looked like a contemporary art museum. I followed my mother up the front steps as we pressed the doorbell, and then, when no one answered, she just opened the door. She had obviously been here before.

I followed her through the house, which was filled with 1980s deco furniture and mirrored walls covered in framed movie posters that were also hung along the giant staircase. All the posters featured the same woman's face. I wondered if this was my mother's new friend.

"Sable!" my mother called out at the top of her lungs.

"Out here!" a woman's voice yelled back.

Kaitlyn, my mother, and I all walked out to the backyard, toward a large jelly bean–shaped pool.

"Hi, Deb!" the woman's voice called toward us, and I quickly scanned the pool to put a face to the voice. In the center, on a bright blue plastic raft, I saw a beautiful, tan, topless woman covered in tanning oil. She didn't have the same face as the woman in all the movie posters.

She started waving at Kaitlyn and me with a big, enthusiastic smile, like she was expecting us, then paddled to the pool's edge and climbed out, throwing a towel around her body and kneeling down to greet me.

"Well, you must be Chrysta," she said with a thick New York accent. "I've heard *sooo* much about you."

She turned to Kaitlyn, who was now three.

"And you must be Kaitlyn," she added with a warm smile. She was good with kids.

She leaned back and took both of us in, hands on her hips, thinking.

"I've got something special for you two girls," she said, motioning for us to follow her back into the house and into the large kitchen, where she opened the state-of-the-art 1992 freezer and pulled out two giant ice cream sandwiches.

Kaitlyn and I sat at a kitchen island, on black metal-and-leather chairs, eating our ice creams as my mother, Sable, and I all talked.

It turned out this big house belonged to Sable's boss, the woman in the posters, who was a comedian and famous actress named Lily Tomlin. Sable was supposed to be in Los Angeles for only a few weeks, on an assignment as Lily's assistant, before returning to New York, where she lived. My mother had met her at that first AA meeting she'd attended. There was such an energy between them when they sat next to each other that they wound up holding hands.

Sable walked over to a sound system and put on a record. A woman's voice—the most mesmerizing voice I'd ever heard—came on.

"Debra, you have never played Judy Garland for Chrysta?" Sable asked my mother with a look of exaggerated shock on her face. "We are going to change that this minute!"

Mom started dancing and asked me if I wanted to join her. As I danced with my mother and Kaitlyn joined in, Sable disappeared into a closet and came out holding up a cassette tape.

"Chrysta," she said as she pressed the cassette into my palm, "I want you to have this. It's Judy Garland at the Palace. You have to promise you won't lose it."

"I promise," I said as I watched my mother smile at Sable in a way I hadn't seen her smile in a long time. My mother turned back toward me, sat on one of the black leather chairs, and plopped me onto her lap, kissing my head.

I looked over at Sable's smiling, tan face and her curly black hair and that deep New York accent, and decided then and there that whoever this woman was, I wanted her in my life. I loved the act that Sable was putting on to impress my mother by being over-the-top great with kids. I loved her type A, rough-around-the-edges personality. I loved the way she bossed my mother around. Most of all, I loved that she had somehow brought back the mother I had lost completely for the past few years. I was also thrilled to get to be alone with my mother and Kaitlyn, without Emily, Robby, and Chris. We were our tiny family unit once more, and I was returned to my rightful place as the oldest child, with all the power and attention—even if it was just for the afternoon.

After an hour, my mother said it was time to go home. Sable gave us all hugs goodbye, and Kaitlyn, my mother, and I all hopped back into the car.

"What do you think of Sable?" my mother asked as we were stopped at a red light and she fumbled to get my new cassette tape working in the car stereo.

"I love her," I said, definitively.

She smiled and drove on. I could tell she was thinking about something. I wondered what it was. After a few moments, she looked at me.

"How would you feel if we were to move out of the house with Mommy Fay and Emily and Chris and Robby and then moved in with Sable as Mommy Sable?"

"I think that's a great idea," I said without pause.

I clasped my eight-year-old hands together, closed my eyes, and tried not to cry with joy as I listened to Judy Garland belting out "Over the Rainbow." God had heard my prayers.

A few weeks later, I watched in horror as Kaitlyn wept hysterically while Mom buckled her into her car seat. Mommy Fay, Emily, Chris, and Robby all stood at the edge of the cul-de-sac waving and saying goodbye. Mom had to physically restrain Kaitlyn from climbing out of the car seat to run back to Fay. I sat with my seat belt on as we drove away from the Divorce House, leaving that family behind, and I looked at my traumatized sister, then out the window at Fay, who fell to her knees in tears, her hands over her face. I felt horrible and guilty. I'd prayed for this. I'd told Mom to do it. And at no time, as I did these things, had I really thought about how it would affect poor Kaitlyn or Mommy Fay.

We drove from the Divorce House to a quaint three-bedroom in Studio City with a pool. Mom was thirty days sober and had secured a stable nine-to-five job in a new mortgage brokerage in Beverly Hills with, for once, a fantastic boss, while Sable had quit her job with Lily Tomlin, canceled her flight to New York, and decided to take on the role of stay-at-home parent in this new family unit. Mom had just closed her first mortgage deal, and the commission from that, combined with some savings Sable had, had given them enough for the first few months' rent and a security deposit.

Our new life with Sable was like the first day of spring when the apple blossoms open and the roses bloom. It was filled with mornings by the pool, sipping iced tea and eating meticulously cut tuna sandwiches with no crusts, and lazy afternoons in front of the television watching Turner Classic Movies. Sable quickly introduced me to *Meet Me in St. Louis* and *Funny Girl* and New York City and Broadway, where she took me to see *Phantom of the Opera* and *Cats*.

Sable's true magic was her effect on my mother. Suddenly, my mother got dressed in the morning rather than staying in bed all day. Her flannel pajamas were replaced with silk ones whose tops and bottoms matched. She was on time when she picked me up from school. Lunches were accompanied by love notes in her whimsical handwriting; I opened them at recess, unable to wait until lunchtime. I swam in the pool without any fear of sharks and slept in a room with two giant mirrors on my closet doors and never once worried about Bloody Mary. Kaitlyn, too, was doing well. She missed Mommy Fay often, but she was also able to sleep in her own bed for the first time, across the hall from me. And she and I were bonding in a way we never had. We spent hours in that hallway between our rooms, giggling as we realized the walls of the hallway were close enough to each other that we could climb them, as we raced each other to the ceiling.

I would later come to understand that Sable's mystical effect on my family wasn't some enchanted spell; it was sobriety. Sable was twelve years sober. She had helped bring my mother back into her old AA meetings after several years of relapsing, and returned her to the present, optimistic woman I had missed so much. My mother was also in love with Sable in a way she'd never been with Fay, and Sable's organized, take-charge way tempered my mother's more disorganized, impulsive one. Sable was not open to the idea of a zoo like the one my mother had left behind with Fay. Instead, she agreed to add a single dog, a boxer named Sadie, and finally, at my mother's begging, two Scottish fold kitten siblings who I named Sweetie Pie and Little Owl, and two tiny tortoises, each the size of a fifty-cent piece, which Sable agreed to only because they were very low-maintenance and Mom told her she "needed them for my happiness." One was a Sri Lankan star tortoise, from India, and the other was an African sulcata. Mom named them Machu and Picchu. And we still had Denmark, the only animal that remained from the Fay period.

Sable ran our house like she was the head chef at a very organized restaurant. She was a professional caterer by training and quickly implemented strict rules, including consistent mealtimes and bed-times. She was what my mother called "neurotic," and being intensely neurotic myself, I adored every second of this newly predictable, tidy existence.

My mother was the biggest kid of us all, and like me, she thrived with all this enforced, rigid structure. Sable even got her to adhere to a diet, and my mother finally lost some of the weight she'd been carrying since she gave birth to me a decade earlier. Mom's childlike personality became charming, and harmless, and fun. We were always laughing and playing, as she got us piles of presents because she could afford to again, and she read us *Siddhartha* and *The Prophet*, which she said would be "important for your lives" as we fell asleep at night. I watched her get dressed in bright orange or purple or aqua power suits, or in tight skirts, and head to work every morning. She always had bright red lipstick and perfectly painted bright red nails you could spot from a mile away.

I started to feel pride again, and my anxiety went away. Under Sable's watch, I'd switched schools and finally learned how to read with her careful guidance and a program called Hooked on Phonics. And after carefully hiding my new mom from everyone for several months, telling people that Sable was my mother's "business partner," I even decided to open up to a girl at school named Malena after I overheard her saying that her mother had a "partner" who lived with them.

That day Malena and I talked for four hours straight late into the night, and when I went to school the next day it was with a skip in my step; I was happy to have a real friend who knew the real me. Slowly, all the shame that had knotted up in my stomach about my unconventional family dispersed. My mother, too, was prouder than ever. She and Sable even went on a talk show on national television, to show the world what a happy gay family looked like: exactly like a happy, traditional family. Kaitlyn, too, had started forming pride around our identity. In kindergarten, she sat all her friends down during recess and announced, "You're all going to have to accept me for who I am: I'm a lesbian."

Life felt safe. If you'd told me then that in less than six months Sable would disappear forever from my life, I wouldn't have believed it. I had let this woman into my heart in a way I'd never done with any of my mother's other girlfriends. I loved her just as much as I loved my mother.

On the morning of my ninth birthday, it took us nearly twenty minutes to get through the presents, not just because of how many cards my mother had spent the last two weeks filling with her thoughts about me, but also because she had to take several breaks to collect herself after bursting into tears. She was always spontaneously crying like this in those days, but they were happy, grateful tears. I didn't mind.

"It's from me and Sable," my mother said at one point, handing me a carefully wrapped square package.

"What is it?" I asked, turning it over in my hands, curious.

"Just open it and you will see, Chrysta!" Sable said with her thick New York accent.

I started to tear up as I unwrapped a framed photograph, professionally shot, of two red foxes snuggling in the snow. The red fox was my favorite animal, and I'd seen this gift in a catalog months earlier and had been begging my mother for it almost every day since.

Sable got out her drill and hung the photograph over my bed as I went off to get dressed before all the kids in my class arrived for my birthday party. My mother was anxious but doing a good job hiding it from me. She had an even more special present on the way: my father. My mother had decided not to tell me about this second gift because she was worried he might not actually show up.

Since we'd moved in with Sable, I hadn't seen a lot of my father. I missed him, but I was also okay seeing him less now that my home life had become so beautiful.

After Ziggy died, he had decided to try to get Heather pregnant to bring Ziggy's soul back through reincarnation. This registered as insane to my mother, but it's what came next that really troubled her. Heather did get pregnant, my father was convinced that Ziggy had returned, and Heather decided to put her foot down.

"Jeffrey, either you marry me," she'd threatened, "or I am getting an abortion. I do not want to raise a kid on my own and I need to know you are serious about this relationship."

When Jeffrey refused to marry Heather, she made good on her threat. My father sat in the waiting room at the abortion clinic, in tears as he experienced the loss of Ziggy all over again. A few weeks later, Heather moved to Florida.

My mother decided it was not her responsibility to save Jeffrey, and even if it was, she had to face the possibility that doing so might not be feasible. She was back in her AA meetings and trying to live her life soberly, which hadn't left a lot of room for my dad. Sable also did not have any patience for my father's eccentricities.

When my birthday finally came around, my mother hadn't consulted Sable; she'd just decided to call my father and ask him to come over. Thankfully, he was his fun and endearing self for the afternoon. The party was held outside, and he played his guitar and sang for all my friends, and he chased me around the house with a hose (which Sable wasn't happy about, but it sent me into hysterical laughter).

As we played, Mom went upstairs to find the birthday candles and was startled when she found a woman sitting on the edge of her bed, rifling through my mother's address book.

"Can I help you?" Mom asked.

The woman didn't look up. "How do you know Warren Beatty?" she said. "And Eva Gabor?"

"That's none of your business," my mother said, shocked by the brazenness of this person.

The woman finally looked up, then toward a bronze statue of an angel on my mother's dresser—one of her most prized possessions.

"Where did you buy that?" the woman asked.

Mom breathed in and took in the appearance of this woman, who revealed herself to be Donna, my friend Sarah's mother. Donna was peculiar. She had long, unpainted fingernails that curled at the tips, and she was wearing a tattered purple dress. She wore deep purple eye shadow and had a strong, imposing jaw and long, thinning, dyed blond hair with short, ragged bangs that looked as though she had cut them over the sink.

My mother ignored Donna's question about the angel and walked over to grab her address book out of the woman's hands. She then grabbed the candles she had come in for and asked Donna to leave the bedroom.

My mother returned outside, her red nails gleaming as she clutched my birthday cake, lit with nine candles, and everyone gathered around to sing "Happy Birthday."

"Make a wish," my mother said to me as I stood with my father, my two sober mothers, and Kaitlyn.

Closing my eyes and blowing out the candles, I whispered to myself, "I wish that it will stay like this forever."

Around the holidays, my mother and Sable were asked to appear on a national talk show to discuss our family in front of a live audience. They knew they were taking a risk by going on the show, but they hoped that by increasing the visibility of gay parents they would help defuse some of the fear and hostility around the issue that was rampant in 1993. A group of my mother's colleagues saw the show and were outraged. They teamed up and told the CEO of the mortgage brokerage that it was "us or the lesbian." The CEO, a warm, good-natured man named Charlie, whose mother had survived Auschwitz and who hated bigotry in all forms, told the group they could go fuck themselves. They all left in one mass exodus, and his brokerage went under.

My mother, trying to stay optimistic, decided to invest everything she and Sable had in a new business venture. She was going to make a fortune on gay and lesbian expos. The expo business was booming in the U.S.: businesses could sign up to run booths at huge, multiday events and sell their products or services, network, and get to know a new community. African American expos were huge, but, according to my mother, "no one had done an expo focused on the gay and lesbian community." She thought the idea was ingenious and developed a business plan to launch expos in Los Angeles, San Francisco, Chicago, and New York.

"We are going to show the power of gay dollars in corporate America!" she boasted confidently to me and Kaitlyn. Our oversized Ross Perot T-shirts were replaced with new T-shirts that said, in big rainbow letters, UNITY EXPOS.

It rained in Los Angeles the day of the first big Unity Expo, which

Mom had spent months, and every dime she had, organizing, and the turnout was underwhelming. This meant Mom hadn't made enough in tickets and sales to recoup the losses—or to pay back the vendors, who were angry. She felt sure she could make Unity Expos a success, with enough time and capital, but she couldn't get anyone to fund the project.

Without any other job leads, and unable to open any credit cards because of having filed for bankruptcy back when she was with Fay, she started charging our school tuition and all our family bills to Sable's credit cards, which led to stress and fear, which led to fighting.

Mom asked Sable if she could find a temporary position as a chef (since Sable was a professional cook) or as a therapist (since Sable had several master's degrees in psychology), just to hold us over while she figured out her next move. Sable just froze, unable to muster the energy to go out and get any kind of job. She spent the next several afternoons lying out by the pool in silence while Mom scrambled to find another job.

"Debra, I've never been good in the work area," Sable confessed one morning in the kitchen as I sat scooping Cheerios into my mouth, trying to pretend she and my mother hadn't been fighting, trying to pretend that this, too, wasn't about to come crashing down. "I thought that could be your part in the play."

In January, the great Northridge earthquake of 1994 hit, one of the worst earthquakes in U.S. history. Its epicenter was very close to our sweet little house in Studio City.

At 4:30 a.m., I woke up in my bedroom to everything shaking. My mother ran in to grab me from under my covers, and then we ran in the dark to get Kaitlyn, whose room was across the hall. All the pipes in the bathrooms had broken, so water was spraying all over the place. I stepped over broken glass from fallen TVs and mirrored furniture that had turned upside down and followed Mom, carrying Kaitlyn, out the front door and into the street, where we stood, terrified, with our neighbors in the dark. An aftershock almost as big as the original earthquake came a few moments later, and it felt like the street might split in two under our feet.

After it was over, Kaitlyn and I were too scared to sleep in our own rooms, so we moved our mattresses into Mom's walk-in closet to be close to her and Sable. As we all grabbed brooms and started cleaning up the mess the following morning, I felt hopeful that the disaster would bring the family back to normal.

For several days, terror and love suppressed their fighting, but a few nights after the earthquake, I woke up to hushed but intense arguing coming from Sable and my mother's bedroom. I crawled quietly out of my bed in their closet, past Kaitlyn, who was sleeping deeply, and watched through a slit in the closet door as Sable picked up a giant, heavy quartz crystal from her bedside table and threw it at my mother's head in a rage. The crystal missed my mother's head, but she started screaming in shock, then crying, while Sable continued to rage, and I knew there would be no going back to normal for us.

"Where's Sable?" I asked the next morning.

"She went on vacation," my mother replied, forcing herself to sound upbeat. Somehow, it didn't occur to me then that I would never see or speak to Sable again. Or maybe I knew. I just didn't want to believe it.

We were so behind in our rent that the landlord and his wife started coming by every day to ask us to move out. Mom changed the locks so they couldn't get inside.

One afternoon I watched while she yelled into her giant cordless telephone at Aunt Diane for refusing to help us pack up the house, and I wondered what had happened between my mother and my aunt, who I hadn't seen a lot of in the Sable period. She had a new girl-friend now, a famous comedian and gay rights activist named Robin Tyler, and for some reason, she had largely disappeared from our lives. As my mother yelled into the phone from her bedroom upstairs, she accidentally tripped, falling down the stairs and breaking her knee for the third time.

Mom, now all by herself, nursing a broken heart and on crutches, was also bankrupt with no savings and no credit cards with any room on them. She was too proud to ask Aunt Diane to take us in, and had no second or third girlfriend lined up, not even a car to drive—because Sable came back in the middle of the night and stole it. I watched as my mother stared blankly at that bronze angel statue on her bedside table, a tear streaming down her face, trying not to lose it in front of me. I was overwhelmed because I didn't know how to help.

"It's going to be okay, Mama," I told her as she closed her eyes and started chanting some words I did not understand.

"Namu myoho renge kyo," she sang, trying to keep her voice steady and focused. *"Namu myoho renge kyo. Namu myoho renge kyo."*

THE GUESTHOUSE

After Sable left, we sold all our furniture and whatever possessions hadn't been destroyed in the earthquake in a sidewalk sale, and then moved into a tiny, five-hundred-square-foot guesthouse in Tarzana that belonged to Donna, the woman in purple who had been sitting on the edge of my mother's bed and reading her address book at my birthday party. The "crazy witch," as we called her, lived with her daughter, Sarah, in a dark, one-story ranch house next door that seemed to be perpetually under construction. We didn't have any money to pay Donna rent, so Mom arranged to give her various antiques and artworks she'd collected over the years, starting with the bronze angel. It now sat in the center of Donna's living room coffee table, beside a glass ashtray filled with Donna's cigarette butts.

Donna's house was packed with mahogany furniture, dressers overflowing with old chiffon nightgowns from the seventies, and piles of boxes that made walking through her house and garage feel like making one's way through a mouse maze. I would later come to understand that Donna was addicted to crystal meth, which perhaps fueled the hoarding and explained why she was so irritable, especially if Sarah, Kaitlyn, my mother, or I didn't follow one of her *many* house rules. Donna was insane, but she was also a genius and occasionally lovely, sometimes mesmerizing us with Mozart concertos on her piano or spending hours teaching me how to paint blown Easter eggs and turn them into ornaments. She also had a quirky habit of running on our guesthouse roof in the middle of the night with her much younger boyfriend, Bob, who worked construction and was leading Donna's remodel, along with their two white wolves, Easy and Breezy. While Easy and Breezy were adorable when Donna first got them as puppies, as they grew older, they became utterly terrifying, since, as Donna explained, they were 70 percent wolf; their playful habit of nipping at our heels to say hello was starting to hurt and feel dangerous.

Thankfully, because Donna was an animal lover, we got to bring Denmark and Sweetie Pie and Little Owl along with us as part of our traveling family. (Sadie the dog had disappeared with Sable and the car.) My mother, Kaitlyn, and I now shared one bed and one rusty toilet, and my mother borrowed the handyman's barely functioning old gray Volvo to get around. The new situation made Mom deeply unhappy, and she often wept at night when she thought I was asleep, or raged unexpectedly over small things, like dishes piling up in the tiny, rust-corroded sink, or if Kaitlyn or I was taking too long getting into the car for school.

Chanting *"Namu myoho renge kyo"* was Mom's new "plan." The words were based on the teachings of a thirteenth-century Japanese priest named Nichiren Daishonin. For seven years, in her late teens and early twenties, Mom had devoted her life to Nichiren Shoshu Buddhism, proselytizing the religion around the United States in a senior role in the organization; traveling to Japan seven times to visit its leader, President Ikeda; giving guidance to young women who traveled from all over the country to seek her counsel; and chanting every morning before the sun rose. She painted images for Kaitlyn and me of her life when she was a young woman, waking at dawn in a Japanese monastery overlooking Mount Fuji and watching the sun rise through the fog as she ate a single bowl of rice for the day.

If we chanted these words, she explained—once in the morning when we woke up, and once in the evening before we went to sleep—and if we concentrated all our mental energy on this framed scroll, the Gohonzon, that hung in a frame on the wall above our bed, all our wishes would come true, and we would become enlightened beings and help create world peace.

Kaitlyn and I listened in awe to Mom's stories, though some part of me had started to become suspicious of secret words and magic scrolls, and sometimes I resisted chanting. She'd physically drag me outside to belt out oms to the moon and I'd eventually give in, mostly just to make her happy. The moon brought her peace. She also seemed to believe that our oms would radiate out into the universe and that the universe would respond by improving our finances and getting us out of this "shithole," which is what Mom had taken to calling where we now lived.

Sometimes I tried to lovingly suggest alternatives.

"Mom, what if, instead of chanting, you used our computer to print out a resume, and went to apply for some jobs at clothing stores on Ventura?" I would ask.

"Don't be ridiculous, Chrysta!" she would bark. "Jobs like that don't cover private school! I am way overqualified for those jobs!"

A big part of Mom's stress seemed to be around how to keep us in school. She valued education, and had always dreamed of sending us to the best schools, but she couldn't scrape together enough money to keep both of us enrolled. The first day of first grade, she dropped Kaitlyn at Wilbur, the local charter school, and then drove by a few hours later. Her heart broke when she saw Kaitlyn through a metal fence, sitting alone at lunchtime. Mom couldn't bear the idea of tearing my sister away from all the friends she'd been with for the past few years, especially not after all the other changes in our lives, so after that, she came up with a creative way to keep us enrolled where we'd been for free: by promising to put the principal in her will.

I really didn't mind living in Sarah's guesthouse for the years we spent there, even if it was small and cluttered. It was cozy sharing a bed with Mom and Kaitlyn once again. There was a small loft above us that Kaitlyn and I loved to play in—we'd pretend we were princesses stuck up in a castle—and the backyard had a giant fruit-bearing pomegranate tree that we picked and ate from with relish. I was just glad that my mother was still sober, and that this new place had a back-yard where she could sit and watch the tortoises, Machu and Picchu, grazing in the grass.

There were no rules now that Sable was gone. We could eat waffles for dinner, binge on Fruit Roll-Ups for lunch and Sour Punch Straws for breakfast. We blasted a Spanish dance hit called "Macarena" until midnight for two weeks straight. My mother—possibly because she was too tired to create any rules, or because she hated rules herself—would build pillow forts for us that no one cleaned up, and laugh as we threw rotten pears at cars, or made prank calls to random people in the yellow pages.

All this unsupervised fun helped temper the sadness I felt over the loss of Sable. As the days wore on and Sable didn't return from vacation, I finally realized that people did not just perpetually take vacations, that this was a lie my mother had told me to soften the landing of the truth. Sometimes I thought about asking where Sable was living now, or what had happened with their relationship, but then I would stare into Mom's worn, tired eyes and worry that if I let her know I was sad about losing Sable, or confused by it, she'd start drinking again. I was developing the very misguided belief that I had the power to prevent that from happening.

My mother's mirage of strength was beginning to burn off. I felt I had to be the strong one in the family, in a sense the parent, and deal with any weak or vulnerable feelings on my own. I didn't want to let Kaitlyn see how down I was, thereby suggesting that there was any-thing for her to be sad about. Kaitlyn didn't seem to be suffering at all, nor did she perceive this new home as a downgrade, which was a relief. She was thrilled that she got to sleep in bed with Mom again, and to play all afternoon with me, who she worshipped and idolized.

In a world where I had no one to talk to or process anything with, some of my old, irrational fears and obsessive-compulsive habits crept back in, and I was once more terrified that Bloody Mary lurked inside the mirrors in our house. I did my best to see that Kaitlyn didn't suffer in the same ways I did from our mother's depressed mood, and I helped her get dressed in cute outfits for school and made sure she didn't watch scary television shows. I also trained her in the art of not sharing sad or negative feelings with our mother. I told her she should share them with me instead.

The saving grace for me in all this was that I got to live next to Donna's daughter, Sarah, who was becoming the best friend I'd ever had, right along with Malena, the girl with two moms. Both Sarah and Malena went to school with me, both had complicated families, and all three of us were now happily participating in a musical theater after-school program in which I'd landed the role of Miss Hannigan in *Annie*. Kaitlyn was in the show, too, happily playing an orphan.

I still put great effort into hiding that my mother was gay. Even when we'd lived with Sable, as good as things had been, I had never fully stopped hiding this fact—though I had been comforted when a famous woman on television named Ellen announced to the world that she was a lesbian. I'd listened as grown-ups and kids at school had discussed Ellen's announcement, and I'd kept a tally of who was for it or against it. Two years later, I'd gone to see *The Birdcage*, a hysterical comedy about two gay fathers pretending to be straight for their son. To my shock, everyone loved the movie, but I got the sense that people were comfortable with men being gay if they were stylish and funny, but that people felt there was something more abnormal about lesbians.

Mom, too, now put great effort into hiding her sexuality. After losing her job at the mortgage brokerage, she'd crept back into the closet, which I would later learn was part of why her relationship with Aunt Diane had become so strained. Aunt Diane, and especially her girlfriend, Robin, were gay rights advocates who wanted everyone out of the closet. Mom felt pressure on both sides: in work settings to be straight, and from the gay community to be out. She chose the former, which had led to Aunt Diane and Robin largely disappearing from our lives.

When it came time for the *Annie* performance, my mother did everything she could to make me feel special, including packing the audience with so many of her old friends that I'm sure some of my classmates' family members couldn't get in. My father, who I hadn't seen in a long time, came, as did Mom's old girlfriend Annie, who my mother had resumed a friendship with. There was also my godmother, Damian, and an older grandmotherly-looking woman with gray hair who Mom had met at an AA meeting and convinced to play the part of grandmother because no real ones were available. Then of course there was my mother, her arms filled with bouquets of flowers we could not afford, beaming with pride in the audience as I belted out "Little Girls."

When summertime rolled around, Sarah's mother, who was occasionally attentive and kind, began taking Sarah, Kaitlyn, and me on weekend trips in her RV to a vacant lot she owned in the desert. At night, I suffocated from the stench of Donna's chain smoking in the tiny RV, but during the day, Kaitlyn, Sarah, and I roamed free in the desert, returning with dreams of the three separate mansions we were going to build in the wilderness, the elaborate floor plans in our minds.

When we pulled up in the RV after one of these desert trips, my mother came out of the guesthouse screaming for me and Kaitlyn.

"What's wrong?" I asked, running toward her.

When I got closer, I saw that she was smiling as she furiously waved an envelope in her hand, like it was a deed to an oil well she hadn't known was in her name.

"I pulled off the impossible!" she shouted, gleaming as bright as the sun that was hitting her face.

"What, Mom, what!?" I asked, excited and nervous about whatever was making my mother so happy.

"I got you into an incredible school for the sixth grade, Chrysta," she said, bending down and taking me in her arms. "It's a brand-new all-girls school called the Archer School for Girls, over the hill in the Pacific Palisades. They gave you a full ride on financial aid."

As my mother wrapped me in her arms, I did my best to feign a smile, not thrilled at the idea of going to an all-girls school, since I had secretly started to like boys. But I saw how much my admission meant to my mother, so I gave her an appreciative hug back and pretended that I, too, thought this was the greatest news in the world.

Later that night, Kaitlyn, my mother, and I sat down to celebrate over some tofu sticks and tomato sauce. Kaitlyn and I had recently become vegetarians, after our father's most recent lecture on factory farming.

"There is nothing more important than an education," Mom told me, taking a bite of the tofu stick she held between her fingers and leaning back in her chair. "I remember how proud my father was of me when I got into UCLA," she said.

My mother dove into various favorite memories of her family: about how her grandfather Culbert had gone to Georgetown University, then became a senator in Utah, and then moved to California, where he was elected governor in 1939; how he had been nicknamed the "people's governor" because he fought for the rights of the working class, and against the oil companies and the Catholic Church; how he had appointed the first female, Black, and Latino judges. She also told us about her father, Culbert's son: that he'd gone to Loyola Law School, then became a prominent attorney with Melvin Belli; that he could have kept at it and made a fortune but became a judge instead, preferring to sit at the back of the courthouse with the criminals and prostitutes—the "real people"—rather than up front with the white-collar lawyers.

"No matter how much our family could have used some extra money," Mom said, "Dad always slammed the phone down on the dirty lawyers who had called to try to bribe him to allow bad, wealthy people off. 'Debra,' he used to say, 'if you can't look at yourself in the mirror, then you have nothing—remember that.'"

As Mom spoke about her father, I noticed a sudden vacant sadness in her eyes, and I wondered if there was more to her stories than she let on. Whenever a shadow began to creep in at the edges, I would ask her more pointed questions, but I was always dismissed.

"What's the point of dwelling on dark things?" she'd say. Right now, she told me, we needed to focus on only the future—on my bright, bright future at the Archer School for Girls.

THE SCHOOL PICNIC

The day of the introductory school picnic at Archer, my mother woke me up early with breakfast in bed.

I had grown out of all my clothing, but I knew we couldn't afford to go shopping, so I kept this fact to myself, knowing full well that if I mentioned it to my mother, she would open several new credit cards. I did my best to get dressed in what we had available, putting on an old pair of knee-length jean shorts that Sable had purchased for me two years earlier, which I could barely walk in, and a hideous oversized shirt of my mother's. The suit she was wearing also didn't fit her; her weight had swelled well beyond the sizes she had in her closet.

"Now Chrysta," my mother said as we pulled up to Temescal Canyon Park in the Pacific Palisades, where the picnic was taking place, in Donna's handyman's old car, which we had borrowed. "Make sure you tell everyone that your great-grandfather was governor of California."

"Mom, I'm not going to tell everyone that," I said, as this fact seemed irrelevant. He was not even my grandfather: he was my *great*-grandfather, and this seemed like one too many generations ago to impress anyone.

As my mother looked for a parking spot, I saw rows of Mercedes and large, black-windowed Navigators lining the park's esplanade. A pang of anxiety rose in my throat as I became excruciatingly self-conscious about how old and dirty our car was by comparison.

We began to walk toward a gathering of mothers, fathers, and daughters, my mother standing tall as she held my hand in hers. I became increasingly uncomfortable as I compared myself to the other girls, who wore cool jean jackets and mid-nineties purple-flowered dresses. Then I looked at the mothers, one in particular, who had glanced in our direction.

She was blond, like my mother, but significantly thinner, dressed in jeans and a button-down blouse, her neck and wrists covered in gold, sparkling jewelry. I watched as she scanned my mother's suit up and down and stopped to focus on her lapel; when I followed the woman's eyes, I realized that Mom's suit had stains on it and was ripped at the elbows. Mom was oblivious. She didn't observe any difference between us and them, which only heightened my anxiety.

I paused to look around at the other children, many of whom seemed to already know one another, and then I walked over to a swing set a hundred feet away. Two girls in my incoming class approached me on the swing. They were by far the coolest-looking eleven-year-olds I'd ever seen, smiling as they walked like the stars of a Gap commercial.

I was surprised to see them coming over but also excited, so I smiled in their direction.

"Hi, I'm Gia," said the first one, her face covered in freckles.

"I'm Miro," the second one added. "Like the painter."

I nodded, pretending I knew the reference.

"Your mom told us to come talk to you," Gia explained, making a judgmental face. "I thought that was a really weird thing to do," she added, as if I hadn't understood this with her first sentence.

I looked across the yard and caught my mother's smiling eyes, watching me to see how her plan had worked out.

"Would you mind getting off the swing so we can take a turn together?" one of the girls asked.

I got off the swing as fast as I could, running back to my mother, furious at what she had done. I told her I wanted to leave the picnic—"Now!"

Part of my problem was how I looked: I now had braces, which my mother had paid for with a payment plan that stretched out over several years, and my eyebrows had grown into a unibrow. On top of that, even though I was one of the tiniest girls in my class, I'd gone through puberty early and inherited my mother's giant breasts. At age eleven, I was eighty-five pounds, with a D cup. Had I been sculpted into a statue, I would have toppled over.

We wore uniforms at Archer, which was a relief, but mine were way too large because they were expensive: by buying big, my mother hoped I could wear them for a long time. In the first days of school, the teachers asked each girl to stand up, introduce herself, and explain what her parents did for a living. The room was filled with words like "actor," "producer," and "studio head." Rather than try to explain my parents' occupations, which I wasn't completely sure of, I escaped to the bathroom.

Many of my classmates were not just wealthy; their parents were well-known and powerful, giving them the illusion that everyone lived like they did. If I didn't come to school with a Tiffany's silver bracelet or a pencil case with gold initials carved outside, it didn't occur to anyone that this might be because I couldn't afford those things. Instead, I got a rep for not having any style or knowing what was cool. The same went for where I lived. When I told a girl in my new class that I lived in the Valley, she repeated the words back to me with a gagging face. "Oh God," she said, *"the Valley."* I genuinely thought she might vomit.

Certain places in the Valley—like Studio City and Sherman Oaks—garnered less disdain from my classmates than other places. I quickly got the impression that Tarzana, where I lived in Donna's guesthouse, was among the most unfortunate. I was getting an education at Archer; I just wasn't sure it was the one my mother intended.

I would have felt better, I thought, going to a school with other children whose lives looked more like mine, at least financially, because then I would have fit in. Or at least then I could have more easily hidden the differences. But my mother would hear none of this.

In truth, my peculiarities were more than just superficial, and I'm not sure switching schools would have made me any more popular. I tended to randomly burst into song, on the bus or in the middle of class, and while this was something that many of my old musical theater friends also did, no one at my new school found it charming. I also told everyone in my class that I lived in an underground world called Miss Perfect's Land, where there was a queen cat ruler named Miss Perfect. To me, inhabiting an imaginary world seemed preferable to admitting my real one.

The girls at school were cruel to me, and I just came to accept that I would make no friends. I still had Sarah to spend time with after school, and Kaitlyn, who was becoming a closer friend to me than ever now that she was older.

I returned home one Friday and handed my mother the school calendar, on which, to her horror, she noticed an upcoming event called Father-Daughter Day.

In the time that we had lived in Sarah's guesthouse, we hadn't seen much of my father. He'd come around on the day after Christmas and to see Kaitlyn's and my school play, but as the months wore on, the visits decreased. I had wondered privately if my father came over only because my mother asked him to. Enough adults had come in and out of my life that I was starting not to trust their affections.

When I told my mother that I "didn't care" whether my father came to Father-Daughter Day or not, she seemed to grow restless and sad, and she said he would be there, but I could tell—because she was upset—that she wasn't sure if he would show up.

The morning of Father-Daughter Day, my mother woke me up with a smile and told me Dad was on his way over. I was secretly overjoyed.

He arrived over two hours late and looked as though he hadn't showered or slept in several weeks, and he smelled—a deep, layered smell of incense and dog hair. He was still handsome, but his hair was now long and ratty, and he was so thin that you could see the outline of his bones under his T-shirt. Most disturbing, he had a gray distance in his eyes, like the life spark had been put out.

I'd recently turned twelve, and he had brought a pair of socks from Goodwill as a belated birthday present. He handed them to me, and then gently reached into his dirty pocket and pulled out a wreath of wilting pink flowers, which he carefully laid over my head like a crown. He told me he was going to "initiate me into womanhood" with a special TM ceremony.

"I am going to teach you a magic technique for when you feel anxious," he said.

I smiled, not having the heart to tell my father that he'd already "initiated" me years before. I sensed that this, and the worn socks, were his only gifts to give.

I let him ramble on about his guru, the Maharishi, as I breathed in his dirty smell and observed his deteriorating appearance. Then I felt my stomach drop when my mother reminded us that we really needed to get going.

I wondered if my dad would feel uncomfortable and self-conscious amid the directors and Hollywood producers. I knew my mother was trying her best to help me fit in by giving me a father to bring to school, and the last thing I wanted to do was make her, or him, feel bad about themselves. I could handle the embarrassment, but I worried about how they would handle it.

The next few hours were a blur. I checked out of my body as I watched immaculately dressed fathers pulling up to the two-story school in the Palisades in their perfectly cleaned luxury cars, ushering in their daughters, who were especially primped for the occasion. My father held my hand—a gesture that I could tell made him feel uncomfortable—and I smiled at him, trying to look proud, as I observed how my mother had pulled his hair into a neat bun, and done her best, but failed, to dust off the dirt and dog hair from his clothes.

I will never know what my classmates thought of my dad that day, but one thing was certain: my mother had registered my father's deteriorating appearance.

After she dropped me and Dad off at school, she had come home and gone into the garage that was connected to our guesthouse. There, behind one of her stacked Golden Memory Boxes—one of the only things that had survived all our moves and couldn't be sold—she'd found a tarnished spoon that she was convinced had the residue of speed on it.

Everything suddenly made sense to my mother as she recalled my father's wild hallucinations about being the second coming of Christ and the Ziggy pregnancy. Maybe Jeffrey wasn't mentally ill at all: maybe he was simply addicted to speed. My mother, holding the spoon in her hand, began to doubt herself and wondered if perhaps the spoon belonged to Donna or her boyfriend.

The next morning, at 4 a.m., while Kaitlyn, my mother, and I were all fast asleep, there was banging on the front door of the guesthouse.

"Let me in!" a man's voice yelled.

"Who is it?" my mother asked, woken from a deep sleep and now afraid.

"It's Jeff," the voice called. "I need some money."

My mother stood up, went to the door, cracked it open, and saw Jeffrey with a group of terrifying-looking bikers with Hells Angels jackets on sitting on motorcycles behind him. He was, she felt, visibly high.

"Jeff, get out of here," she whispered, shooing him with a few five-dollar bills she had on hand, worried he'd wake us up.

The spoon was definitely Jeffrey's, my mother concluded.

The following day, she got a phone call from an old friend named Jules Buccieri. My mother, father, and Jules had once been close friends. Jules was much older than my parents and had served as a kind of spiritual "teacher" to them both. He'd owned one of the first vegetarian restaurants in Los Angeles, as well as a famous antique store, where throughout the seventies and eighties he'd hosted "gurus" and "channelers" like Yogi Bhajan, Ram Dass, and Ramtha; my mother and father had sometimes attended these events together.

Jules, who was usually calm and meditative, was in a rage, screaming that he was going to call the cops and have Jeffrey put in jail. He explained that my father had been crashing on his couch and that $10,000 in cash that Jules kept hidden had gone missing. He was sure Jeffrey had stolen it.

My mother begged Jules not to press charges. "I believe Jeffrey is a drug addict," she told him. "I have a plan," she assured him before she hung up.

Her plan, she felt, would get Jules his money back and save the father of her children. Oddly, this new belief—that Jeffrey was addicted to drugs—had given my mother new hope. Now there was a diagnosis she could understand. She'd gotten enough junkies sober in her day, herself included. What Jeffrey needed to become the perfect family member, she now believed, was an intervention, and then rehab and an introduction to a twelve-step program. But how could she afford rehab? And even if she found a way to get the money, how would she convince him to go?

My mother took a deep breath, picked up her large white cordless telephone, and decided to take her chances, dialing the number of the woman she always assumed was the cause of Jeffrey's suffering.

She knew she was taking a great risk. It was an even bigger betrayal, she knew, than the time she had planted a gun on her sister to get her locked away and convince her to get sober. But that decision had saved her sister's life, and her sister had eventually forgiven her, even if their relationship was not as close now as it once was.

The phone started to ring. Debra was shocked when a soft, compassionate-seeming, rational-sounding woman's voice arrived on the other end of the line.

"Hello, this is Jeannie Pechin," the woman said. "May I ask who is calling?"

"Hi, Jeannie," my mother answered. "This is Debra Olson, the mother of Jeffrey's two children, Chrysta and Kaitlyn."

As my mother waited anxiously for the woman to speak from 2,500 miles away, in a bucolic home on a hill that overlooked the glittering ocean waves of the eastern end of the island of Maui, Jeannie Pechin stood looking out the window, repeating the idea back to herself: "grandchildren."

DONOR 150

The first time my father donated sperm to the California Cryobank behind my mother's back was sometime in November 1985, one year after I was born and three and a half years before Kaitlyn arrived.

That first day, after finding out that my mother went on TV and mentioned his name, he'd gone straight from his strip-o-gram job to the Cryobank, walked inside the building, and taken the elevator up to the ninth floor. He'd approached the front desk, which looked like it could have belonged in any office building in 1980s America.

"I'd like to donate sperm," he told the man sitting at the desk.

"Have you donated before?" the man asked.

Jeffrey explained that he'd been in this room one year earlier with a woman named Debra; that was all he had to say and the man remembered him instantly. My mother had been the pickiest woman the Cryobank had ever dealt with. She hadn't even considered using one of their donors—she'd made it clear that they were not up to her standards—and when she brought Jeffrey in for testing, she was so beside herself at the genetic perfection of the man she'd found for the job that she couldn't help but boast to everyone who worked there about him.

"Yes, of course, good to see you!" the man said now. "Well, since you've already gone through our screening process, all we have to do is fill out a profile, and we can get started with your first donation today."

The man took out a clipboard and explained what he explained to all his donors: that Jeffrey's identity would remain completely anonymous, and that the questions he was about to ask were meant to give prospective parents the information—nothing more—that they needed to make a decision about the genetic father of their child. Most of them, he explained, would never even tell their children the truth about their genetic makeup.

Given that my father wanted his donation to be a secret from everyone in his life, he was comforted when the man explained that Jeffrey's name and photograph would never be given out. From here on out, he would be known only as Donor 150.

"What month and year were you born?" the man asked. "And how old are you?"

"November nineteen fifty-six," my father answered. "I'm twenty-nine."

"What is your height?"

"Six feet."

"Weight?"

"One sixty-three."

"Eyes?"

"Blue."

"Hair color?"

"Light brown, sandy blond."

"And your ethnic origin?"

"WASP," my father answered.

"The religion you were born into?"

"Episcopalian."

These answers were true.

Then came a question about his education. My father had never graduated from college, even though his parents had offered to pay for it. The closest he'd come was attending the unaccredited Maharishi

University in Italy, where he'd lasted only a few months, studying Transcendental Meditation and "yogic flying" before he returned to the United States, after having a mental health crisis.

"Bachelor's degree in philosophy," he answered. It wasn't so much a lie, he felt, as a generous interpretation of the facts.

Next up was a question about fertility.

"Do you have any children?"

"Yes, one," Jeffrey answered. "She's a year old, and very healthy."

The man wrote this down, and then followed with several questions about Jeffrey's physical health, what exercise he practiced regularly, and his diet. In response, Jeffrey explained that he was extremely physically healthy; that he enjoyed swimming, weight training, and karate; and that he was a vegetarian.

"Any history of genetic diseases?" the man asked.

"None."

There were no questions about mental health.

"What is your current or most recent occupation?"

"Dancer," Jeffrey replied. (He left out that he was a strip-o-gram dancer.) "You can also put that I'm a musician, a private fitness and nutrition instructor, and a writer," he said.

There were several more questions, mostly about his family history, such as the heights, complexions, and eye colors of his parents and grandparents (most were tall, fair, and had blond hair and blue eyes); their educations (his father had graduated from Harvard and Yale and his mother from Wellesley); and how old they were when they died and what they had died from (most had been in their seventies or eighties and had died of natural causes). Having completed his questionnaire, the interviewer handed Jeffrey a final page titled "In your own words" that he was meant to fill out about himself.

Jeffrey took the paper and sat down in the waiting room to write.

"Why do you want to be a donor?" was the first question.

Jeffrey paused for a moment, looking around the room. His eyes landed on a binder filled with profiles of the other donors available through the Cryobank. Curious, he picked it up and flipped through the pages, studying what other men had written about themselves. Most of these donors, Jeffrey observed, had science backgrounds. Almost the entire binder was filled with students from UCLA medical school. Only two donors mentioned being artistic, or playing music, and of those two, both were short. No one discussed spirituality.

I'm going to get chosen off the hook, Jeffrey thought with a smile as he put the binder down.

He reread the question: "Why do you want to be a donor?"

"I feel I was blessed with a very good physical body + mind," he wrote in his small, careful handwriting. "I know for one reason or another people need healthy genes. I am glad to share with others in any way I can."

"In your own words, describe your personality and character," was the next question.

"My deepest aspiration in this life is spiritual," he answered.

"If we could pass on a message to the recipient(s) of your semen, what would that message be?"

"This earthly life is transitory," Jeffrey wrote, "and the joys of this world are ephemeral, short-lived. Everyone wants to be happy, but look beyond the surface of this life to find a deeper experience of a happiness which won't die when your body does—within the hidden depths of your own soul. And don't rely on hearsay—question your most inveterate beliefs. If you do, you'll find a love and joy beyond your wildest dreams, which you may share with all those around you. Keep your mind open, and if sincere, great fortune will come."

Jeffrey finished his application and returned it to the man at the front desk.

"Oh, and there's something else," Jeffrey said, reaching into his pocket and pulling out a photo of me at six months old—blue-eyed, blond, and smiling happily—that my mother had given him. "I know you won't be using my photo on the application," he said, "but if you want, you can attach a picture of my daughter, Chrysta, so parents can see what she looks like."

The man happily took the photograph from Jeffrey and added it to my father's profile. The man then escorted Jeffrey into a tiny room with a large sink and a stack of *Penthouse* magazines. Fifteen minutes later, Jeffrey left the building with a twenty-five-dollar check.

For the next eight years, my father donated sperm to the Cryobank two or three times per week, making $300 to $400 per month, which was enough to pay for gas and weed and his rent when he had an apartment. Early on, Jeffrey was paid per visit, regardless of how much viable sperm he produced in a sample. Later, the Cryobank changed its compensation model and began paying only for the visits that resulted in a certain baseline amount of viable sperm, which the clinic could then split into somewhere between three and seven ampules of sellable sperm. If Jeffrey abstained from sex for several days and used vitamin C supplements, he found that some months he could make up to five accepted donations per week. In the beginning, the Cryobank paid him twenty-five dollars per visit, and then that number was raised to thirty-five dollars, and eventually to fifty dollars. Each donation would be broken into several ampules, and then sold individually, for around $100 to $150 per ampule. In total, Jeffrey donated sperm around five hundred times and provided the Cryobank with enough ampules for thousands of babies.

Sometimes, when the Cryobank hadn't seen Jeffrey in a few months, they'd call him to say that they'd sold out of his samples and needed him to come in to restock. He had been correct in his assumption that he'd be in high demand. Heather had once told him, when they were dating and she still worked for the Cryobank, that Jeffrey was their most requested donor by far, and that at one point there had been a six-month waiting list for his sperm.

There were many reasons why women chose Donor 150.

Some chose him because of his physical description. Jeffrey's height, weight, and eye color reminded one woman of her father; another liked that he'd written that he "tanned easily" because she always burned.

Other parents chose him because of the answers on his "In your own words" page. His artistic and musical nature was a deciding factor for many, while for others it was his love of animals, or the fact that his parents had gone to prestigious colleges. For yet others, it was his spirituality. One lesbian couple in the Midwest—the first lesbians in their small town to ever start a family—were so in love with Donor 150 after reading that his greatest aspiration in life was spiritual that they added their names to the six-month waiting list and refused to consider anyone else.

Other parents didn't pick Donor 150 at all; their doctors did. Or they were encouraged to try him out by the staff at the Cryobank after they had failed to get pregnant with other donors.

"Donor 150 has been very successful in the past," the nurses and doctors would tell them. "He's also very kind, and *very* good-looking."

It wasn't just the staff at the Cryobank who promoted Jeffrey. The head of the Cryobank, Dr. Cappy Rothman, was also quite fond of him. When Cappy threw a party to celebrate the Cryobank's second office opening, Jeffrey was the only donor who was invited to attend. My father would later recall dressing up in a suit for the occasion and being ushered by Cappy around the room like a trophy wife, the handsome, put-together, impressive exemplar of what you got when you bought sperm at Dr. Rothman's Cryobank.

Cappy also recommended Jeffrey privately. After a wealthy, influential heterosexual couple was devastated to find out, after years of trying to conceive, that the husband was infertile, they wanted assurances that they were selecting the "best" donor, so they called Cappy directly.

"Dr. Rothman," the husband had said on the phone. "If you were going to use one donor out of all your donors, just tell us: which one would you choose?"

"Donor 150," Cappy replied, without a pause.

Of course, being on a six-month waiting list meant that Jeffrey's sperm was not exclusive, even if you had a lot of money and influence. And as the Cryobank grew, the quantity of children being conceived with Donor 150's sperm was sometimes a question that came up with prospective parents.

"When there are thirty confirmed pregnancies," the Cryobank staff assured parents, "we will retire the donor."

The truth, however, was that no one was keeping tabs on who got pregnant after those packages on dry ice arrived in doctor's offices or, later, directly on people's doorsteps. The sperm bank industry had zero government oversight to compel, for instance, the fact-checking of information in donor profiles. The Cryobank was the first sperm bank in the world to make direct deliveries to people's houses. For many parents, especially LGBTQ parents who valued their privacy during a time when their creating a family was so taboo, this was the reason they chose the California Cryobank to begin with. And business was booming: the Cryobank would eventually become the sixth-largest customer of FedEx in all of Southern California.

Meanwhile, as the years wore on, all over the country, day in and week out, dozens of mothers-to-be who had been inseminated with Donor 150's sperm nine months earlier welcomed children into the world, praying and hoping they'd made a good genetic choice for their new family.

Some parents—especially those who were single mothers or part of a lesbian couple—kept Jeffrey's profile in a special place, intending to take it out and read it aloud to their children when they were old enough to understand what a donor was.

Other parents—especially those in heterosexual marriages with an infertile father—often stuffed the paperwork into a box in the attic or the basement or into the trash, and vowed never to speak a word to their children about it. For this group, which was the largest segment of customers for the California Cryobank in the eighties and early nineties, the fact that their children had a donor at all was a secret they intended to keep.

Jeffrey kept his double life as a sperm donor well hidden from everyone and made a point of never revealing his secret to my mother, or to his own family.

Jeffrey's mother, Jeannie, was traditional. She was the kind of woman who wore pastel-colored earrings to match her pastel-colored purse and shoes; who mailed handwritten thank-you cards after being invited out for dinner; who fundraised for the Humane Society and the SPCA and belonged to tennis clubs and sipped martinis over lunch with friends. She fed the birds every morning, as her dad had done; she was gentle and now led a quiet life. She was not someone who often discussed personal matters, and certainly was not confrontational. She was a WASP.

Jeannie had been vaguely aware of us throughout the years, but the one or two times Jeffrey had attempted to bring us up with her, she had discouraged her son from discussing the topic. Early on, when my mother was pregnant with me, he'd tried broaching the subject.

"Hey Mom," he'd said, "a woman approached me to be a donor—to help her have a kid." He'd explained that he'd had no romantic interest in her and that they had a written agreement that stated he would have no financial responsibility for the child.

Jeannie had been silent on the other end of the phone.

"Oh Jeff, this worries me," she'd finally said. "I just want you to know if you get married to someone, that's one thing, but anything could happen. You could be liable. These children won't have a dad."

Jeffrey tried to defend the idea but this simply was not the way Jeannie had hoped he would give her grandchildren. She made it gently clear that she didn't want to hear any more about it.

When Jeannie picked up the phone the day that Debra called her, my mother launched right into telling her all about Kaitlyn and me. She hoped that if Jeannie heard details about us that endeared us to her, my mother would have more leverage when pleading

Jeffrey's case. After pulling Jeannie in, Debra moved on to the story of the tarnished spoon, the Ziggy pregnancy, Jeffrey's deteriorating physical appearance, the erratic late-night phone calls, and the stolen money.

Jeannie sat listening. Of course she was concerned about her son. After a few moments of silence, she told my mother that she would pay for a rehab for Jeffrey on one condition: that my mother could get him to sign himself in to one.

Jeannie likely had her doubts that this would work, having already tried many strategies to help her unpredictable and complicated son. She loved Jeffrey and it's possible she harbored some guilt for decisions she'd made that she felt had contributed to his struggles; for example, guilt that her marriage to her first husband, Jeffrey's father, had failed so horribly. Jeffrey's father was charming and quite the ladies' man but he liked women a bit too much. He also had anger issues, which, when he drank, sometimes made him abusive toward her in front of the kids and sometimes toward the children, too. Jeffrey's father had been a soldier in World War II, his father had been a general, and as his father had done to him, Jeffrey's father had treated Jeffrey and his older brother like they were cadets in the army. Jeannie's second husband had been much kinder to her, but he, too, drank, and he had little patience for young Jeffrey's rebellious spirit. It also didn't help the new marriage that Jeffrey didn't get along with his new stepbrother.

Jeannie had agreed with her husband to send young Jeffrey to boarding school soon after the new marriage began. (Jeffrey was the only child of the three who was sent away.) He'd called every night, begging to come home, but Jeannie had refused, not because she was heartless but because she didn't want to ruin another marriage, and also because she herself had gone to boarding school and it had been good for her. Jeffrey felt like he'd been sent away from the family to the Gulag. He made no friends while he was at school. Then his heart broke into a million pieces when his beloved childhood dog, the one family member he'd felt safe with emotionally, died. Soon after

Jeffrey was sent to boarding school, the dog had escaped from the house and got his paw stuck in a tree. Jeffrey felt that if he'd been home, he would have realized the dog was missing and been able to save him.

Jeffrey had never been quite right after boarding school. Jeannie had tried to support him when he asked her to pay for him to study Transcendental Meditation in Italy instead of going to a proper college. He had returned home from that trip emaciated, and then swallowed a bottle of aspirin, hoping to kill himself, but instead he just developed a painful ulcer. He began hearing voices, so Jeannie sent him to Delaware, to be with his father, hoping her ex-husband could help their struggling son "straighten up and fly right," in his words. Jeffrey's father found his son a holistic therapist out on a farm; Jeffrey spent months working with the man, talking about life. This approach seemed to be helpful to Jeffrey, who saw the therapist as the kind of gentle father figure he'd always needed. But a few weeks in, Jeffrey became so passionate about gardening that in a manic state in the middle of one night, he dug up his father's entire property. After that, his father took Jeffrey to the Cleveland Clinic to figure out what was happening with his son. After a forty-five-minute exam, the doctors diagnosed twenty-year-old Jeffrey with paranoid schizophrenia, prescribing pills that made him feel terrible and which he later refused to take. Jeffrey felt that the diagnosis was ludicrous. How could they know he was *that,* whatever *that* even meant, in forty-five minutes? Apparently, Jeannie was also confused by the diagnosis.

She didn't share any of this story with my mother that day on the phone. Mental illness was not the kind of thing Jeannie would dare to discuss publicly. It also wasn't something Jeffrey cared to discuss—certainly not that first day at the hair salon with my mother, or on his donor profile, or after all those vials of sperm had been sent all over the country to prospective parents. He didn't believe the diagnosis was true, so why mention it to anyone?

A few days after Debra's call with Jeannie, my mother picked up the phone and invited my father over to our guesthouse, saying she had something to show him. When he arrived, she pulled out several brochures for rehab facilities. His mother then called in, to tell Jeffrey she would pay for his treatment. It felt to Jeffrey like an ambush, not too unlike the time when he was eleven years old and his stepfather had called him in to show him the glossy pamphlets for boarding schools spread out all over the dining table.

Jeffrey went insane. His relationship with his mother was already strained; he felt this would create a permanent rift between them.

"How dare you call my mother!" he screamed at Debra from the driveway as I sat in the house, listening through a cracked window. "How dare you! You broke our agreement!" he shouted. "I am not a drug addict! What proof do you have that I am a drug addict? You told my mother I was a drug addict? Because of some fucking spoon? You set me up!" he raged. "You are just trying to lock me up in some jail cell so you can tear me away from all my animals!"

I had never seen my father in such a state. Two words kept playing over and over in my head: "drug addict."

At twelve, I was still sheltered, but I'd overheard enough grown-ups in AA talking about drug addiction to know that it was a very bad thing for my father to be.

It was the next thing he said, though, that really hurt.

"Go find a new father for Chrysta and Kaitlyn," he yelled.

He got into his car, screeched away, and drove out of our lives.

As my mother came back into the house, I crawled into bed next to Kaitlyn, closed my eyes, and pretended to be asleep. I felt tears coming on as Mom slid the covers up and got into bed next to me in her pajamas. The last thing I wanted to do was give her one more thing to feel sad about. She loved me so much and there was nothing that made her sadder than me being hurt. I cried quietly into my pillow, listening as she started to cry quietly herself, and thankfully, she didn't hear me.

It would be several years before I saw my father again, and I sensed the finality of his departure already. While my mother had, over time, attempted to distance us from our father, she'd never been able to cut the cord completely—always bringing him back into the fold whenever she felt we needed a dad. No matter how many times she swore she was done with him, she never was.

I lay in bed and promised myself I would never let my mother see how devastated I was. The last thing I wanted was for her to force him back into our lives artificially, just because she sensed I needed him to be there. If he didn't want to be my dad, I didn't want to coerce him into the role. However much my mother had spent to purchase my father, that money was gone.

PART THREE

COOL SHOES

The foils in my hair burned my scalp with the same degree of pain as the panic attack now coursing through my body.

"Breathe," I told myself as I looked over at my mother, who was elated by my transformation.

We were in an expensive hair salon in Santa Monica, and all I wanted to do was run outside and hide as I sat under a fan blowing desert heat all over my head and face.

"Mom," I whispered, sweat beading down my forehead as I looked around at all these fancy people next to me getting their hair done, and then at the holes in my mother's pantsuit, which had once been small and hardly noticeable, but which were now visibly apparent to anyone who looked at her outfit. "How much are we paying for this?" I asked.

"Stop worrying, Chrysta!" my mother snapped. "Trust in the universe!"

The problem was, I had just overheard the receptionist tell someone their bill was "five hundred dollars."

I didn't trust in this universe because here my mother was God, and you never knew how things were going to turn out. I had gone to enough supermarkets with my mother, watching her shovel packages of expensive health foods into the shopping cart—sometimes two shopping carts—to know that it was always a gamble once we got to the checkout line whether the credit card would clear, or someone would remember she'd written a bad check, and we'd have to pick through the cart to see what—if anything—we could afford as people waited in line behind us.

"Mom, are you sure you have enough money in your bank account?" I probed as my brown hair slowly turned platinum blond, like my mother's, under the tinfoil flakes that I kept batting out of my face so that I could see.

"My God, Chrysta!" she barked. "Our financial worries are behind us!" This last sentence was belted out so loud that the entire salon turned in our direction. Mom was incapable of not making a scene wherever she went.

She had been saying we were in the clear financially for over a year, but I was skeptical. Out of the blue, one of her old multilevel marketing friends had called with a shiny new opportunity. All I knew was that the man who had reached out had a criminal record, had served time for fraud, and had well-known Mafia ties. But to my mother, these details were a technicality.

"We're going to make millions!" she'd said to me and Kaitlyn right after she hung up the phone, getting out of bed and out of her pajamas. "This time it's real, baby. We're going to be millionaires!"

While I sat in bed, dubious, Kaitlyn started jumping up and down on the bed, giggling, as she and my mother listed all the amazing things they would buy with our millions of dollars, like two kids writing a wish list to Santa.

"Can we get a new house?" Kaitlyn asked.

"Yes, with a giant pool!"

"And a car?"

"Two cars! Three!" Then, as if she had just remembered something, my mother shrieked, "We'll finally get our hippopotamus!"

"Oh my God! Really?" Kaitlyn asked.

"Really," my mother replied. "What should we name him?"

For my sister, who was now eight and a half, every daydream was still possible.

"How, exactly, are we going to make millions?" I asked. At thirteen I felt like the only adult in the room.

"I'm going to sell the internet to people who can't afford it!" my mother said.

"How?" I inquired.

"I don't know the small details—my God, Chrysta, just be happy!"

And yet, overnight, the wheel of fortune that was our life together took a big spin and landed once more on a gold star.

My mother went from being clinically depressed, in bed all day eating popcorn in her flannel pajamas and watching the news, to getting up early to make coffee and dress in old, brightly colored suits that had collected dust and stains, and then—to my utter amazement—to leading giant meetings on a stage at the company's new headquarters in Valencia, first with a few dozen people in the audience and then hundreds. Her work ethic was incredible when she was inspired.

"We're going to make millions!" she'd shout from the stage like Tony Robbins as I sat on the floor beside her, pausing from my math exercises to stare in shock as these grown adults cheered for my mother. Her confidence was contagious and people wanted desperately to believe what she was saying. As I watched these people get sucked into the show, I grew increasingly aware, probably unlike them, that my mother had been down a hundred similar roads before, only to discover there was no pot of gold waiting for her at the end. I felt physically ill thinking about how they would feel about Mom when they realized it, too.

What especially boggled my mind was that after several months of these motivational talks, after my mother quickly became the company's highest earner and was practically running its West Coast division, she could barely explain, even just to me, how the company worked.

It was 1997, and Futurenet was a multilevel organization with the mission to sell everyday people the internet through an inexpensive electrical box, a "WebTV," they could plug into their televisions. My mother's job, as far as I could tell, was to sign people up under her as "distributors" who would sell WebTVs. In other words, another pyramid, but my mother felt that this was a "legitimate multilevel business," if there even was such a thing.

Some of the questions from audience members concerned me, such as "Why wouldn't someone just sign up for the regular internet, instead of this extra contraption?" or "Why won't people choose to buy a WebTV at the store, instead of through us, since it's available down the street for almost the same price?"

The details were so difficult to comprehend that my mother couldn't figure out how to operate the box. Thankfully, she never had to demonstrate how a WebTV worked—her motivational talks were not technical demonstrations, and she had a miraculous ability to distract from the harder questions with answers that led back to what people wanted to believe: "We're going to be rich!" Other times Kaitlyn and I would be dragged along to the houses of people she was trying to sell a box to, and I would watch in horror as she sat prodding at the buttons unsuccessfully until she finally called in Kaitlyn or me to help her get it working.

Despite my skepticism and worry, the checks started rolling in, just as Mom had said they would, and she began spending them with all the eagerness of her former self.

One day she scooped us up from school in a brand-new white Mercedes and took us home—not back to Sarah's guesthouse, but to a massive house in Tarzana, down the street from Sarah's, with a giant swimming pool and a custom fourteen-foot teepee she'd just had shipped in from a Lakota tribe.

"I always dreamed of having a real teepee," she said to me proudly as she stood next to it. "We will sleep under the stars outside in the summer, Chrysta, and stare at the Sturgeon Moon, just like the Native Americans. It's going to be glorious."

She started assembling a new menagerie of animals. We still had Denmark and Sweetie Pie and Little Owl, but then she got Kaitlyn two

Chihuahuas, Jack and Mary, who were attached to my sister at the hip, as well as two chinchillas, Timmy and Tundra. My mother also got a pair of ferrets, which were illegal to own in California and smelled like mildew, and several ducks, which followed Mom around in a little line. (She told me and Kaitlyn she was their "mommy duck.") Then came chickens. Then she surprised us with a basket of baby rabbits on Easter, which she thought were the same sex, but clearly weren't, because we woke up one morning to find dozens of baby rabbits hopping around our backyard. We couldn't give them away fast enough; every few months, we'd come outside and find a fresh dozen babies. It turned out they had built a rabbit colony under our yard.

On my fourteenth birthday, my mother presented me with that same silver Tiffany bracelet that all the other girls in my class had.

I saw the gleam in her eyes as she held out the light blue box, and I carefully slid the chain out of a tiny blue pouch delicately laid inside. As I held the chain in my hand, staring at a dangling heart she'd had inscribed with TO CHRYSTA, WITH LOVE, FROM MOM, I felt incredibly guilty. I had asked my mother for one of these bracelets in one of my weaker moments, and now I regretted it because I should have known that whatever I asked for she always found a way to give me.

"Mom," I said, squeezing the bracelet in my hand as I felt both moved by the gift and also distressed at the idea that she was spending money so carelessly on things we didn't really need. "What if Futurenet doesn't work out?"

I'd asked the same question when she'd brought me to our new home for the first time. I'd thought we were just coming here for an open house, as a weekend activity, like going to a museum, taking a tour of a place we'd never be able to afford and, for a few fun hours, pretending we'd be moving here.

"I just signed a two-year lease and put down forty thousand dollars toward purchasing it!" Mom announced, triumphant. "Do you like it?"

Seeing my face, she took me in her arms and gave me a tight hug.

"Relax, Chrysta. Just enjoy your life for once!"

I did like the house. It was giant and had an eighty-year-old sweet gum tree in the backyard that dropped yellow and gold leaves in the fall. This was somewhere I'd enjoy living, and where I'd feel proud to invite friends. But I had no friends at school, and whatever impulse drew me to fantasize about living in a place like this made me feel like one of the millions of children who stare at the television screen watching the Oscars, imagining being up there one day.

"Mom, I don't think that was responsible," I said, now exasperated.

"Chrysta," my mother said, angry. "Just leave the adult responsibilities to me, the adult, okay?"

I sat on the marble floor in the foyer of our new house, motionless, trying to process the irony of this statement.

"Money is just energy," she said as she flicked her hands in the air.

"Yeah, and it's really bad energy when you don't have any money," I retorted.

I still hadn't made a single friend at Archer.

My dream of having my best friend, Sarah, join me at school had quickly turned to heartbreak. Her mother had managed to get Sarah in for seventh grade on a scholarship, but a few days into her first year, Sarah had taken me aside and said, "Chrysta, I love you, but I think I need to spread my wings and take a little break from our friendship so I can make some new friends."

I'd spent the rest of that year eating alone at lunchtime, as I had the year before. I did my best to act as if this was my own choice and not the result of having no one else to spend time with, and I often returned home in tears to my mother because the girls at school had become so cruel.

They'd be mean about the oddest things. They made fun of me when I stared in wonder at green pasta because I'd never seen that before.

"Oh my God," two of the girls had said, laughing at me. "She's never heard of pesto!"

It was the cruelty around my mother that hurt the most, though.

Mom had taken to calling other parents to see if they could drop me at home when she had to work late, and many kids at school liked to tell me how weird their mothers thought my mother was.

For two years, I had gone to great lengths not to let my mother know that I'd been suffering at school, not wanting to add to her many burdens, and not wanting her to get involved. But one afternoon in the beginning of eighth grade, it got so bad that I burst into sobs in her arms when she walked out to greet me at the bus stop in front of our house.

"Honey, what's happening?" she asked, confused, as I buried my head in her arms, crying hysterically, harder than she'd ever seen me cry, so hard I could barely breathe.

"Hannah told everyone that my mom's a lesbian, like that was a bad thing," I said, barely getting the words out as I choked over the sentence. "Then everyone started saying I was a gross lesbian, too."

My mother held me sobbing in her arms as rage filled her body, and before I could stop her, she ran toward the bus stop, where Hannah and several other kids from school were waiting for their parents.

Hannah, a smug thirteen-year-old who was physically almost twice my size, with big, curly red hair, looked my mother straight in the eye as she approached. Standing with one hand on her hip, Hannah stared and smiled, as if to taunt my mother with a "You wouldn't dare" kind of look.

I watched from our front door in horror as my mother pushed Hannah against the bus, holding her forcibly while she put her finger right up to Hannah's nose.

"Listen, you little fuck," my mother raged as several kids watched, jaws agape at the insane scene unfolding in front of them. "If you ever say anything that hurts my daughter again, you'll be sorry. Do you hear me?" she screamed.

The smug look on Hannah's face was replaced with fear, and she burst into sobs, promising my mother whatever she wanted if my mother would just leave her alone.

My mother returned to me, triumphant. I felt angry at myself for telling her what had happened. In the past few years, since the Sable breakup, she had drifted so deeply into the closet with her sexuality that sometimes she told Kaitlyn and me that she wasn't really a lesbian. All the pride and openness she'd been able to gather during the Fay years, and then with Sable, had eroded. I felt the Hannah incident had been the final nail in the coffin of that part of herself.

That night, I sat in my bedroom, under my canopy bed, worried about my mother. At one point the door opened and she walked in, her eyes filled with pain.

"I just got off the phone with Hannah's mother," she said, smiling, lying down next to me. "Hannah feels terrible for what she did, and she is going to apologize to you tomorrow at school."

The next morning, I faked a temperature and skipped school for the rest of the week, and the week after that. Kaitlyn skipped, too. I think Mom was as excited as we were to have us play hooky as we drove to and from Valencia for her Futurenet meetings.

I didn't have the heart to tell her when, the following Monday, the bullying only got worse, because now everyone said my mother was "a lunatic," and "a child abuser," and a few other names that I managed to block out of my memory.

It was some time after the Hannah incident that my mother looked down at me with my single eyebrow and my mouth full of braces and my hideous clothes and decided it was time to turn me blond. She also had my braces removed and took me on my first shopping spree at Neiman Marcus in Beverly Hills—or Neiman Markup, as she called it with a laugh.

For once my mother's plan worked. I went on a school trip to Washington, DC, no longer wearing her too-big tie-dyed shirts or hand-me-downs from Sarah. I had newly blond hair, my braces were finally off, and I was wearing a new (drastically overpriced) outfit that my mother had purchased, including a pair of black leather Mary Janes with a slight platform sole and a Velcro strap that I had noticed some older girls at school wearing. I had started to grow into my breasts, and I looked like a different person. Not beautiful—I would never feel beautiful, even if attention from boys did increase—but, at the very least, put-together and, dare I say, almost cool.

On the trip, all the most popular girls in my class, one by one, noticed and complimented me on my outfit, but especially on my shoes. They ran up to me and linked their arms in mine as we walked through the tulips blooming among the historic statues. I had put on a new pair of shoes and, like they were a pair of magic ruby slippers, not only were all the girls in our class who had tortured me for years now inviting me to eat lunch with them, but they were linking their arms in mine like we'd been best friends the whole time. That something as ridiculous as a pair of shoes could so greatly alter how people treated a person shocked me. It made me furious. And worse: it made me desperately want to learn how to replicate this magic.

As chance would have it, I was assigned to sleep in the same hotel room as Gia, the girl who, two years earlier, had approached me on the swing set, coldheartedly asking if I could get off so she could take a turn with her friend. She was also one of the girls who had made fun of me for not knowing what pesto pasta was, for my too-large tie-dyed T-shirts and my vintage cat-eye glasses. She was the most popular girl in our class by far and, aside from Hannah, the person who had been the cruelest.

Now, as we lay next to each other in our pajamas, sharing a bed in a hotel room, she took a deep breath and decided to tell me about something she'd never told another friend: that her father had just gotten engaged to a woman much younger than her mother, and she worried that he was going to start a new family with his new wife, leaving her unclear where she and her mother fit into the picture.

As my new friend spoke, I felt sorry for her, and I forgave her for all the horrible things she'd done to me. I felt that perhaps she'd been cruel to me because of her own complicated life at home.

As we lay next to each other, I thought about my own father. I hadn't spent much time thinking about him since he'd disappeared. I felt sadness creep up in my throat, and I briefly considered discussing with Gia what had happened. It would have felt good to tell someone what was going on with me. But my father wasn't a Hollywood producer; he was a "drug addict." And my mother wasn't young and thin and put-together, like Gia's mom; she was older, and eccentric, and a lesbian. I felt that if my new friend knew anything true about me, she would not want to be my friend anymore. The risk of self-disclosure was too great, especially now, when I was on the verge of being accepted.

As my friend fell asleep, I lay awake, staring out the window at the sparkle of Washington, and I briefly let my mind drift to Dad, wondering where he was, and what he was up to. I wondered if he was lying there thinking about me, too, or if he ever thought of me at all. I doubted it very much.

CAMARILLO
MENTAL INSTITUTION

While I'd been immersed in the drama of junior high school, another drama had been secretly unfolding in my mother's life. In February 1998, the FTC had filed a lawsuit in the U.S. District Court of Los Angeles against my mother's employer, Futurenet, claiming the company was a pyramid headhunting recruiting scheme. Though there was no evidence of this, Mom was positive Bill Gates was behind the lawsuit. If people used their television as their monitor, her theory went, then nobody would need his personal computers. Futurenet battled the case in court, and for a year, Mom stayed optimistic, but eventually it became clear that the business and my mother's latest dream of financial freedom were dead.

Mom was apoplectic at the unfairness of it all. The lawsuit represented, for her, all the injustices of capitalism. She would shout, or cry, and then shout again, irritable at the smallest provocation. Then she'd watch the news, and whatever was happening around the globe was more evidence of what a terrible, horrible world we lived in.

As Futurenet quickly disintegrated, my mother did what she often did when she saw no way out and a terrible financial crash approaching: she decided not to think about it.

Instead, one day she came home with a distraction: a woman named April, who she had met in the audience at one of her motivational talks.

Kaitlyn and I were playing video games on our mother's bed when she brought April over for the first time, entering the room with a look of excitement as she introduced us to her new "friend." I observed April's short black hair, which was styled in a sharp bob, and her plump lips covered in poorly applied maroon lipstick. She had a loud, unsettling laugh. As I took in her appearance—her white leather jacket with rhinestones and tassels and her matching white rhinestone-covered cowboy boots—every intuitive nerve ending in my body set off alarms.

As soon as April left our house that night, I told my mother we needed to sit down for a serious talk.

"I don't like her," I said.

"Oh Chrysta, you are so judgmental," Mom replied. "What's wrong with April? Tell me. She makes me laugh."

"I just don't like her," I repeated sternly, trying to be intimidating. "You will not date her. Do you understand?"

I watched and felt helpless as the look on my mother's face said she would not be abiding by my demand.

Mom had been single since Sable, and I preferred it that way. There were too many variables that came with Mom's relationships. I had no idea that Futurenet had fully crumbled, or that my mother was already running out of the money from the last check that would ever arrive in our mailbox from Futurenet—she hadn't wanted to worry me, and she certainly didn't want to say "You were right all along." Mom's problem wasn't making money—she was very clever at finding ways to make money; her problem was keeping it. I suspected that things were amiss, that my mother was in a particularly vulnerable state, and the appearance of this new woman rattled me.

After she met my mother, April left her husband, and at the same time, my mother told our landlord to start using her $40,000 down payment on the house to pay the next several months' rent.

I had very good reasons for being terrified of April, even if I couldn't explain them with words. It turned out that behind that obnoxious laugh, and inside the pocket of that ugly rhinestone jacket, was a tiny pouch of cocaine, my mother's "drug of choice"—a substance she had been proud to stay away from my entire life, even through the party house years. She'd spent the seventies on cocaine, and she knew that going anywhere near that drug would be a life sentence. But now that realization seemed far off in some other reality. *What's the harm of one night of fun?* she'd asked herself as she snorted a line and picked up the phone to order some wine from the liquor store down the street.

I'd come home from school, and Nina Simone would be playing full blast, and Mom would be dancing around the house and doing the dishes, or vacuuming, in the most delightful, carefree mood I'd ever seen her in. Everything was hilarious. I was, briefly, thrilled to see her this way. Maybe Futurenet had won the lawsuit, I thought, and Mom was feeling celebratory.

The next day, she'd wake up grouchy, raging at the smallest provocation. It went on this way for months. If I complained about how she was acting, she would either get irrationally angry or she would burst into sobs, feeling sorry for herself and uttering nonsensical things like, "Maybe if I wasn't here at all, then you'd be happier."

The mood swings made no sense, and the only explanation I could come up with was that my mother had returned to drinking. She insisted she hadn't, and because I could find no wine bottles under her bed to prove my theory, I ignored my intuition and chose to believe her.

If my mother wasn't drinking, I told myself, then things at work must be pretty bad. I knew about the lawsuit, but Mom was trying to appear as if everything was going to work out. I understood how much stress she was under caring for Kaitlyn and me, and I felt guilty for the burden. Here she was with two children, no income, and a massive overhead that included private school, whose financial aid had been revoked when she started making money a year earlier. We also had this grand house and a new car, not to mention a need to purchase enough food to feed three people—four if you counted April, who I made no effort to hide my disdain for—and our small animal kingdom.

I tried to keep the peace and do my best to make my mother feel that she was not failing us. I took over more of the responsibilities of caring for Kaitlyn after school and on the weekends. The semblance of normalcy that I knew to impose included starting Taco Tuesdays (something I'd heard that other families did) and implementing a chores system (that my mother tried but failed to follow).

She sometimes tried to oblige my "highly neurotic" personality, as she'd taken to labeling it. One day she came into my room, very proud of herself when she handed me a large pile of hundred-dollar bills, and told me to hide them from her for a "rainy day."

I was elated as I tucked the bills carefully away in my closet, next to my school uniforms, feeling that finally we were going to have a "savings plan," as I'd heard that other families did. A few days later, she came into my bedroom in a wide-eyed, manic state and demanded I tell her where I had hidden the money. I refused, and we got into a screaming fight until, defeated, I walked into my closet, pulled the bills from their hiding place, and handed them back.

My mother had gone into overdrive to find new work. Each week for a year she had a different career. One week she was an art dealer. The next she was selling a private island to a billionaire.

In a ten-minute period, she would speak with said billionaire about how gorgeous the island was, accept a conference call with an ambassador to the UN to discuss an international peace conference she was cohosting with Ted Turner in New York, and get advice from our handyman, Chacho, about how to steal registration stickers off other cars because she couldn't afford to buy new ones for her Mercedes.

The contrasts in our life weren't new but seemed harder to understand.

We managed to stave off the first few eviction notices by scrounging enough money to cover the late rent, or transferring the bills from one credit card to another. But when we could no longer pay, the notices began to arrive along with the angry landlord and his wife. Mom would jump up at their knocking, at first frightened, and then feign that this, too, was another "adventure." She'd usher us into her closet, or under the kitchen table—whichever was closer.

We'd hear thuds on the door and "I know you're in there! Open up!," from which my mother tried to distract us with talk of her dreams of the condo on Little Exuma Island that she was going to get as part of her commission as soon as her next deal closed.

"Are there dolphins on the island?" Kaitlyn would ask, getting excited.

"Definitely," my mother would say.

Kaitlyn and my mother would sit on the floor of the closet, talking about collecting seashells in the Bahamas, while I listened to the banging on the front door and wondered how long this could go on before we would be thrown out by a sheriff.

Once, when my mother was out and Kaitlyn and I were home alone, we heard that familiar banging on the door and slipped off as quietly as we could to hide from the landlord. There, on the floor, we found a stack of mail and a Martha Stewart catalog. Kaitlyn reached over and started to flick through the pages, and I looked over her shoulder at the perfectly decorated children's bedrooms and the dining tables set with immaculate glassware and flowers, ready for a feast.

"Is this what a normal house looks like?" Kaitlyn asked. It was the first time I realized that Kaitlyn was even slightly aware of how not normal our home had become.

"I guess so," I said, taking the magazine from her hands. Turning the pages, I daydreamed about what it would feel like to live a life as neat, and tidy, and contained as the ones in the catalog.

When the landlord finally gave up and we came out, Kaitlyn ripped out a dozen pages and taped them to her bedroom wall. She would stare at them at night as if they were her favorite teenage heartthrob or band.

On the weekends, too tired and depressed to get out of bed, my mother started to just hand me the car keys. Off Kaitlyn and I went with a group of my friends, driving along the freeways of Los Angeles, a gaggle of fifteen-year-olds and a ten-year-old girl in a car.

With my mother checked out, I began getting into some trouble, spending time with a group of older boys I'd met at a skate shop who went by the collective name the Moose Crew, as they liked to crash private school parties with a loud moose call to announce their arrival. The Moose Crew had guns, dabbled in drug dealing, and stole cars from car dealerships. I had started to drink, like all my other friends at the time, but I'd stayed away from drugs, including weed, because my mother always told me I had an addictive personality, and I believed her. Still, I was attracted to people who partook in dangerous, illegal behavior, even if I wasn't partaking. One afternoon, the summer before my sophomore year, I showed up at home in one of three brand-new stolen white Escalade SUVs, with one car blasting Eminem so the entire neighborhood could hear. Several boys stepped out, wearing jeans sagging below their butts and giant oversized T-shirts and gold jewelry, but instead of flipping out, my mother opened the front door and, always delighted by youth, invited them all inside with a smile.

On my sixteenth birthday, I woke up to balloons and a sign that read HAPPY RETIREMENT.

It was only when I pointed out the mistake that my mother realized she'd bought the wrong sign. Kaitlyn doubled over in laughter, like it was the funniest moment thus far in our entire lives. I was not amused.

I opened present after present, looking up at my mother's childlike eyes, and I wondered who she'd borrowed money from, or what credit cards she'd maxed out. I wanted to scream and shake her violently for spending what little money she had. She was deep in denial and in a fantasy that we could live an abundant and lavish life, that we were just like the other families at Archer, that the rest of it, the reality, was "just details."

Kaitlyn and I started to feel like we lived in an insane asylum, and we wasted no time telling Mom this. In one of her more lighthearted moods, she thought this label was hilarious, and began answering the home telephone with a loud "Camarillo Mental Institution! How may I help you?" Camarillo was the name of the mental hospital all her friends went to when they were trying to kick heroin and cocaine in the seventies.

I wished that April would just go away. I assumed that if she was gone, my mother's problems would magically stop—the same way they'd miraculously ended after we left Mommy Fay. I was elated when, almost two years after April entered our lives, the most unexpected person imaginable—an eleven-year-old named Lizzie—did what I couldn't do, and rid my family of April once and for all.

Kaitlyn had become best friends with Lizzie on the swing set at school, because the two of them were always the last ones to be picked up. Lizzie had black hair, fair skin, and piercing blue eyes. She was much taller than Kaitlyn, and a bit self-conscious about her weight, about which she was bullied at home and at school. Kaitlyn, meanwhile, was the tiniest girl in her class, with blue eyes and almost white blond hair. Genetic opposites, the girls felt like sisters.

Lizzie swore like a sailor, and she knew so many movie references that she gave the impression she'd been raised more by television than by parents. She could make Kaitlyn and me laugh to the point that we both fell on the floor with physically painful convulsions, and in the years when I'd had no friends, I'd spent hundreds of hours at sleepovers with her and Kaitlyn—bossing them around with a clipboard in my hand at all times while I wrote, directed, and produced holiday musicals for them to star in, which my mother happily filmed while high.

One afternoon when Lizzie was over at our house, she decided to play an innocent prank on April, hiding outside the bathroom door and jumping out when she opened the door. The prank landed a little too well, and April was so terrified that she shouted and reflexively jumped, knocking out Lizzie's front tooth with a large portable telephone that April was holding in her hand.

Lizzie ran to show my mother what had happened. Mom was furious and I watched with glee as April tried to defend herself. My mother apparently had a line, and knocking out a kid's tooth was slightly over it. She kicked April out of the house that day for good.

Sadly, my fantasy that Mom would return to her old self was just that. She was using cocaine daily, on her own, often while washing our school uniforms in the garage after Kaitlyn and I went to sleep, or in the car when she was in line to pick up Kaitlyn from school. She'd be waiting for Kaitlyn to come out, feel suddenly tired and overwhelmed, and then pull out her little glass vial, the size of a quarter, tap a bit of cocaine into her palm, scoop it up with her red-painted fingernail, and put it in her nose, feeling instantly happy and in control. Back when she had given me those hundred-dollar bills to hide from her, it was an attempt to keep herself from buying more drugs. She knew that what she was doing was dangerous, but the cravings were greater than her willpower.

With April gone, if my mother wanted some company to use with, she now had Lizzie's mother, Madeleine. Mad, as we appropriately called her, was from the South and had dated Roman Polanski as a teenager. She wore all black and sunglasses indoors and loved drugs as much as my mother did. She was straight, and married, and adored my mother. The two, in Mom's words, were "crazy as bedbugs" and "sisters from another mother." They were nonromantic soul mates. Of all the women who had entered our lives through the years, Mad was the craziest, and the one who would stick around.

When my mother was nursing a terrible hangover or exhausted from trying to figure out how to keep us in school, she would drop off Kaitlyn at Mad's for several days. Mom was happy for the relief, and Mad was happy that her daughter had someone to play with while she and her husband nodded out on an opiate cough syrup called Tussionex. Lizzie and Kaitlyn would stay up until 4 a.m. playing Barbies, then play hooky from school, and always got up to something mischievous or weird with no parents in sight to rein them in. Once they were playing Chumash Indians in Mad's car and accidentally put it in gear. Thankfully they managed to put it back into park before it rolled down Lizzie's driveway. Other times they'd wait all day by our front gate for Leonardo DiCaprio from *Titanic* to drive by, because our handyman, Chacho, had told them he would.

At around the time she met my mother, Mad was spending a great deal of time driving up and down the California coast with her husband, going to pharmacies with called-in prescriptions from Dr. Jane Sneider, a.k.a. Madeleine, for the heavily regulated Tussionex. She had been arrested five times and had two felonies on her record, one for "impersonating a doctor," the other for tax evasion. (Her husband was known as the best sight-reading pianist in Hollywood, and he made a fortune as a studio musician, but the pair spent their millions as quickly as they came in and never got around to filing their taxes.)

"Mad, I just got some heroin," my mother said with a smile to her best friend one afternoon. "Have you ever chased the dragon, like in the song?"

Mad had snorted heroin but never smoked it. The two moms drove to a McDonald's parking lot in Studio City. There they lit a flame under some tinfoil where the brown tar was sitting while my mother sang the words to her favorite Steely Dan tune.

"The water may change to cherry wine," she sang as the smoke filled her lungs, and then, as she exhaled, "And the silver will turn to gold."

As the brown tar heroin flowed through her lungs and a euphoric calmness swept over her, all those worries about money and the future evaporated. In that moment, my mother didn't even have to worry about Kaitlyn and me, or where we were, or who we were with. All the chaos had, for ten minutes, turned to gold.

SENIOR YEAR

One Saturday afternoon I fell asleep while watching TV in my room, and I was terrified when I awoke to find a man sitting at the edge of my bed.

Startled, I jumped up, and then realized it was my father.

"Hi, Chrysta," he said in a kind, loving whisper.

He had combed his hair and put on an old but clean shirt. He looked much better than he had the last time I'd seen him, though he was still too thin. His face was now wrinkled, making me suddenly aware of how much he'd aged.

It had been four years since I'd seen him. He pushed my hair to the side and smiled as he looked into my eyes with a gentle expression. My mother had told me so many different stories about why he had disappeared over the past four years that I didn't know what to believe. Now he was sitting on my bed, looking at me with an expression I hadn't seen him wearing since I was a little girl, when I really believed that he loved me.

I smiled back. I wondered if he was off drugs now and had come to apologize for leaving and to make up for all that lost time. Out of the corner of my eye, I noticed a woman sitting across the room in a chair. I hadn't realized she was there.

I turned to stare at her, wiping a tear from my eye and sitting up straight. She was physically beautiful, dressed in a long hippie skirt, with a pink flower in her hair. I turned back to look at my father, and realized with disgust that our tender exchange had been a performance. My father hadn't come here because he missed me at all; he had come to show this stupid woman with this obnoxious pink flower in her hair—the same kind he used to give to me—that he had a family he cared about, and who cared about him.

I stood up and walked out of the room without saying a word.

He started to show up at our house once again, now to shower, or to raid the fridge, or to swim in the pool that was infested with mold because my mother couldn't afford to maintain it, and I would just leave whatever room he entered. Dad responded to my new attitude of ignoring him when he came over or rolling my eyes when he told jokes by calling me a "spoiled brat."

Because all our money was being funneled into Mom's cocaine habit and she was too tired and hungover to take care of a menagerie of animals, one by one, our pets all disappeared onto that "farm," and we were finally forced to leave our big house in Tarzana. We moved in with the mother of one of Kaitlyn's friends—a gorgeous, straight, dark-haired and dark-skinned wealthy divorcée named Joanna Staudinger, who was the epitome of Mom's type. Joanna had a heart of gold and was happy to let us stay with her for the next six months while Kaitlyn and Joanna's daughter, Sarah, finished seventh grade together. We were at Joanna's the morning of 9/11, and the five of us all sat in her TV room in our pajamas watching the news, afraid and confused. It was incredible the way massive world disasters always coincided with our family ones. After a few months at Joanna's, with Kaitlyn and me waking nightly from nightmares of bombs and terrorists creeping into this house, we moved on. Mom was butting heads with twelve-year-old Sarah, and you can have a sleepover for only so long.

For the next few months, we sublet a few downtrodden rentals in Santa Monica that made my mother increasingly depressed when she realized we could not afford even the smallest of apartments in the neighborhoods she wanted us to live in. We finally settled into an empty unit in an office building in the Pacific Palisades, which she'd driven by one afternoon and seen a FOR RENT sign in front of. It had a balcony with a view of the ocean and where my mother could do her meditations. Our neighbors included a marketing agency and a private gym. How my mother paid for this new living situation, and how we were allowed to live in a commercially zoned building, will forever remain a mystery to me.

My mother and I each converted an office into a bedroom, and Kaitlyn took what was previously the conference room, complete with a large plate glass window that looked out on what would have been the reception area. To bring us good luck, Mom painted her entire room bright orange. With her cocaine addiction in full swing, her new favorite activity was hanging out with François, her hairdresser, and breeding Bengal kittens in our shared walk-in closet to give to friends. (The only animals from our previous life who were still with us were Machu and Picchu, who were now giant and roamed our office home freely.)

I didn't bother to decorate my room because I knew it was only a matter of time before we were kicked out of this place, too. I also didn't bother to get attached to the cats. Kaitlyn had not learned her lesson, and she loved these new baby kittens with all her heart as she took to snuggling with them to sleep. Her pick of the litter was Oliver, who was bright orange and the most confident of the bunch.

Mom became involved in a merry-go-round of consulting jobs. At one point, she was negotiating a business deal to sell a Modigliani painting to a billionaire, which fell through at the last minute, to her astonishment, after the painting was inspected and deemed a counterfeit. At another job, she was helping to orchestrate a "global peace conference" with the United Nations for the following summer, and she would somehow manage to bring Kaitlyn and me with her to Geneva, Switzerland, for the several-days-long event, where we would sit in a large hotel suite with Jane Goodall, Linda Evans, Amma the "hugging saint," and several other women my mother would explain were world leaders, who were there to discuss storming the capital and handcuffing themselves to the gates of the White House.

With money tight, Mom explored moving Kaitlyn and me to a small, off-the-grid town in Colorado called Crestone, which she told us was the "spiritual epicenter" of the planet. A close friend of hers named Hanne, who was married to the under-secretary-general of the United Nations, lived there. Our mother dragged Kaitlyn and me on several trips to Crestone, where we attended an endless procession of spiritual ceremonies of various origins, and where, one night when I was not present, Mom supposedly witnessed the Dalai Lama's lama, who had just been snuck out of Tibet to escape death threats from the Chinese, "levitate" on a mountain, which seemed dubious to me, as my mother was known to exaggerate.

When we returned from Crestone, my father began showing up at our office apartment with regularity, to eat our food, ramble about 9/11 conspiracies, and lecture my mother about animal cruelty when he found an uncooked chicken in the fridge. I had no insight into where he went after he left, who his friends were, if he had any friends or a place to live. I didn't ask and, truthfully, didn't want to know. (The one constant in his life was that he, too, always had animals—about four dogs at that time—and he explained that he couldn't get a job because then he would have to leave them by themselves.)

Even though we often lived together in a small apartment, many parts of my parents' lives were hidden from me. I had finally confirmed that Mom was drinking when I walked into her bedroom one evening after returning from a friend's house and found Kaitlyn sitting on the edge of the bed, crying hysterically, and then turned to see Mom, belligerent, with a bottle of wine in her hand.

"Don't look at me like that, Chrysta!" she said, pugnacious and laughing. "The world is going to shit and I need to drink to deal with it all."

A few days later, Mom vehemently denied that we'd seen her drunk. She told us we'd made the whole thing up.

"I've been sober for almost ten years!" she shouted. "It's you two who are the alcoholics!"

Now seventeen, I had started drinking more on the weekends, along with all my friends, but I was hardly an alcoholic, and I had still never touched a drug, not even weed. Kaitlyn had never taken a sip of alcohol. I wondered if it was true that I had an alcohol problem, and I decided to cut back.

My father's life as a "drug addict," meanwhile, appeared to be reaching a crescendo. Once I watched him pour Campbell's chicken noodle soup into the coffee maker after my mother asked him to make her a coffee. Another time he came into my bedroom and threw an old 1980s issue of *Playgirl* at me. Not knowing what this was, I opened it, right to a picture of my dad, fully naked, with an erection. I ran into my mother's bedroom to tell her what had happened, and I found her in her pajamas on the bed, screaming at a bill collector. I turned back to look at my father, who was laughing, and all I could think was how much I hated them both.

It was now the summer before my senior year of school at Archer. College was a topic on everyone's mind, and at the suggestion of a kind and attentive English teacher, Ms. Pavliscak, I'd decided I wanted to be a writer, and to go to a school called Barnard because it had a strong creative writing program. The school's other most enticing feature was that it was in New York, as far away as I could get. The only time I'd ever been to New York was with Sable, and the city had remained in my mind forevermore as a magical place, perhaps because I'd never felt more safe and emotionally free than I had felt then. Some part of me fantasized that in New York I would return to that carefree person I had been back then. Maybe I would be walking around Central Park, and I would run into Sable, and she would tell me that she'd been waiting for me, and missing me, all these years, and she would explain what had happened with her and my mother's relationship. And in this fantasy, maybe suddenly everything that had happened since would make sense, and I would convince Sable to come back home, and we could go back to living as we once had: as a perfect little family unit.

Kaitlyn and I had grown apart during this time. While I worked a hostess job at a nearby restaurant and spent the summer with friends to get out of the apartment as much as possible, Kaitlyn had become a permanent guest at a rotation of friends' houses. She adapted very well to other people's families, always a good influence on other children, with her focus on schoolwork and tidiness, and with being appreciative at dinner. The parents must have known that something was going on at home when Kaitlyn sometimes stayed with them for weeks at a time, but they never let on that they knew, and they took her in with kindness and compassion.

I had no idea how bad things were with Mom, or that we were about to reach our lowest point as a family, but I would soon find out, starting with our removal from the Archer School for Girls.

I came home from a friend's house one morning a few days before school was meant to start and could tell something was wrong. My mother had been told by the principal at Archer that if all her debt wasn't paid off and the first semester paid in full by the first day of school, Kaitlyn and I would not be able to go back. Mom hadn't shared this information with me, but I had observed over the past few years that affording private school for us was bringing her great anguish, so I'd suggested on numerous occasions that she move us to a local public school. There was even an arts-focused magnet school called LACHSA that seemed like an incredible free alternative to Archer.

My mother would hear none of this. Archer was more than a school to her. As the stresses of life had slowly chipped away at her dreams of how our family would turn out, keeping us in private school was a symbol to Mom that she'd done something right. Even if she couldn't pry herself off drugs, or keep us in a fancy house, or give us a normal father, or live up to the image of the mother she'd always hoped she would be, and even if something happened to her, she knew we'd be okay because she had set us up for success in life with a good education.

Upon entering our apartment, I realized that Kaitlyn was overdue from a cruise she had been on with one of her friends' families, and I asked when she would be coming home.

"Jessica's father has offered to adopt Kaitlyn," my mother blurted out after a long pause.

I just stared at my mother with a blank expression.

"In return," she concluded, "he has agreed to pay for you to complete high school at Archer."

I couldn't believe the words that had just come out of my mother's mouth. Never in my entire life had I felt more rage toward her.

"You are going to give my sister away, like she is one of our animals—is that it?"

My mother was not able to take this. Her eyes darted back and forth—she was very high, but I assumed she'd just been drinking.

"If you'd taken better care of Kaitlyn," she said snidely, "instead of being out all the time with your friends, this wouldn't be happening!"

My heart started beating quickly as I suddenly thought about sweet, innocent thirteen-year-old Kaitlyn, the look of confusion she had given me when I walked in on Mom drunk. I wondered if I had been selfish these last few months, always gone from the apartment instead of at home, caring for Mom and Kaitlyn. I felt overwhelmed and physically dizzy. I tried not to cry.

"Mom, I'll be better," I said. "I'll take care of Kaitlyn. I'll stay at home."

My mother left the apartment and drove her now much older white Mercedes to the large estate where Kaitlyn was staying. The way my mother tells this story is that she burst through the front door calling Kaitlyn's name. No one was around so she walked through the home to the backyard, where she found my sister in a bathing suit by the pool. Her friend's father, a big-time Hollywood producer, was feeding Kaitlyn grapes, one by one, a situation Kaitlyn was too young to understand was problematic. Nothing seemed to have happened, but the scene alerted my mother to the possibility that this would not be a good living situation for Kaitlyn long-term.

"You will not be adopting my daughter," Mom said with indignation as she stole a purple grape from the father's hand. "Sweetheart," she whispered, turning to Kaitlyn, "go get your stuff. You're coming home."

When Kaitlyn and my mother got home, I smiled at my sister as though nothing had happened, asking if she wanted to watch a movie or paint our nails together. Then I looked up at Mom, and I saw pain and shame in her eyes, which refused to meet mine. I knew then that it wasn't that Kaitlyn was too much responsibility for Mom. On some level, she must have felt she wasn't doing a good job as her mother anymore, and that someone else—someone with more money—could do better.

A few days later, she woke us up and told us to get dressed in our uniforms.

"I found a way to pay for school—you're going."

I should have questioned this statement, but our mother was always figuring out how to save the day at the last minute, so I didn't. She dropped us off, and we slipped into school with the rest of our classmates. I was secretly elated that I'd be able to graduate with all my friends after having been with them since the sixth grade.

Thirty minutes later, in the middle of morning meeting, which the entire school attended, a loud commotion was heard by everyone, reverberating through the hallway and into the auditorium. A woman was screaming, and while no one else knew who it was, I certainly did. The assistant principal appeared and motioned for me to follow her outside. Hundreds of teenage eyes, filled with curiosity, stared in my direction as I made my way out of the auditorium, where I was greeted by the image of my mother screaming at the principal. Mom had not figured out how to pay for school—she had simply taken her chances that the administration would not have the heart to pull us out if we showed up. She was wrong.

THE INTERVENTION

After Archer, my mother miraculously got me into another Westside private high school called New Roads. She had used her most powerful weapons—her telephone and her inability to hear the word "no"—to cold-call every private school she'd ever heard of until she landed on New Roads, a brand-new high school in Santa Monica that was dedicated to offering a progressive, independent education to students from families who might not otherwise be able to afford it—a goal it accomplished by requiring the wealthy parents to pay more than they otherwise would. The cofounder and principal of the school, an eccentric, idealistic man named David Bryan, was having trouble recruiting enough students to fill out the grades, so to my mother's great astonishment, he took pity on our situation and let me finish my senior year there on financial aid. I cringed as I overheard her on the phone, between sobs, using words to describe me like "honors student" and "artistic genius," the latter of which I most certainly was not, though I had always been hardworking in school. Since New Roads started with ninth grade and Kaitlyn was going into eighth, she was sent to the local public school down the street, Paul Revere, with the plan that she would attend New Roads the following year.

For the next few months, I focused on getting good grades, spending time with Kaitlyn, and keeping our apartment clean. I turned in my application to Barnard and hoped and prayed that soon I'd be in New York.

As the holidays came around, I was growing increasingly concerned about Mom. We were still living in the office building, but eviction notices had started to appear on the front door and Kaitlyn and I took to hiding in the closet once more when the landlord came by. I noticed that Mom didn't have the same confident look in her eyes that she'd be able to find a way out. She talked a lot about her generous life insurance policy, how "if anything ever happened" to her, Kaitlyn and I would be taken care of financially.

Two days after Christmas, I came home from a friend's house and heard mumbling and frantic voices I didn't recognize coming from my mother's bedroom. Turning the corner, I came upon Kaitlyn, sitting at the edge of our mother's bed. Mom was sitting across from her on her unmade bed, in her red silk bathrobe. To Mom's left was Madeleine, sitting on the sofa. Madeleine's giant green eyes had the heavy look someone gives you as they prepare to break the news that a family member has terminal cancer, or just died in a plane crash. Beside Mad sat a white-haired couple in their sixties who I had never met before. Everyone had that same look except for Mom, who sat doodling on a notepad like a middle schooler who didn't feel particularly in the mood to pay attention in class.

"What's going on?" I asked.

"We've been waiting for you to begin," Madeleine said quietly.

"To begin what?"

"Please have a seat, darling Chrysta," the white-haired woman said with a thick Irish accent, introducing herself as Fianulla. "Your mother has something she'd like to tell you."

I cautiously sat down in a chair borrowed from the kitchen table.

My mother sat up straight, suddenly present and excruciatingly cognizant. "I am not doing this! No way! I've changed my mind!"

"Changed your mind about what, Mom?" I said, now angry. "What the hell is going on?"

"Debra," Fianulla's husband said a bit sternly. "It's important that you tell the children the truth." There was a long, painful pause as he and my mother stared each other down. "All of it," he added through pursed lips.

Mom's eyes darted to each of the adults before moving back to me and my sister, calculating.

"Kids," she began slowly. "As you probably know, I've been drinking."

She stopped and looked around, trying once more to find a way out. She was cornered on every side.

"In addition to drinking," she said in an oddly nonchalant way while she kept doodling on the notepad in her lap, "I'm also addicted to cocaine."

My mother continued speaking, but all the words after "cocaine" blurred into one.

I realized now that my mother had lied to me, countless times, about what was really happening to us, often blaming me for many things that were not my fault, or responsibility. What hurt me most was that, right in that very moment, I could now see she was high as a kite.

"When did you start doing it?" I asked.

My mother proceeded to downplay her problem, but I was done believing anything she said, and realized that for her to be cornered into telling me a truth this ugly, things must be bad.

"Is that why you almost gave Kaitlyn away?" I asked.

I was cruel to my mother. Worse than I'd ever been. I began screaming every horrible thing I could think of. But in that moment, all I wanted was to crawl into the bed with Mom and get under the covers and cry in her arms, while she tickled my back and assured me that everything would be okay. Yet the woman sitting across from me, while she looked like my mother, was not her. I didn't know how long it had been since I'd seen her.

Madeleine, who not too long before had chased the dragon over a piece of tinfoil with my mother, was now a year sober. She interrupted my rant, worried that if I continued, my mother would change her mind and run straight out that door to get more drugs.

"This is an intervention, Chrysta," she explained matter-of-factly.

"Your mother doesn't want to get sober, but she is going to die if she doesn't get help, so she has agreed to go to rehab for ninety days. You two won't be able to talk to her while she's gone, but you can come stay with me, or be here by yourselves. It's up to you." Then Mad said solemnly, "It's her only shot."

I'd already lost one parent to addiction; I told myself maybe I could handle losing both of them. I looked over at Kaitlyn, sitting quietly in front of me, almost invisible, and my heart broke. I stopped screaming, and I tried to pull myself together, for my little sister.

I turned to stare at my mother, who grew still for several beats.

"The tortoises!" she yelled.

Everyone looked at one another, like she had finally cracked, as she continued.

"I cannot go to rehab! What will we do with Machu and Picchu? Who will take care of them?"

And there, at my feet, like he'd been waiting on cue to make an entrance, strolled one of our two tortoises, about fifteen inches long, a prehistoric creature, crawling on the carpet, likely in search of a scrap of lettuce.

"Debra," Madeleine said in exasperated disbelief, "we'll find someone to take care of the tortoises."

Mom spent twenty minutes making excuse after ludicrous excuse as to why she could not check into rehab—the legitimate one, of course, being that she could not leave her two children by themselves.

Madeleine interrupted with the final knockout argument. "Debra, let's face it. You are not exactly being an effective parent right now."

Not liking this comment one bit, yet exhausted from fighting, my mother gave in and started to pack her things—albeit in between several long visits to the bathroom.

While my mother packed, Madeleine and I decided that Kaitlyn would go to her house for the evening and I would stay with a friend. We could make it through one night, we reasoned. Then we'd figure out what to do for the other eighty-nine days.

The next morning, as I rode up the cold metal elevator back to our office apartment, the smell of the salty, overcast Pacific Palisades ocean was boggy and overwhelming. I opened the front door to the empty waiting room area, which was eerily silent and void of life, apart from a dying Christmas tree in the corner.

I glanced around, plugging in the lights on the Christmas tree, and began straightening up. Kaitlyn was supposed to sleep at Madeleine's house for a couple of days while I stayed here alone, but after one night away, she felt homesick and decided she'd rather live with me.

I peered through the giant glass wall overlooking Kaitlyn's conference room turned bedroom, where the two of us would sleep that night. The room had a TV with a VCR and I figured I would make popcorn, and we'd watch something wholesome, maybe *Funny Girl* or *Singin' in the Rain.* For a few hours, we could melt away in this nineties-era office apartment and check out with Barbra Streisand and a little Technicolor tap dancing.

I walked into the kitchen to see if there was anything to eat and was met with a note from my mother on the counter, written in her big, eternally optimistic handwriting, carefully placed next to the keys to the Mercedes and one single crumpled twenty-dollar bill.

I held the twenty in my hand and my anger toward my mother was suddenly dwarfed by shame. On the one hand, all she had left was twenty dollars; on the other, she didn't think twice before giving it, like everything else, to her two daughters. Then, as if this was some hysterical test by the universe, I tried to fathom how I could make twenty dollars last for Kaitlyn and myself for twelve weeks. How many months, legally, could Kaitlyn and I hide under the table or in the closet when the landlord showed up?

My eyes moved to the car keys. My mother knew I was a terrible driver. After failing my driving test twice, the last guy had just taken pity on me and given me a pass, even though I'd almost run someone over while demonstrating a left turn.

It then occurred to me that my mother may have left behind a bag of cocaine to celebrate with when she got out of rehab. Seconds later, I stood in the depths of my mother's closet, taking in the overflowing shelves. I stared at her jackets and old purses, and all the wood and plastic hangers bursting with silk and cotton tattered clothes purchased in better times. I began digging desperately, opening zippers and looking underneath hats and around pens and belts. I told myself that if I could find every morsel of the demon that had taken my mother away from me and flush it all down the toilet, send it out into the choppy ocean three blocks away, then everything, somehow, would be okay. But as I shoved past shoulder pads and through every pouch and crevice like a deranged animal, I found nothing. I felt an avalanche of grief sweep over me and then heard the front door opening, then click closed. I knew Kaitlyn was home. I took in a deep breath.

She can't see me like this, I told myself. *She needs a mother right now.*

I walked out into the living room, and there, standing in the doorway right next to the twinkling dying Christmas tree, was my skinny blond sister, holding her overnight bag in one hand and a stuffed animal in the other. She put on a big brave smile as I walked over and gave her a long hug.

"Are you hungry?" I asked.

"Yes," Kaitlyn said. "Starving."

We walked into the kitchen and I inconspicuously tucked the twenty-dollar bill, my mother's note, and the car keys into my pocket so Kaitlyn wouldn't see them. I opened the pantry and saw a few cans of SpaghettiOs and a bunch of almost empty boxes of Cap'n Crunch.

I made a mixture of the cereals out of what we had left, which wasn't much, split the contents into two bowls, and then, thankfully, found enough milk in the fridge to fill both.

We can get through this, I thought. In truth, the money would last less than a day. And the monster that took my mother would come for me. Soon I would be getting drunk in math class, falling off my chair onto the floor, laughing as I took another sip from a plastic Starbucks cup filled with a Jägermeister iced chai latte. And after I found myself falling into a relationship with the dreamiest boy at my new school—whose family was just as dysfunctional as mine, albeit very rich—my new boyfriend would spin into a drunken rage one bright, sunny afternoon, his face covered with blood, as I screamed and stood at the edge of a cliff, terrified, with the glistening waves of the Pacific crashing down below.

JAMES

There were all kinds of practical matters that had to be taken care of after my mother left for rehab, which didn't give me a lot of time to sit around and wallow in self-pity. I had to take out the Christmas tree because it was emanating a terrible smell, and I had to go to the market because we were out of food, including cat food, which made me realize I had to get a job because twenty dollars would probably feed us all for only a few days.

I set off for the Third Street Promenade in Santa Monica, a few miles from our apartment, and politely left my resume with store owners and managers. The only person who called me back was a manager at Abercrombie & Fitch, who offered me a job folding clothes for $6.75 an hour. Putting aside the terrible perfume that I'm sure they were pumping through the air conditioner's grilles and the trendy music that torturously played on repeat, the worst part about my new job was that employees were required to purchase the brand's clothes to wear on the floor. This meant that after taxes, my paychecks were barely going to be enough to feed the cats, let alone me and Kaitlyn. Worse still, my first check would not come until I'd been working for two entire weeks—and I needed money now.

On my way home from my first day of work, fate was waiting for me in the guise of an eighteen-year-old boy named Eli, who lived across the street from our office apartment. Eli was one year older than me, had been raised by a struggling single mother, and, like me, had grown up broke among mostly wealthy private school kids. Ambitious and always starting new businesses, Eli had launched a successful print magazine by the time he was fifteen and had a side hustle where he sold fake California driver's licenses. Eli's IDs were better than anyone's—they scanned and had the hologram. Driving past Eli's parked car as I pulled up to my apartment, I had an idea for how to make some money.

A few days later, when school resumed after winter break, I packed Kaitlyn's lunch with whatever leftovers I could find in our fridge, dropped her off at Paul Revere Middle School, and drove up Sawtelle Boulevard toward New Roads in Santa Monica.

Eli sold his IDs for $150, but I figured the kids at my new school could afford double that. I walked onto campus and quietly spread the word that I was trying to "get a fake ID," but needed four other kids to go in with me, or my hookup "wouldn't take the order." It was a lie, but I figured getting caught buying a fake ID would be less legally problematic than selling them. I told everyone the IDs cost $250, and two days later, I gleefully walked across the street from our apartment, handed Eli $600 along with the passport photos of the seventeen-year-olds in my class who had just had their pictures taken at the local pharmacy, and walked home with $400 in my pocket—enough for a few weeks' worth of groceries and plenty of Abercrombie & Fitch clothes to wear to work.

At home waiting for me was a large package from Barnard. I knew before opening it, because of the substantial size and weight of the envelope, that I'd gotten in. Inside was an acceptance letter and a generous financial aid package. My heart sunk in on itself. This should have been incredible news—it meant a ticket out of this life and to a new, possibly much brighter one at an esteemed liberal arts college in New York. But how could I possibly leave Kaitlyn alone with our mother?

I had been trying my best not to let my mind wander to my mother. She had not called since she left, which Madeleine explained was the "protocol." My mother's silence had in some ways made it easier for me to be in denial about what had happened. I desperately needed a distraction—anything to take my mind off the situation—and I soon found exactly that in a problematic crush I had developed on a troubled sixteen-year-old at school named James.

James was medium height, with the build of a soccer player, dark olive skin, and long, multilayered eyelashes. In addition to being objectively the most handsome teenage boy I had ever seen, James was exorbitantly wealthy. He displayed a combination of arrogance, aloofness, and disinterest whenever I walked past him that made me think the closest I would ever get to being in a relationship with him was creepily having his photograph taped to my wall. I would have done that, too—in fact I tried, except his photo was oddly missing from every yearbook I got my hands on going several years back. I'd open to the page with his name, and there was just a blank square where his picture was meant to go, next to everyone else's photos, because, I later surmised, he had never bothered to show up on picture day.

Nine times out of ten, James did not show up for school. For months since starting at New Roads, I had sat in English class staring idly out the window at the designated parking spot that James's parents had paid for, feeling a pit in my stomach because the spot was so often empty. Once or twice a week, he'd speed in and park on an angle in his silver BMW sports car, throw a soccer bag over his shoulder, and walk into class, only to leave again thirty minutes later, like whatever rules that applied to everyone else didn't apply to him. The one time I'd built up the courage to speak to James, it hadn't gone very well.

"I'm Chrysta," I'd said, holding out my hand and trying to be casual when I found him sitting in the grass next to another kid I knew. James looked me up and down with a completely flat expression, then stood up and walked away without a word. I'd spent the next three days trying to unwind the encounter to figure out what I'd done to offend him.

"He's just weird. Don't take it personally," his friend said.

"How does he get away with skipping school all the time?" I asked.

"Oh, you know. His parents just keep buying the school new buildings," he responded.

For the first few months of school, every morning I'd spend hours getting ready in the mirror, on the off chance I might finally get James's attention. Each day I'd come home disappointed when I hadn't, and then spend hours staring in the mirror, trying new makeup or a different way of styling my hair, none of which made a difference. James was out of my league.

When school resumed after winter break, one of the guys who had purchased a fake ID from me invited me to a get-together at James's house. I tried to act casual as I accepted the invitation. Kaitlyn had gone back to stay with Lizzie and Madeleine for a couple of weeks, so I had the apartment to myself. I ran home after school and spent two hours getting ready, hoping the right combination of clothes, blow-dried bangs, and eyeliner would finally catch James's attention.

That night I walked through a giant mansion in Brentwood with a meandering staircase and several rooms that weren't in use and out to the back, past what felt like an acre of perfectly manicured rose gardens, to where a group of kids from school were hanging at a table by a large pool, passing around a joint. James was sitting at the end of the table in a ridiculous sun hat, next to an empty seat, which I promptly plopped myself in. He looked up at me with a smile and held out the joint.

"No thank you," I said timidly and a bit embarrassed. "I don't smoke."

"Suit yourself," James said with a British accent, even though he was not British. (This was a curious quirk of James's that he employed often, without explanation.) He passed the joint to the guy next to him, then looked at me sideways, like a science experiment he was suddenly curious about.

I am nothing like my mother, I thought resolutely, as I watched the joint being passed in a circle by each person's pinched, careful fingers. I looked back at James and realized, to my great shock, that he was staring at me, and smiling.

"I think it's time we initiate her," he said to the group, standing up.

"No, please don't," another guy at the table said.

"Yes, initiate me!" I replied, unsure what that meant but inebriated by the idea that James might do anything to me.

Before I had a chance to reconsider, James lifted me into his arms and threw me into the deep end of his pool, fully clothed, with my shoes on. I screamed, then paddled quickly toward the edge.

"Let me help you up," he said, holding out his hand with a gentle, concerned expression. It was a trick and he forcefully pushed me back into the pool, laughing hysterically. No one else thought it was funny. The friend who had invited me to the party shook his head, then walked over and reached down to help me out. James was laughing and smiling at me flirtatiously.

I knew I should be angry. My phone and shoes were ruined, and I could not afford to replace them. Perhaps if I'd been raised in a slightly less dysfunctional situation, I would have taken this experience as a red flag and quickly swerved out of the way of James and his fancy sports car. Instead, I thought it was the most romantic moment of my life.

"Can I borrow some sweatpants or something?" I asked. James motioned for me to follow him. We walked through the kitchen and past James's father, who looked me up and down in a way I found disturbing while he chatted on the phone and arranged an elaborate Italian take-out meal on the kitchen island. At this point I was introduced to James's mother by her voice only, as she yelled at her husband over a loudspeaker.

"My mother likes to communicate with the family over speakerphones that she had installed in every room," James explained. "She gets anxiety leaving her bedroom."

James's home couldn't have looked more different from mine, with rose gardens, a staff of housekeepers, and pantries and a kitchen brimming with fresh food, yet I found something oddly familiar in its sheer level of dysfunction.

He led me up the stairs to his bedroom, where he tossed me a pair of sweatpants and a T-shirt. The room looked as though it belonged to a ten-year-old child, not a sixteen-year-old boy. James still slept in a twin bed, right next to his younger brother's identical twin bed, with matching *Star Wars* comforters and several stuffed animals laid out on the pillows in their perfectly washed and pressed pillowcases.

He sat on his bed and motioned for me to sit next to him.

I froze, in disbelief that this was happening. He laughed, and I started to doubt myself. I wondered if maybe this was all a game, like the pool. Then he kissed me.

Things began to progress, at which point I pulled away. It wasn't that I didn't want to go further—I did. But that strategy with boys hadn't worked out very well for me in the past. I watched as James's face changed to anger, his eyes glinting with fiery light as if he wanted to strangle me right there on his *Star Wars* comforter.

"Why don't you get out of here?" he said, now with a look of disgust as he walked out of the room and down the stairs. It made no sense to me, and I drove home that night deeply confused.

The next day at school, wanting to maintain some level of pride, I ignored James. This strategy worked brilliantly. He walked up to me during a free period and announced, with a thick British accent, that he was "in love" with me. This was more shocking than being thrown into the pool.

Shortly after, James and I began dating exclusively, engaged in a dance that I had no idea would soon turn dangerous. My mother was right that I had an addictive personality like her and my father, but my drug of choice was a person.

Being in a relationship with James was like walking through an active war zone, set with booby traps and bombs hidden in the most obscure and unexpected places. Once we were playing Monopoly at his house, having what I thought was a great time, and I won. James exploded into a rage and threw the dice at my forehead so hard that I bruised. In a state of shock, I broke up with him. He pretended not to care, told me I could walk home because he would not give me a ride, and then followed me slowly in his car as I walked down San Vicente Boulevard toward my apartment. When he realized I was serious about breaking up with him, he pulled over and started crying, begging me to take him back, saying he felt horrible for throwing the dice and would never do anything like that again.

Looking at James in tears, I felt there was some part of himself he had no control over. When he got angry, it was like a switch flipped, and some monster he didn't understand and could not control took over his body. I wondered if his problems—of which there were many, including drug use, failing grades, and a constant rotation of medication and psychologists—were all the result of bad parenting, if perhaps all he needed was some unconditional love to help him heal. I excused every bad behavior as beyond his control.

Another red flag I ignored was that James really seemed to like drinking and getting high. Several times I caught him snorting his crushed-up prescription for Adderall. He would appease me with promises to quit, which he, of course, never did. In the morning before school, he had a habit of pouring out half of his venti iced chai latte and replacing it with Jägermeister. I agreed to try it with him one morning after sleeping at his house the night before, and as the alcohol kicked in and James sped into his designated parking spot, I felt like the coolest girl in school. I'm not sure if it was the booze or the high of having James as my boyfriend, but for the first time in years, I felt a sense of ease and well-being. When I fell off my chair in math class an hour later, laughing hysterically as the room started to spin, I thought to myself, *Wow. This is the best day of my life.*

Our pattern of extreme intimacy followed by separation had begun and our fights became physical. I started drinking with James before school and took great care to hide the bruises that started appearing on my arms. James would get angry and punch or lightly strangle me, I would break up with him, he would make a grand gesture, and I would take him back. The combination of adrenaline and dopamine plus alcohol was so consuming I could think of nothing else and didn't even care that my mother wasn't around. In some ways, I was relieved as there was no one to stop me from being in this relationship. When my old friends, who I rarely spoke to now, expressed concern, I dismissed them as jealous, and we grew even further apart.

During our calmer moments, James's anger came in sideways. He began teasing me about things that he felt were wrong with me—calling me pudgy, for example, and a "piglet" when I ate with too much enthusiasm, even though I was five foot six and weighed 115 pounds. As "in love" as I increasingly felt with James, I felt equally less confident in myself and attempted to diet for the first time in my life, a process that filled me with self-loathing as it was much more difficult than I had imagined. While I tried my best not to eat, I did worry about feeding our many animals after the money from the fake IDs ran out, and I started slipping cans of cat food from the pantry at James's house into my purse. One day James caught me. In addition to "piglet," he gave me the nickname "mooch." When my second paycheck from Abercrombie came in, he told me to prove that I loved him by buying him dinner, so I spent almost the entire paycheck treating him to a meal.

I had not seen Kaitlyn in a couple of weeks, as she was splitting her time between our place and Madeleine's house, but she called one night asking if she could come home early. "Of course you can," I'd told her, a pang of anxiety hitting my gut as I knew this would cause problems in my relationship with James. I told him I had to take a break from seeing him after school for a few days to be with "my family."

I hadn't explained that my mother was in rehab. James didn't even know where I lived, as I'd made him drop me a block from my apartment on the one day that I didn't have my car with me. He'd sensed I was hiding things from him, though his suspicions as to what I was hiding were grossly inaccurate. When he started asking me questions about my home life that I didn't want to answer and insisted on coming over to meet my family, I decided to end the relationship then and there.

Later that evening, I tried my best to take my mind off James and be there for my sister. Kaitlyn and I were painting each other's nails on my bedroom floor and watching *Gidget* when I looked out the sliding glass door to the balcony. I screamed when I saw a figure in a hoodie approaching from outside. James had scaled the sixty-foot side of our office building apartment.

"What the hell are you doing here?" I asked as I cracked the door open. "Are you insane?"

"I needed to see you," he said, agitated, looking past me to see who really lived here with me—some secret boyfriend, he was sure. "Can I come in?"

"No, you cannot come in! My mother is sleeping!" I lied.

"I don't believe you," he said, peeking past me. "Who really lives here?"

He pushed me aside and walked in, seeing Kaitlyn on the floor in her pajamas.

"Well, hello," he said with a British accent, smiling and realizing that I was not secretly living here with some older man but in fact with my thirteen-year-old sister.

I had no choice then but to tell James everything, since he could very plainly see as he traipsed through the apartment that my mother wasn't home.

"Wow. This place is a total shithole," he said, walking around and checking out every room like this was some kind of archeological dig, like, *Oh, I see: this is how the other half lives. Fascinating!*

Rather than be insulted at James's tactlessness, I just felt grateful that he knew the truth and still liked me. He came back into my bedroom, sat down on the floor, and motioned for me to join him. Then he smiled at Kaitlyn and put his head on my knee like a puppy.

"Oh, Goosey," he said, using the new nickname he'd given me.

He proceeded to move in with me and Kaitlyn, preferring our "shithole" to his Brentwood estate, and the three of us became one utterly ridiculous, dysfunctional little family.

In the mornings, I'd make Kaitlyn and James toast and eggs for breakfast and pack Kaitlyn's lunch for school, and then we'd take off in James's BMW. We'd drop off Kaitlyn at Paul Revere Middle School and then get drunk on the way to New Roads. I was too buzzed to consider how reckless it was for James to be driving.

Things weren't rosy between us for long. Soon James grew irritable and physical, sometimes in front of Kaitlyn. There were high highs and low lows in this new family unit, which was perhaps not too dissimilar from the family I'd been raised in, except now I was the mother, and I was the one fucking up.

One Saturday, just as I got off work, I received a phone call from a blocked number.

I picked up the phone as I started the car. "Hello?" I said.

"Hi, Beanie," I heard my mother say.

My stomach dropped. I had put my mother into a box deep in my psyche. Hearing her voice on the other end of the line pulled the lid off, and all my mixed emotions—my fear, my rage, the black hole of hopelessness I felt about the future—rose to the surface and overwhelmed me.

"Hi, Mom," I said, my voice as loving and supportive as I could make it sound.

My mother explained that she was doing well, but was sick of rehab and wanted to come home early. She had gotten into an argument with the head of the program—something to do with her having snuck in her blow-dryer.

"I think you should stay, and do whatever they tell you," I told her, not ready for her to come back.

After the call, I drove toward the Pacific Coast Highway in a daze. As I stared at the glistening sun over the ocean, not looking at the road, I slammed right into a car stopped at a red light at fifty miles per hour, totaling my mother's car. She returned from rehab the next day.

I sat with Kaitlyn inside a small, artificially lit room, in a circle with fifteen teenagers, aged twelve to eighteen. I didn't want to be here, but I had no choice. After Mom returned home, she'd seen the bruises on my arms and then gotten into a big argument with James when she told him he would no longer be living at our apartment. The police were called, and after James arrogantly refused to leave, placing his feet up on our kitchen table with a shit-eating grin on his face, he was escorted out of the apartment in handcuffs. My mother got a restraining order against him after he proceeded to scale our building again later that night. I'd continued dating him secretly through graduation and into the summer, until an acquaintance called to share that James had been cheating on me with someone else, which led me, finally, to break up with him. It took more self-control than I felt I had not to pick up the phone when he called, which was constantly, and I was in a very dark space.

My mother felt that I needed help as much as she did, and her solution was to force me to sit in this room with all these strangers, twice a week, until I realized that alcoholism was "a family disease," and that I was sick, too.

I looked around the sparsely lit room. On one side was a cheap picnic table with sugar cookies laid out carefully on it, and there were several posters taped to the walls.

In bright red letters, one poster read, WHEN YOU DON'T KNOW WHERE TO TURN...BECAUSE SOMEONE DRINKS TOO MUCH...ALATEEN CAN HELP. LEARN MORE BY ATTENDING A CONFIDENTIAL MEETING IN YOUR COMMUNITY. 1-800-ALATEEN.

On another wall, straight across from me, was a green poster with bold white letters: THE THREE CS, it read. WE DID NOT CAUSE IT. WE CANNOT CURE IT. WE CANNOT CONTROL IT.

I stared at that poster for quite some time as I wrestled uncomfortably in my metal chair, looking around the room at all the other uncomfortable faces. *What did these people know about my life?* I thought, irritated.

All I could think about was James. Was he thinking about me? I had not gotten a single missed call from him in several days, and it was driving me crazy.

A woman leading the group, with a wise face and a gentle, loving voice, picked up a piece of laminated paper and read a set of questions, which were meant to help the kids in the room decide if this program had anything to offer them.

"Do you constantly seek approval and affirmation?" she read off the paper.

Yes, okay, sure, I thought.

"Do you have a need for perfection?" she read.

I looked over at the cookies. I could smell their frosting from ten feet away, and I wanted to grab one. It had been months since I'd allowed myself a bite of anything that delicious. I was not a piglet, I had told myself, as the weight fell off me.

"Do you confuse love and pity and tend to 'love' people you can 'pity' and 'rescue' as you did with the problem drinker?"

I sat there, dumbfounded. The woman in the chair across from us was describing me.

She continued speaking, but I didn't want to hear what she had to say. I was angry at my mother for what had happened, and I felt that it should have been her sitting here, not me. I nudged Kaitlyn to get up so we could slip out of there and head home.

A largely uneventful and depressing summer passed by as I worked a hostess job, stayed home to keep Mom company, and mentally prepared for Barnard in New York. Mom had insisted that I go, that she and Kaitlyn would be just fine, and she helped me fill out the paperwork for student loans to bolster the financial aid. Mom was doing okay but I felt incredibly guilty about going to New York. Being newly off alcohol and drugs and without a car to drive had certainly left her on edge. I wondered how long she could stay sober, and how Kaitlyn would manage without me.

The night before I was set to leave, I just couldn't stand the discomfort I was feeling, and I decided to text James, to ask him if he wanted to say goodbye. As soon as I hit Send, I regretted it, but within five seconds I got a text back: "leaving now, be there in 10."

I told my mother that I was going to see some friends, then walked out of our apartment and took the elevator down to greet James. It wasn't a complete lie—I had arranged to see one of my old high school friends, who was set to pick me up in thirty minutes. James pulled up, and I got into the car. I figured I would say a quick goodbye, give him a hug, and then have him leave before my friend arrived, since she would not be thrilled to come face-to-face with him.

Things didn't go as planned.

James and I hugged, then a tear dripped down his face, and he told me he was sorry for everything that had happened. I told him I was sorry, too, and would miss him. We had a lovely ten-minute talk, and then I told him I had to go, but that I was happy I had gotten to see him. I grabbed the passenger door handle to leave.

"What are you doing?" he asked.

"What do you mean?" I said. "I have plans to see Anne. I just wanted to say goodbye."

"I thought we were spending the evening together," he said. I could see that switch flipping inside of him, that he was trying very hard to keep himself from exploding. "I thought I could take you out to dinner," he said, voice trembling.

I knew I had made a mistake, and tried to calm him down.

"I just can't," I said. "I already have plans."

Before I could get the passenger door open, James started the car and sped out onto Sunset Boulevard.

"James, what the hell are you doing?" I could see there was nothing I could say to deter him. I'd never seen James so angry. He started crying hysterically, and then banging his head insanely on the steering wheel, pulling his hair out so that strands of it were suspended in mid-air as he sped far beyond the speed limit. He turned to me and I saw that his head was bleeding.

"James, please calm down," I begged. "We can go to dinner. We can do whatever you want. Please, just stop the car."

He couldn't hear me, he was in such a manic rage. He screeched up a canyon onto a private road, barreling up to the top, way past where there were houses, to a clearing at the end. Then he got out of the car and came around to open my door. I held it closed.

He wrestled the door open and pulled me out by the arm.

I screamed for help, but there was no one around. He threw me down in the dirt in front of the car.

I quickly pulled out my phone and tried to dial 911, but he grabbed the phone aggressively out of my hands, and threw it off the cliff next to us.

"Please take me home," I begged. I started crying. "Please, James. I'm scared."

"Stay there," he demanded as he walked back toward the driver's side and got in. I wondered what he was going to do—if he was going to run me over.

I started to scream again, but all I could hear was my own voice echoing through the canyons. There wasn't a house anywhere nearby and no one was coming to save me. It occurred to me that James might actually kill me. That I might die.

I held back tears and steadied my voice.

"James," I said quietly, walking slowly toward where he was sitting in the car as he turned it on. "C'mon, James," I said. "I'm sorry that I told you we couldn't spend the night together. We can. I'll spend the whole night with you. Can you just please calm down a little and turn off the car?"

My speech wasn't working. He gave me a skeptical look.

"I'm sorry we ever broke up, James. I really am," I said. "I've missed you so much."

As I said these words, I noticed James's face start to shift.

"James, I love you," I said.

He looked at me skeptically again, trying to suss out if I was telling the truth.

"Please," I continued gently. "Let's just get back in the car, and spend the night together."

James turned off the engine, stepped out of the car, and put his hands down at his sides, staring at me.

I tried my best not to show anything but tenderness on my face, even as I was suddenly repulsed. I knew if I made one wrong move, the window to save myself might close. I walked up to him, and kissed him.

He picked me up and threw me into the back seat of his car, taking off my clothes. I tucked all my trembling terror away and acted the part of remorseful girlfriend and let James have sex with me.

Afterward, James smiled lovingly as if everything was perfectly normal between us. He got in the driver's seat and started the car, and as I moved back in the passenger seat next to him, he began whistling as he drove back down the canyon.

"I love you, Goosey," he said with a British accent.

I held James's hand and told him that my mother would be worried about me by now, and I asked if he could drop me at home just so I could lie and tell her I was going out with friends. To my astonishment, he dropped me at my building. I gave him a kiss and exited the car, and headed slowly toward the door. When I was out of sight, I ran to the elevator and rode it up to the apartment.

I didn't want my mother to know I had just seen James or what had just happened, so calling the cops was out of the question. I felt somewhat responsible, because James had been leaving me alone. I was the one who had reengaged with him. I had played the game of back and forth, intensity and withholding, and I felt I had, in some ways, made him feel this insane about me.

Not knowing what else to do, I walked into my bedroom and called James's father.

"James just went crazy," I told him. "I thought he was going to kill me. He's in his car waiting for me downstairs from my apartment, and if you don't come get him right now and keep him away from me for the next ten hours until I leave for New York, I'm going to call the police and tell them he violated the restraining order."

I hung up and watched from my balcony as ten minutes later, James's father showed up in a large black SUV and demanded that his son follow him home. I went back inside and sat at the dinner table with my mother and sister, who had no idea what I'd just been through. I picked at my plate, trying to understand what was wrong with me. For most people, such a traumatic experience would have shaken them to their core and possibly scarred them in a deep way. For me, it all just felt kind of normal.

PART FOUR

HELLO, I'M YOUR SISTER.
OUR FATHER IS DONOR 150.

It was a late Sunday afternoon in 2005, and my father stepped out of the car he had been living in, stretched his arms, and closed his eyes briefly in the mild November sun. He gathered his rescue dogs, Junior and Trixie, for their daily stroll to his favorite coffee shop, Abbot's Habit.

Jeffrey was forty-nine now, and his once thick sandy-brown hair was beginning to gray around the temples. It was much thinner than it once had been, and filled with knots he didn't bother to brush out as he pulled it back into a ponytail. He wore a necklace he'd purchased for a few dollars at the Mystic Journey Bookstore. His clothes, which were now a decade old, were filthy and covered in dirt and stains.

Jeffrey entered Abbot's Habit to stand in line as his dogs sat by his feet, scratching fleas and rummaging for leftover snacks on the unswept concrete floor. Jeffrey ordered a coffee and a pastry. It was their routine. Jeffrey would wake up, usually in the late afternoon, come here, tell jokes to the baristas, who knew him by name, or chat up the locals' dogs, who came in with their owners. Occasionally, he'd find someone interested in sitting down to discuss various conspiracy theories. His most recent obsession was that no plane had hit the Pentagon on 9/11—that it had all been made up by the "people who were taking over the world."

I was now living far away in New York, a junior at Barnard, while my mother was in our office apartment five miles north of Venice, which she'd somehow managed to hold on to. She was coming up on three years sober and passionately fundraising for a vegan congressman from Ohio named Dennis Kucinich, who she was convinced could be president. Jeffrey knew nothing about my mother's stint in rehab or her problems with drugs and alcohol. Mom wasn't someone who shared that type of information. Jeffrey was unsure what change had occurred in Debra, but she had resumed driving to Venice to check on him whenever she hadn't heard from him for a couple of weeks.

Jeffrey's sperm donation days were a distant memory now. He made his meager living by setting up a blanket along the Venice boardwalk and putting up a handmade sign offering to crack tourists' backs or necks for ten dollars. At night, he'd grab a bite to eat at the Hare Krishna center, always with his dogs in tow, and then walk around the streets of Venice until sunrise, feeding whatever stray animals he saw hiding under old boxes or in gutters. At any one time, he might be caring for a family of pigeons, three families of rats, a baby raccoon, a raven with a broken foot, and two feral kittens. He had always suffered from strange sleep patterns and terrible insomnia and liked to say he was nocturnal, like his animals.

Jeffrey grabbed his hot cup of coffee, then sat down at an empty table, where he noticed a copy of the *New York Times*.

He was looking forward to reading the Sunday paper because he had been closely following the coverage of the Iraq War and wanted to see what this week's news would bring. He sat back, unfolding the crumpled front page, and saw the headline: HELLO, I'M YOUR SISTER, it read. OUR FATHER IS DONOR 150.

Jeffrey spilled his coffee all over himself and the paper. He nearly fell out of his chair.

Was this a dream? A hallucination? A bad trip? He looked at the clock above the barista stand and around at the other people. They were all real. He was here, awake, and yes, this was a story about Donor 150—him!—on the front page of the *New York Times*.

Maybe there is another Donor 150, he reasoned, skeptical that this story on the front page of the newspaper of record could be about him.

There are probably other sperm banks with a Donor 150, he thought. *Surely I am not the* only *donor with that identification.*

Jeffrey started reading.

"Like most anonymous sperm donors," the piece began, "Donor 150 of the California Cryobank will probably never meet any of the offspring he fathered through sperm bank donations."

"Holy shit!" Jeffrey said out loud. "Donor 150—from *the California Cryobank!"*

There was no question.

"There are at least four [children], according to the bank's records," the piece continued, "and perhaps many more, since the dozens of women who have bought Donor 150's sperm are not required to report when they have a baby."

"Wow," Jeffrey said out loud, shaking his head in disbelief as he read. "Wow. Wow. Wow!"

The article, written by journalist Amy Harmon, told the story of two of Jeffrey's genetic daughters, born to different mothers and living in different parts of the country: Danielle, who was sixteen, and JoEllen, who was fifteen. They had been connected through a website called the Donor Sibling Registry, which enabled parents or offspring to enter their contact information and search for parents and children who had registered under the same donor number and sperm bank.

"For children who often feel severed from half of their biological identity," the piece explained, "finding a sibling—or in some cases, a dozen—can feel like coming home. It can also make them even more curious about the anonymous father whose genes they carry."

Jeffrey sat, processing.

He recalled a "flash" during a spiritual experience many years earlier when he had seen his picture printed in thousands of newspapers all around the world. Though he trusted this vision wholeheartedly, he had never been able to figure out why, exactly, he was on the cover of these global media outlets. Now it occurred to him that *this* was the story he had envisioned.

"I am now the most famous anonymous sperm donor in the world!" he said aloud to himself, sitting a little taller in his seat. For Jeffrey, this moment affirmed his every vision, every religious experience, all the eccentric behavior that other people didn't understand. It affirmed walking into that hair salon two decades earlier and the choice to donate sperm secretly for as long as he did. It was all part of some greater destiny he was only now beginning to comprehend.

The piece went on to explain that Danielle and JoEllen now spoke on the phone and emailed each other regularly. It also described a more general phenomenon among biological siblings that included a "sense of familiarity that seems largely irrational, given the absence of a father, unrelated mothers, and often divergent interests."

Danielle was described as having a lot of anger toward her parents, since they'd only recently told her she was the product of a sperm donor. She was also angry at the prevalent idea, which her parents shared, that "biology doesn't matter. If it really didn't matter to them," she was quoted as saying, "then why would they use [donor insemination] at all? They could just adopt or something and help out kids in need."

Jeffrey sat in his chair feeling empathy for Danielle for having been lied to all her life. During his childhood, he himself had been lied to by his parents on numerous occasions, and thinking about it even now made him angry.

He read that, for Danielle, getting to know her half sister "had eased her frustration of knowing only the scant information about her biological father contained in the sperm bank profile—he is 6 feet tall, 163 pounds, with blond hair and blue eyes. He was married, at least at the time of his donation, and has two children with his wife. He likes yoga, animals, and acting."

Jeffrey laughed at himself for his decision, somewhere along the line, to start referring to Debra in his profile as his "wife."

While most of the Donor Sibling Registry's matches thus far had been between half siblings, the piece noted that the registry especially welcomed donors.

Jeffrey sat, holding the paper in his hands, and pondered the idea of coming forward as the man behind Donor 150. He would later describe his intentions for doing so as largely selfless: he related to Danielle's anger at being lied to and wanted to help bring his offspring closure by being able to meet their biological father if they wished to.

There was just one big problem that made him pause: my mother.

She had absolutely no idea that Jeffrey had ever donated sperm to anyone other than her. She was in the process of saving up to buy Jeffrey a motor home so he wouldn't have to live in his car. He was certain that his motor home would no longer be on the table if he went public.

NEW YORK, NEW YORK

For winter break of my junior year of college, I returned home from New York for two weeks, grateful to see that my mother was doing better than I had seen her in a long time. She was happy, present, and dating a new woman, her first girlfriend in years, who I loved from the second I laid eyes on her.

Kathy was a large woman, with short brown hair, freckles, and a childlike button nose. She wore the same black leather jacket every day, spoke in a thick French-Moroccan-Israeli accent, and had a heart of gold I sensed immediately. She ran a car dealership in the Valley, where she made a stable living, which meant that Mom was now driving a comical rotation of used cars. I could tell, from Mom's sudden lightness of mood, that Kathy was also helping to pay some of our bills.

When I met Kathy for the first time, right after my mother and I returned home from the airport to our office apartment, she strangled me in a tight hug, laughed a jubilant, guttural laugh, and slipped a hundred-dollar bill in my pocket.

"Now you spend this on something fun, you hear me, Chrysta?" she'd whispered. "And don't tell your mother!"

I laughed and promised I wouldn't.

I turned to get my first good look at Kaitlyn and realized in horror that she was who I should have been worrying about.

Kaitlyn had always copied me, as younger siblings often do. When I wanted to surf, she wanted to surf. When my computer password was Oliver, her computer password was Oliver. It had sometimes annoyed me, but mostly I was proud that she looked up to me. But now I felt ashamed of myself as I looked at the bones jutting out of her chest. She was five foot six and couldn't have weighed more than ninety-eight pounds. My stomach dropped as I pulled her toward me for a hug, feeling as if one touch could crush her. *This is my fault,* I thought.

Moving across the country had given me the chance to rebuild my identity from scratch, with a biography no one knew anything about. On the outside, I was doing okay, getting straight As in school and even making it on the dean's list as I held down waitressing and babysitting jobs. But inside, I was struggling with sometimes severe depression. And the truth was, leaving home had not really allowed me to escape any of the demons of my childhood.

I had, in my constant striving for outward perfection to find love, honed a strict dieting regimen, and had dwindled down to ninety-five pounds myself. My greatest accomplishment in college was not my high grades, I felt, but being able to fit into a pair of black pants I had owned since I was twelve. I spent hours every day obsessing over my appearance: I kept a journal of how many calories I'd eaten, worked out between classes in the school gym, and took the subway to spend what little money I had sitting under bright lights with a disgusting-smelling cream all over my body to get a fake tan, caring little about the fact that skin cancer ran in our family. When my willpower to not eat was almost overcome by my hunger, I found anorexia websites online to help motivate me and keep me focused. I'd become a shell of a human being in an effort to appear more attractive to men, or perhaps in an effort to feel in control of a life that felt largely out of my control.

Kaitlyn had also developed an inability to get close to people. She'd inherited the best physical attributes of both of our parents, and she was now, more than ever, stunningly beautiful. She had flawless tan skin, a soft face with large blue eyes, and our mother's enormous breasts. Her beauty had brought her a lot of male attention, but no one was able to get past her iron-clad, avoidant defense system. The exception was a much older man who was the heir to a massive fortune. Kaitlyn became enamored with him as he showered her with gifts and attention. But he'd quickly turned psychologically abusive, and the relationship raised concerns among several friends' parents. Mom was concerned as well, but even though she was now sober, she'd lost credibility in Kaitlyn's and my eyes and had trouble controlling either one of us.

Looking back, I wish I'd been able to tell my sister that her boyfriend was a loser and pedophile who should be in jail, but at twenty-one, I was just as mixed up about men as Kaitlyn was. I had continued to date James through college, and was only ever able to stay away from him for a few months at a time.

The day before Christmas, our mother suggested we go visit our father. Mom would have preferred to continue having our father come to us, as he'd always done, but because driving in general now gave him profound anxiety, the only option was to go out to Venice.

We pulled up to a vegan Indian restaurant our father had selected and sat inside for nearly two hours, sipping lukewarm water out of plastic cups and growing hungry at the smell of curry and lentils passing our table.

Finally, he arrived, saying that he'd "overslept," without showing a hint of self-consciousness that it was 8 p.m. He greeted Kaitlyn and me with stiff, uncomfortable hugs, then smiled, at which point Kaitlyn and I noticed that most of his teeth were missing—all but the front two. His face, hair, and clothes were all extremely dirty. He clearly had not abided by our mother's many requests to get cleaned up before this visit.

He told a joke to lighten the mood: "You guys should come to my music show on Venice Boulevard. The audience consists mostly of my dogs and cats, and occasionally someone walks by."

Kaitlyn and I looked over the menu, pretending that nothing was wrong or shocking about how Dad looked. Then we caught each other's eyes with a mix of shame and guilt that we even cared what anyone thought. I hoped my father hadn't sensed it. I got the feeling that this was his one and only Christmas celebration this year, and I felt deep sadness thinking about how lonely he must be.

My mother, visibly uncomfortable at Jeffrey's appearance, especially his missing teeth, tried to steer the conversation away from government conspiracies and to lighter topics. She filled in our father on how college was going for me, and what classes Kaitlyn and I were taking, but he had trouble participating in these conversations. He seemed nervous but he made no mention of the *New York Times* article. He still wasn't sure at that point, a month after he'd read it, what he was going to do, and I wonder if seeing us at Christmas made him pause, or if he gave any thought to how coming out with the news would make all of us feel.

When the meal ended, we walked outside to our car to retrieve some gifts we had brought for Dad.

I stood in the cold parking lot, across from my father, watching as he opened a card we'd filled out on the way over and gently unwrapped several sweaters, some jeans, and a warm hat, which Mom had bought for him weeks earlier. He seemed increasingly uncomfortable accepting each of our gifts but said thank you in a small, quiet voice. Then he turned, and I watched as he fumbled into his own car, which was parked next to ours.

He pulled out two pairs of used socks, which he handed Kaitlyn and me, along with a few spiritual brochures from the Hare Krishna temple up the street.

"Merry Christmas," he said with a look of self-consciousness that broke my heart. We took his gifts with big smiles. I wanted to crawl out of my skin for bringing him anything. Our gifts had clearly made him feel bad.

I peered over at my father's car, inside of which I noticed several dirty blankets among piles of empty cans of food, several sleeping cats, and a large bird in a cage.

"Is that where you live, Dad?" I asked, realizing, for the very first time, astonishingly, that my father was homeless.

My mother followed my gaze, then looked at my father. She scrambled to change the subject, but before she could, Dad replied, casually, "Yep, that's where I live, with little Junior and Trixie and my cats—my little family."

On the ride home, Kaitlyn and I were quiet, staring out the windows as we drove past strip malls, gas stations, and bus stops.

My mother looked back at Kaitlyn, and then at me beside her up front. We didn't need to say anything. Mom knew what we were thinking.

HAPPY VALENTINE'S DAY

It was Valentine's Day 2007, and more than a year had passed since that painful December evening when the four of us stood exchanging gifts in the Indian restaurant parking lot. Things were looking up for Mom as she sat at a new desk, staring out a charming Cape Cod–style window at a pair of deer walking through her new backyard.

After several years of living in our office apartment and almost being evicted several times, she had just moved Kaitlyn and herself into an adorable house a mile from the beach. There was even an empty bedroom made up for me, which Mom hoped I would occupy as soon as I graduated from college later that year.

The house, in the hills of the Palisades, butted up against a mountain, where wild animals constantly came prancing down to say hello through the window. Of all the animals that had come and gone, we now had only Oliver, Kaitlyn's pick of the litter of twelve Bengal cats my mother had bred.

Mom had magically gotten a new job—doing exactly what was unclear, even to her—and it was now paying her a small fortune each month. Being my mother, she was spending every penny as soon as it came in, sure that this time, unlike every other time, the money would continue to roll in.

Her employer's name was Bob, but she simply called him her "fairy godfather." All she had to do in return for this lavish new life that she had somehow hustled into existence was occasionally pick someone up from the airport.

"What does this fairy godfather do?" I asked over the phone when I heard about this arrangement, getting nervous when Mom excitedly emailed me details about an upcoming vacation she was planning, and I noticed the prices on the accompanying receipts.

"Something in finance," she said with a laugh. Clearly she had no idea.

"What are the people like that you pick up from the airport?" I followed with, hoping to get some glint of information that would explain our mysterious good fortune, which felt precarious, as always.

"I don't ask a lot of questions, Chrysta," she said. "I think he just wants to help us. God looked down and said, 'This little family has struggled enough. It's time to give them a break!'"

As I sat in a freezing dorm room on the Upper West Side of Manhattan, slowly, painfully, gaining weight with the help of a school psychologist who I'd agreed to see after a Barnard nurse expressed concern about my weight, my mother sat three thousand miles away, watching those deer.

Then her phone rang.

"Happy Valentine's Day," said Jeffrey, in a giddy mood.

For a moment her heart sang. Was it possible Jeffrey was calling to wish her a happy Valentine's Day? That would be so thoughtful, and so unlike him. But then again, she told herself, they *had* been getting along great recently.

"Happy Valentine's Day to you, too," she said, grinning into the phone.

Jeffrey grew quiet.

"Let me ask you something," he finally offered.

"What?" my mother said, now almost flirtatious in her tone, she was so delighted to be having a normal conversation with Jeffrey, one that didn't involve a conspiracy theory or a scheme.

"Have I been a good father to Chrysta and Kaitlyn?"

Debra paused, in shock.

Jeffrey barely ever asked about us kids—not in the past, and certainly not now. Debra always took the lead, filling in our father on our lives. He certainly had never openly reflected on whether he'd been a good parent. That kind of self-analysis was not in his nature, or if it was, it was deeply buried. He usually just called when he was mad, usually at her, or to rant about someone else who had wronged him.

"Yes, Jeffrey, you've been an incredible father!" she said, trying to butter him up, hoping he'd become even more interested in playing the role of "good father." *Miracles do sometimes happen!* she thought to herself.

Debra just sat there holding the phone, and after several long seconds of silent daydreaming, she descended back down to reality and impatiently asked, "What's up, Jeffrey?"

"I want you to go get a copy of the *New York Times*," he said.

"Why?" she barked.

"Just go get the *New York Times*!" he repeated, without giving her any indication of what this was about.

Annoyed but curious, she threw a robe over her flannel pajamas, carried her hot cup of coffee outside to her car, and drove down to the local Pacific Palisades newsstand, where she got out, sipping the coffee in her mug, still in her pajamas, and scanned the shelves for the *Times*.

That's when she saw it.

On the cover of the paper was a photograph of Jeffrey, sitting on a park bench on Venice Beach, with his arm around a young woman who looked exactly like Kaitlyn, and a lot like me, but who was not either of us.

In big letters stretched over the photo was the headline SPERM DONOR FATHER ENDS HIS ANONYMITY.

Debra nearly collapsed before grabbing the paper to read.

"There is no established ritual for how an anonymous sperm donor should contact his genetic children," read the first line. "But for Jeffrey Harrison, Valentine's Day seemed as good an occasion as any."

My mother's shock turned to rage.

The front-page article told the story of a man—the father of her children—who had made a modest living for almost a decade anonymously donating sperm to the California Cryobank and was once one of its "most requested donors." He was now taking the unusual step of being the first anonymous sperm donor in history to publicly give up his anonymity, inviting all his biological children—every child of "Donor 150"—to come get to know their biological father in sunny California.

"He didn't even have the balls to tell me himself!" Debra screamed into the air as the owner of the newsstand watched this crazy woman talking to herself.

As she held the paper, a deep sense of betrayal washed over her.

Maybe she and Jeffrey hadn't been lovers, but they had become close friends over the past twenty or so years. And she had loved him, platonically but also as a member of our small family. Indeed, next to me and Kaitlyn and her dead parents, my father was likely the only other person she had ever loved consistently through the years. Whatever Jeffrey had symbolized as the father of her children was so durable it eclipsed every romantic relationship she'd ever had, not to mention the evidence at hand of what kind of dad he had been to us.

How could he betray her, and us, in this way?

My mother had worked hard to give us a strong feeling of belonging to a family, even if it hadn't been a "normal" family. She felt she'd failed us in so many ways, especially with her alcohol and drug addiction. But perhaps her greatest shame was over the one thing she really had no control over: having been a lesbian, and having to have children in this different way, and not giving us a father in the "real" sense of the word. Sure, she knew she had not been the mother she had set out to be. But recently, she had thought it was all working out.

Now she realized it had *all* been a fantasy. There was nothing normal about this family. About her. About Jeffrey.

Our mother knew how much Kaitlyn and I were struggling, each in our own ways. She saw the anger we sometimes harbored toward her. She saw the eating disorders and was trying to get both of us help. She could see we were attracted to toxic men, that my drinking was beginning to resemble hers, and that Kaitlyn, while a straight A student at the top of her class, had paralyzing paranoia and obsessive-compulsive tendencies, not to mention still had to sleep next to her mother. Mom was doing her best to intervene with our struggles, with little luck.

She wondered, as she looked down at Jeffrey's photograph, if it was possible that some of our struggles were biological. Was it *all* her fault, because of how she'd raised us? Surely picking a short, balding genius would have been better than this?

She resolved in that moment, standing at the newsstand with the nearby ocean breeze flittering the pages in her hand, that she would do whatever she had to do to keep this information a secret from us forever. The problem was, the *New York Times* story was just the beginning. Hiding the truth about our father would soon become a full-time job.

Dozens of news articles and interviews with Jeffrey followed that front-page *Times* story. Local TV stations made the trip to Venice Beach to get to know the quirky homeless sperm donor as he walked them around his eccentric world on Abbot Kinney.

A Japanese TV station made a docuseries about Jeffrey called *Mr. Perfect.* A film crew from Canada had even flown out to make a documentary about several of Jeffrey's biological children coming to Venice Beach to meet him for the first time.

Jeffrey said yes to every interview with enthusiasm, and was elated at the idea that he would star in a movie alongside three of his biological children.

After years of living on the streets, using drugs, and experiencing waning interest from women, Jeffrey felt he mattered to the world again. Producers ate up his colorful routines and idiosyncrasies, like his going to feed the pigeons on the beach at dawn every morning, or bottle-feeding sick raccoons he'd found on the street. He began referring to himself as the "soul caller," explaining how he'd gone into deep meditations with every single donation, because even as sperm, his offspring already had consciousness. Being the soul caller was a more meaningful vocation, to be sure, than sitting in a cubicle and selling out to corporate America, he felt, and all the media coverage gave him an invigorated sense of importance amongst all his friends. He even got an attractive younger girlfriend, who lived on the streets, like him.

Kaitlyn and I had no idea any of this was going on, but Mom was so stressed about covering Jeffrey's tracks that she started to act erratic and unpredictable. She was in such a state of anxiety and panic that I started to worry she had relapsed.

The situation was so much worse than she could have predicted. She watched clip after clip of news interviews with my father. In one, when asked about his alternative lifestyle, he made a joke that while to the world's eyes he was unsuccessful, to biology he was "doing quite well." Just as he said this, a piece of metal attached to the roof of the motor home she had bought for him, where the clip had been filmed, broke off and fell behind him. It was too much for Debra to handle. What if her friends saw this? What if Kaitlyn and I eventually saw this?

Soon after she watched the newsclip, she learned about a Facebook group that was connecting all the children of Donor 150. She barely understood what Facebook was, but the idea of these brothers and sisters meeting online, on a website she knew Kaitlyn and I used, caused Mom's descent into a full-blown nervous breakdown. The lid to the little box she had put Jeffrey in for the past decade had suddenly started flashing neon.

Her first course of action was to threaten Jeffrey.

"If you ever mention my name or my kids' names, even once, in an interview or to any of your degenerate sperm children," she yelled at him over the phone, "I'll send my friend Al, who is in the Mafia, to pay your dogs a visit."

My mother loved animals and would never deliberately hurt one, but she knew what to say to contain Jeffrey. She also wasn't thinking straight. There was really no telling what she would or wouldn't do to protect her children.

Things quickly spiraled from there.

During one especially manic episode, my mother drove across town to Abbot's Habit, the coffee shop she knew Jeffrey frequented, and accosted him loudly.

"Get in the car, Jeffrey!" she commanded. "We're going to the court-house and getting married!"

In Mom's crazed state, she imagined that if my father married her, and later we found out about the rest of the siblings, we'd still feel "special."

When that plan didn't work, she tried to cut Jeffrey off, curiously announcing to me over the phone that we would no longer be going to visit our father over Christmas. It was March.

"I want you to block his phone calls and his emails, do you hear me?" she demanded.

"What did he do?" I asked, now very curious.

"That's none of your business!" she shouted.

At that point, I barely heard from my father except for the occasional text to say "Happy birthday," and I saw him only when my mother arranged for a visit. In truth, seeing him was painful for me, and pretending he didn't exist was an easy salve.

I was in my last semester of college and felt I had grown in some areas of my life. My eating disorder was now fully under control, and after a few what I would call relapses with James, I had finally cut my-self off from him for good. I was now dating the first guy I'd ever been attracted to who was emotionally available and kind to me. His name was Max, and he was a friend of Kaitlyn's and a few years younger than me. He had grown up in Brentwood, not too far from our new place in the Palisades, and we'd met over the winter break at a party in L.A. He was very handsome and six feet tall, with sandy-brown hair and lake-blue eyes.

As Max and I began a long-distance relationship, chatting on the phone between classes, the situation between my mother and father escalated.

After several months of my mother not speaking to my father, he called her and, in a sheepish and apologetic voice, asked if they could talk, in person, in Venice.

My mother had never heard Jeffrey apologize for a single thing in all the years she had known him. Curiosity got the best of her and she drove over to Venice to see what he had to say, imagining him on his knees, begging for her forgiveness and to return to his rightful place as father to her children and no one else's.

Upon her arrival, she was blindsided by a Canadian movie producer who had been sitting there beside Jeffrey outside his motor home. The producer jumped up to sell my mother on why she should participate in the documentary he was in the process of making about Jeffrey and "all of his children."

"His children!" she screamed. "Those are not his children!"

A week later, she served Jeffrey a stack of papers three inches thick from a lawyer, threatening to sue if he ever mentioned any of our names in the documentary or in any of his other media appearances. Afraid she might do it, or send the Mafia after his dogs, Jeffrey abided by these demands.

But the worst was yet to come.

Several months after serving Jeffrey the papers, my mother received a phone call.

"Debra speaking," she said.

"Debra, this is Wendy."

"What now?" Debra asked.

"I have something important I have to discuss with you," Wendy replied.

My mother had first spoken with Wendy shortly after the Valentine's Day *Times* article.

Wendy was the founder of the Donor Sibling Registry, which she had created because her son, who was ten and the product of a sperm donor, wanted to see if he had any biological siblings and potentially find his father.

When Jeffrey had initially messaged Wendy after the first *Times* story ran, she'd been elated. Not many donors had come forward at that point, and none had come forward with such a large group of off-spring. She'd been charmed by Jeffrey's phone calls and emails initially, and she had helped facilitate his connecting with half a dozen of his biological children registered on the site. She'd also introduced him to the *New York Times* reporter because, Wendy imagined, this heart-warming tale about Jeffrey meeting his children would raise awareness about what these donor-family ties could be, to hopefully open the door for other donors to come forward and maybe also help parents to not be afraid of these relationships.

She soon regretted that decision.

Jeffrey had started to ask Wendy for money for small things, like a new cell phone, which she gave him, feeling bad that he was so down on his luck. Then he'd started telling her about some of his conspiracy theories, like one about Nazis breeding cows, that made her eyes glaze over. Shortly after that, some of the donor siblings and their parents told her stories about Jeffrey's eccentric behavior.

"What does the sperm donor say to his offspring the first time they meet?" he'd asked one nervous and excited daughter during their first phone conversation.

"What?" this twelve-year-old had asked in return.

"Hey, squirt!" he said with a laugh.

Upon hearing this repeated to her by said twelve-year-old's mother, Wendy wondered if she'd made a giant mistake introducing Jeffrey to these sweet, innocent kids.

My father, meanwhile, had started to ask Wendy some concerning questions, like how much money she thought some of the children's parents had. He got angry and argumentative when Wendy wouldn't give him more financial support. He felt that after the *Times* story ran, Wendy owed him for giving her website so much publicity.

It had started to feel to Wendy like Jeffrey saw meeting his biological children as an opportunity to find someone to lift him out of his difficult circumstances. She worried about how confusing his motivations would be for the kids. As Jeffrey did more press, she also worried about all the other families out there who had used donors, her own son being the product of one, and whether Jeffrey was the right poster child for what she had wanted to be a comforting story about new kinds of families.

Today Wendy had a new nightmare on her hands that she needed to discuss.

When Wendy called, my mother was in the middle of getting a massage, lying on a masseuse's table in her bedroom under a white sheet, feeling uncommonly relaxed.

"A few weeks ago," Wendy said, "I was contacted by a lawyer who told me he represented a prominent family with twin girls from Donor 150. The parents were considering making contact with Jeffrey, and possibly helping him, whatever that means, but they wanted more details from me about him, and to know whether I think he's 'a man of character,' before they reveal themselves."

"Okay," my mother said, her anxiety building and wanting Wendy to get to the point.

"Well, at first I was excited by the opportunity for Jeffrey," Wendy continued. "I think you and I both agree that there's a kind and gentle person inside of him, but that perhaps he's been a little hardened by years of living on the streets. So, well, I kind of made a mistake, and I called Jeffrey to let him know that a prominent family with twins wanted to make contact and help him. I thought maybe hearing that would calm him down so he'd be more tactful with his media appearances. But the thing is, well, Jeffrey immediately assumed it was the Olsen twins—I guess because he thinks they look like Chrysta and Kaitlyn—and now he's been going around Venice telling everyone he's the father of the Olsen twins, trying to sell the story to the *National Enquirer*. He just sent me a cease and desist letter from some con artist lawyer demanding I verify it's them, or he'll sue me. This situation is a nightmare."

"Jesus," my mother said, feeling nauseated at the idea that Jeffrey would think to hurt another family in this way.

"Thank God it is not the Olsen twins," Wendy said after a long pause, intimating that she had since found out the identity of the family in question.

"Well, who the hell is it?" my mother asked.

"I'll tell you who it is, but you have to promise you won't share this information with Jeffrey."

"Of course, I promise." She was not prepared for the last name Wendy was about to lay on her.

Upon hearing it, Mom dropped the phone on the floor. Her masseuse went back to massaging her shoulders.

"Don't touch me!" Debra snapped. She stood up from the massage table, then lay down on the cold hardwood floor of her bedroom, unable to move for almost two hours, as she mentally ran through the horrible implications of what she had just learned.

FAMILY MEETING

"Girls, we need to have a serious conversation."

My mother was standing in front of the television, dressed in her usual attire of flannel pajamas and a cashmere bathrobe. She'd blocked the view of my favorite scene in *Gentlemen Prefer Blondes*—the moment in the courthouse when Jane Russell pretends to be Marilyn Monroe—and Kaitlyn and I were not in the mood for one of our mother's random, usually completely exaggerated panics about nothing.

"C'mon, it's almost over," I moaned.

"Move out of the way," Kaitlyn added, holding a new Bengal kitten Mom had just bought from a breeder and named Tonga.

Our mother didn't budge. The wild-eyed look on her face, something between fury and hysteria, told us she was serious. It was September 2007 and I had moved home after graduation. I was twenty-three and a few months sober after one too many blackouts and a handful of nervous breakdowns. My mother had recognized the signs after I'd moved back, asking me to go with her to an AA meeting.

That seat my mother told me she had been "saving for" me was difficult to occupy at first. However, I had begun to recognize that I shared many traits with both of my parents, despite my resolutions to myself that I would be nothing like either of them. A lot of people would have looked at my life after college, having racked up some abusive relationships, an eating disorder, and the occasional blackout-drunk morning-after experience, and said, "That's what college is all about! You weren't an alcoholic!" And certainly many of my friends felt that way, especially the friends who enjoyed drinking with me. But I knew where that story went: I was the third-generation result of those rationalizations, and I wanted a different life. At twenty-three I decided to get sober as a way of escaping, if that was possible, my genetic inheritance.

I'd spent the past several months in AA meetings, sometimes three per day. Alcohol, I realized, had been a solution, not always a problem, for me. It had helped me get through difficult emotional experiences I otherwise could not have navigated. It had given me a base of okayness during dark years, enabling me to function and feel "normal." It had served as a kind of liquid courage when I socialized or entered relationships, because those things brought me such severe anxiety.

My mother, still employed by her fairy godfather and in preparation for my return from college, had moved out of the house with the deer overlooking the mountain and into a slightly larger two-story Colonial with blue shutters and a bright red front door, located in a charming pocket of West Hollywood. Given the regularity of the fairy godfather's paychecks (though we still had no idea what he did), my mother had enough extra money coming in that she let me decorate the entire house with new furniture. My mother and I, to my great shock, were having a lot of fun together.

Not only did I have my own room, but there was an unused bedroom that I got to turn into a studio dedicated to painting, an old interest I was now reexploring. I felt too emotionally unstable to try to secure a steady job, so I babysat at night for extra money and spent my days entirely focused on getting sober. My mother was happily single, and by all accounts several years sober herself.

Unlike the twenty-three years behind me, these days, home had started to feel—could I say without jinxing it?—normal.

Kaitlyn was on her way to her first year of college, having followed me to Barnard in New York, and she, too, seemed to be doing a little better as a result of our mother being in a better place. She'd gotten serious about her piano playing, writing music and performing, and she was even starting a band with my boyfriend, Max, who played the guitar and was an incredible musician himself.

All was looking up until I noticed my mother's erratic body language as she walked Kaitlyn and me into the living room and sat us down on our new white couch. The last time we'd been assembled for a "conversation" was five years earlier, during Mom's intervention. My anxiety started to boil.

"Girls," Mom said before pausing to rummage for the right words.

Then, for maybe the first time in my mother's life, she was just silent.

I looked around the living room to take account of which pieces would sell for what, wondering if we would have enough time to prepare the house for a yard sale by the coming Saturday, before we lost this house.

Surely we could get at least $500 for Kaitlyn's black Yamaha piano? If I washed the slipcovers, the couch I was sitting on might fetch double that.

No, we were not losing the house. We could keep the couch, and the piano, for now. And yes, Mom was still sober.

"Last February," she finally uttered before taking a deep breath, "on Valentine's Day, I found out that your father was secretly a sperm donor and that you have a few biological brothers and sisters spread out across the United States."

I looked at Kaitlyn, who looked back at me, lost over how she was supposed to feel. Whenever anything bad happened in our lives, Kaitlyn would always look immediately to me, completely disconnected from her own inner voice, searching my face for clues as to how we were going to react.

My mother looked directly at me, on the verge of tears, and continued, "You were the first, Chrysta. Don't worry."

"Well that's comforting, Mom," I said.

A picture formed in my mind of the last time I had seen my father.

During our dinner, he had told us one of his own favorite jokes, which I must have heard ten thousand times, but which now took on more significance: "I've been working hard my whole life," he'd said with that giggle of his. Then the punch line: "On my suntan!"

As our mother paced back and forth, now in tears, I realized why she had insisted we not visit our father this past Christmas, and why she had told me to block his number. Then my mind moved on to the siblings. How many were there—really?

The way my mother had said "a few" made it sound like there could be a whole lot more. A dozen? Two dozen? More than that? And what did they look like? How old were they?

The thought of new family members brought a new burden of responsibility to a family that already had more than its share.

"There's more," my mother said, now looking directly at me again.

She held a painful silence for several minutes as she tried to force the words out. I struggled to calculate what more there could possibly be.

"I think your boyfriend might be your brother."

MY BROTHER,
MY BOYFRIEND

The days after my mother told Kaitlyn and me about our father and that I was dating a boy who was potentially my brother, I was in a haze.

I had been avoiding Max for several days as I weighed my options. I was horrified by the now frequent flashbacks of the *many* times we'd slept together. I remembered sitting in his parents' kitchen once while his mother, who was standing at the counter making us tea, periodically glanced at me with pursed lips and raised eyebrows. When she saw that I had caught her looking, she barely feigned a smile. It seemed at the time that she did not approve of me as a girlfriend for Max, though the reason was unclear. Now I wondered if some part of her had known.

I desperately wanted to call Max to tell him what I knew, to see what he thought, and for him to either confirm it to be true so we could process it together or for him to tell me it was wrong. Then again, I didn't know if Max was my brother, or if he was even the product of a sperm donor.

My mother explained that Max's parents had confirmed to Wendy that Jeffrey was the father of their twin girls, but they had said nothing about Max, who was a few years older. He certainly looked like my father. Max was also almost a foot taller than the dad who had raised him. Either way, it didn't feel like it was my place to break the news to him that he might not be his father's son. He loved his father, and he looked up to him.

I remembered when, a year earlier, Max and I had been at a party in New York and someone had come up to us and asked if we were brother and sister.

I felt a stomachache coming on. I couldn't believe Mom had sat on this information for months before telling me.

I told Max over the phone that I had met someone else and ended the relationship.

Meanwhile, a few days after my mother broke the news about our father, one of our biological sisters in the Donor 150 Facebook group, a twenty-year-old named Rachelle, sent me a friend request and a message on Facebook.

Apparently, while my father had respected my mother's legal demands not to mention our family in any of his media interviews, he had told all his new children about us.

"I hate to break this to you," Rachelle wrote to me on Facebook that day, "but your dad was an anonymous sperm donor, and I am one of your half siblings."

Along with the note came an invitation to join her in the Donor 150 Facebook group.

I paused for a moment, then automatically, without thinking, clicked on the group's photos. All the known siblings so far were there happily standing together at a playground, with faces that looked just like mine had during those vulnerable years around puberty.

Seeing that I was online, Rachelle excitedly started typing questions for me while I scrolled through the profiles of each one of my biological siblings, these sweet-awkward-innocent boys and girls who looked to be in their early-to-mid teens and who appeared identical to me and Kaitlyn.

"Did you do musical theater as a kid?" Rachelle typed.

"Yes, I did," I wrote.

"Was there a particular type of math you loved in high school?"

"Yes, there was," I typed, not getting into details.

"Have you struggled with anxiety, or depression?"

"Yes," I said, without adding that right at this moment, I was struggling with severe anxiety and looming depression.

I needed a drink, but I knew that was out of the question.

Rachelle tossed the questions to me like this was a Ping-Pong match that I hadn't signed up to play. I could see she was enthusiastic about connecting with her big sister, but I was overwhelmed by her eagerness, and also a bit irritated that she'd taken it upon herself to break this giant secret to me, since she had no idea whether or not I already knew.

Then again, she did have my father's DNA, I thought, and he was never great at dealing with sensitive topics.

Maybe I can do this, I thought to myself. *Maybe I can be friends with these people.*

With each photo I clicked on and each tiny bubble that popped up to show that Rachelle was typing, I began to feel this was all too much for me. My hands began to shake. I was experiencing a full-blown panic attack. I could not handle one new family member, let alone a dozen of them.

I called Kaitlyn into the room to show her the messages; she, too, grew visibly uncomfortable. We sat for a moment wondering how many siblings we might have. There were, at this point, only seven people in the Facebook group, but in my gut, I felt the number could be much higher. What were the chances, statistically speaking, that there were only a few, and one of those just so happened to be my boyfriend?

"I don't ever want to talk to these siblings," I said.

"Neither do I," Kaitlyn replied.

"Let's make a pact," I told her. "We will never talk to, look at, or think about these people again."

"You don't have to convince me," she replied with a laugh. "Just because we share the same DNA with them does not make them our family."

My mother was thrilled to hear that we could just forget the whole thing ever happened and move on with our lives.

In the years that followed, aside from exchanging the occasional text messages, I lost touch with my father. In the past, when people asked me about my dad, I'd always struggled to explain the situation, telling them either that my parents were divorced or that I had a distant relationship with my father. I had inherited my mother's struggle with shame, in her case over her sexuality, which meant I was careful about who I disclosed personal details to. Sometimes, with those I felt safe with, I'd say that my dad and my mom had been "friends who decided to have a child together," and that he was "still around," which always prompted a set of questions that were difficult and painful to answer truthfully, even with close friends.

Now when people asked me about my dad, I had a new answer.

"Oh, he was an anonymous sperm donor," I'd say, as if that's all he'd ever been to me.

THE GOLDEN MEMORY BOX

A few weeks after we'd learned about the siblings, my mother called me up to her bedroom and told me she had just received news that Mommy Fay had died after a battle with cancer. Hearing Fay's name, which I hadn't heard spoken in years, jarred me, but I wasn't sure how to feel. I had so carefully tucked away every memory of the time we lived with Fay that I couldn't access a single feeling as I sat on my mom's bed, comforting her.

Later that evening, as I got ready for bed, I suddenly remembered, in vivid detail, the morning I'd walked into Debra's bedroom and met Fay for the first time, the sun from my mother's window lighting up Fay's smiling face as she held baby Kaitlyn, just a few days old, in her arms. I had other memories, too: I saw myself sitting happily in the front seat of our moving truck as we all drove to the house in Hidden Hills, and then I saw Fay's tear-filled face four years later, and there was another memory I'd completely forgotten: little Kaitlyn screaming and hysterical as we got into Mom's car to leave our family with Fay and start a new one with Sable.

My hands started shaking once again as I crumpled to the bathroom floor in a burst of sobs. Until this moment, I had looked back on our years with Fay as pure misery; certainly my mother had been in a terrible state during that time, and a part of me had known we would be better off not living in that house with Fay and her family. I couldn't

212

rationalize why I was so upset now. I thought I had moved on from Fay, but it was now clear that eight-year-old me hadn't moved on so much as compartmentalized the experience.

At the funeral, my mother, Kaitlyn, and I all sat at the back of a Catholic church in the Valley, lost among hundreds of strange faces. A priest in a white robe went up to the altar and began discussing Fay's life as I stared at a photograph of her beautiful, smiling face on a giant poster at the front of the room. It was a photo of her as a young woman, and I recognized it; my mother had taken it. I looked up toward the front pew, where I registered the backs of the heads of Emily, Chris, and Robby. Part of me wanted to walk up to the front and sit down next to them, but I felt that those first few rows were for family, and I no longer qualified.

At one point Emily, now in her mid-twenties like me, turned around, and we caught each other's eyes for a moment. She tried to summon a smile. She had the exact same face as her six-year-old self, just older now and red and streaked with tears. Emily had often been a monster to me during the four years that we lived together, but now I remembered sliding down a waterfall together on a trip to Maui, and standing in our nightgowns and reaching up to steal the tops off all Fay's chocolate puddings in the fridge.

What did it mean to be in someone's family? And at what point had I stopped qualifying? Two years later? Five years? The day my mother, Kaitlyn, and I drove away to live with Sable?

I had promised myself I wouldn't give more thought to my biological siblings, the strangers my father had helped create, but now I began to wonder: were they more my family than the three children sitting ten rows in front of me? Emily shared no biology with me, but we shared a history, and parents, even if for only a few years.

After the funeral, I told my mother that I needed to see a therapist. I had spent the past several months in various twelve-step meetings, and every free moment browsing the self-help sections of bookstores, searching for answers to questions I didn't know how to ask. Every day, I seemed to find new parts of myself, old grief that was sitting there just waiting to be excavated and explored.

Anything could set me off—a random photograph of Annie holding me over her shoulder as an infant while she smiled lovingly into the camera, or of Sable hugging me at a Yankees game. And yet if I saw photos of my father, I felt nothing. I'd pore over my mother's photographs of my early childhood, through the old memory boxes, sifting through thousands of pictures she'd taken of him standing next to me, and not a single memory was attached to a single photograph. I wondered if something was seriously wrong with me, if I was experiencing the first symptoms of mental illness.

My mother knew only one psychologist, an old friend of hers who she hadn't spoken to in years. In addition to having a degree in psychiatry, Ingrid had been my mother's first AA sponsor back in 1979, before she had me and in her first attempt to get sober. Somehow it didn't occur to my mother that this history was a conflict of interest. Mom wanted desperately to help me with what I was going through, but she had never really dealt with her own trauma, so she didn't have many tools to be able to point me in one direction or another.

In my early childhood, Ingrid had been around quite a bit, often taking my mother and me on hikes in the mountains for hours. She'd let me borrow her smooth, giant walking stick made from a branch. She'd spend time bending down and answering all my many questions, pointing out the scientific names of specific rocks, plants, and birds. Among all the early women who were present during my childhood, Ingrid had been one of my favorites. She was someone who I had sensed genuinely loved and cared about me, without any ulterior motives.

I drove to Ingrid's small first-floor apartment in Santa Monica and knocked. Ingrid opened the door and greeted me with a tight, stiff German hug. She was much older than the last time I'd seen her, but she looked the same, with her blond hair pulled into a tight bun on the top of her head. I walked in, and immediately remembered all the smells of this tiny apartment, which I hadn't been inside in over fifteen years. There was a cramped hallway stacked with books, which were also on shelves lining the walls, and then a small living room in the front, with a large window and an old, musty red velvet couch. I sat and looked down at the large glass coffee table in front of me; it had a tray inside that was filled with sand and seashells.

Sitting across from Ingrid, I told her how good it was to see her. I told her about discovering that my father had been a sperm donor and about all the many complexities I was trying to grapple with.

"You know," Ingrid said early in the conversation, "your grandfather's horrible death was very painful for your mother."

I sat up in shock, then did my best to relax my body so that Ingrid couldn't see that I knew nothing about my grandfather having a "horrible death." My mother had never told me anything about how her father died, although I knew that he had been pretty young. Why had I never asked my mother this simple question?

"Yes, it was horrible," I responded after several long seconds. It was a lie, but I knew that if Ingrid thought she was sharing any family secrets that my mother didn't want me to know, our conversation would be over. "Go on," I said.

"Well," Ingrid said, leaning forward in her chair, an arm upon her knee. "I think your mother never got over losing her dad in that way, and in some ways, she was trying to turn your father into him."

Was it possible that giving us a father was less about Kaitlyn and me and more about her? That my mother needed him around more than either of us did?

"You have to understand," Ingrid told me, "your mother's father was a serious alcoholic, and her mother was a deeply unhappy woman who wasn't cut out for motherhood. Debra largely raised herself. All those years that she bounced from one religious cult to the next, what she was really doing was trying to find a loving family. Then, after her father died, her traveling around the world to meet with gurus, all of that, it was all about her finding a father to replace him."

Ingrid paused and smiled. "Of course," she added, "there's no greater father figure than God."

"Do you believe in God?" I asked.

"I don't spend a lot of time worrying about what happens after we die," she said to me with a loving smile. "What happens here on earth is mysterious enough."

How many more secrets did my mother have? How many painful truths had she carefully hidden from me?

My mother always told me only the good stories: how much she loved her father, and what an incredible relationship they'd had; about her grandfather, and what an incredible mark he'd made in public office. Of course, all those stories had been true, but the bad stuff was true, too. I also wondered about the why of it all. Why, especially, had my mother struggled so much with her addictions? Ingrid had been a drug addict just like my mother, but unlike my mother, Ingrid had stayed sober for the long haul. Why was it so much more difficult for my mother to do that?

"You have to understand," Ingrid said again, "being homosexual in the nineteen fifties was considered a mental disorder, right up there next to being a pedophile. The American Psychiatric Association didn't officially remove it from that classification until nineteen seventy-three. For many of us who grew up in the fifties and sixties, we really had to be loaded to allow our sexuality to be what it was. We were violating every social norm and we had to wipe out the brain tissue that cares about that. Many of us got involved with heroin and cocaine to black out all of our moral societal judgments just so we could be ourselves. For Debra, it was worse in some ways because all she ever wanted, more than anything else, was to make her father proud. Even from the grave. And he didn't approve."

Though this explanation didn't take away the harm Debra had caused, I did feel a softening in my heart. I'd come of age several decades after my mother, in the 1990s, yet I had still felt, when I was younger, that having a gay mother was something to be deeply ashamed of.

"As children, we inherit our parents' unresolved psychic trauma, whether through genetics or osmosis," Ingrid said to me, "and in your case, perhaps some of your inherited work might be to process your mother's shame around her sexuality."

I knew Ingrid was right. I still needed to examine my own biases and internalized and culturally supported homophobia. Why was having a gay mom such a source of shame for me? In watching my mother's endless cycles of coming out, only to retreat back "in" again, my developing brain had certainly gathered that there must be something wrong with being gay; otherwise she wouldn't hide it, and kids at school wouldn't treat me differently because of it. But knowing this intellectually couldn't erase the sting of shame I still felt all these years later. I still carried shame about so many things—not just about Mom's sexuality, but about our financial struggles throughout the years, about the unusual makeup of our family, about my parents' drug addictions.

After an hour's chat, I gave Ingrid a hug and thanked her for her time.

"I hope I've been helpful," she said.

"Yes, very helpful," I replied, feeling a bit guilty because I had tricked Ingrid into telling me things she shouldn't.

As I was by the door, Ingrid said something else.

"You know, Chrysta, we never took much that your mother did very seriously: the careers, the relationships, the political positions—all of that, because we knew she wouldn't stay interested in whatever it was for long. But there's one thing she never lost her enthusiasm for, and that's you kids. No one had ever seen Debra want anything as much as she wanted to be a mom. My mother never loved me, and I don't think Debra's mother loved her. But if there's one thing I know, it's that your mom has loved you girls with all her heart. I think she did the best she could with the tools she had."

I smiled, feeling in my heart this statement to be true, and then turned to walk out to my car.

When I got home, my mother was standing in the kitchen, waiting for me with a curious smile on her face.

"How did it go?" she asked.

"Great," I told her, saying nothing more for several beats as I stared into her eyes, her delicate soul, trying to decide whether to pry about what had happened to her father.

"Mom, can I ask you something?" I said a few seconds later, unable to stop myself.

"Sure, Beanie. What is it?" she said, unsuspecting.

"How did your father die?"

My mother's gentle demeanor turned to a fluster of rapid-fire eye movements and intense shaking. It was a specific emotional state I had never seen her in, one too complex to decipher. She was upset, and angry. She paced the room, screaming and waving her hands in the air. I thought I might need to call an ambulance.

"Was that why you went to see Ingrid? To be an investigator in things that are none of your business?!"

She continued to pace.

"How dare Ingrid share my own personal business," she said with indignation. "How dare she!" she yelled, growing louder and angrier.

"Mom, it is really not Ingrid's fault," I said, trying to help her see reason. "She didn't know she was revealing a secret to me. But Mom, what happened?"

My mother refused to discuss it. She stomped purposefully out of the room, presumably to call Ingrid to let her know their friendship was over.

Two weeks later, she walked into my bathroom as I was getting ready for bed. She took a deep breath and crouched down on the floor next to where I was standing.

"I will tell you what happened to my father," she said.

THE POOL INCIDENT

One of my mother's favorite early memories of her father, she told me, took place on a warm summer night in 1955, at her childhood home on Bowmont Drive in the canyons of Beverly Hills. She was six years old and in her favorite orange pajamas, sitting two feet away from her family's small black-and-white television. She sat up on her knees as a familiar tune lit up an image sketched into her soul and memorized: a white picket fence encircling a sweet, one-story ranch house, the home of her favorite TV family, the Andersons of *Father Knows Best*.

This must be what normal families look like, she often thought to herself as she watched the Andersons sit down to pray before a family meal. Often she would look up from the television, taking account of the fact that she was eating a Swanson TV dinner she'd prepared for herself while her parents screamed in the next room. Debra would try to make sense of why things were so simple for the Andersons and so complicated for the Olsons. She sometimes wondered if God had placed her in the wrong family. Maybe there'd been some mix-up in heaven.

Tonight, though, her parents weren't arguing. The house was eerily silent.

"Deb!" her father called out suddenly from the back garden. "Get out here right now!"

"Coming, Daddy!" she yelled back, up on her toes as fast as her small body could manage, heart racing with the thought that something terrible might have happened.

"Hurry!" he yelled. "Faster!"

Debra's feet pitter-pattered their way through the house, across the never-ending beige carpet. She made it through the open screen door and onto the concrete pavers outside, almost tripping over the ledge, and then spotted her father, John, standing ten feet ahead, right next to their large turquoise pool. He was shirtless, barefoot, wearing only a pair of his brightly colored above-the-knee shorts.

John smiled, a glint of laughter in his eyes. "Look," he said in a whisper as he pointed up.

Debra followed her father's gaze, up toward the black night sky, past a million glittering stars, until she saw the reason for all the commotion: a massive, glowing circle of white in the sky—the most beautiful full moon she'd ever seen.

"That's called the Sturgeon Moon," he explained, sitting down in the grass as he motioned for Debra to lie down next to him. Tonight, to Debra's great relief, her father appeared to be sober. She nestled in his arms and breathed in the sweet smell of laundry starch that still clung to his skin after a long day at work as a judge.

Together the two stared up at the moon for quite some time. Debra could hear the faint sounds of crickets in the bushes nearby, intermingled with the melodic notes of a saxophone playing in the distance.

There was a magic to Coldwater Canyon in 1954, before the freeways and city lights dimmed the sparkling night sky across Los Angeles. Back then, the family's only neighbors were Frank Sinatra and Dean Martin. The canyons above Beverly Hills were mostly just wild nature, an oasis of oak groves, mountain lions, and long winding dirt roads that Debra felt belonged exclusively to her.

"See that star?" John said to Debra, pointing into the distance. "See the bright light shining on it?"

Debra nodded.

"That star died before the cavemen were even here. And that one"—

he pointed to another, hardly visible star in the distance—"that star died when dinosaurs were roaming the earth. That's how long it takes a star's light to get to us."

A few moments passed quietly before Debra decided to ask her father a question that had been gnawing at her recently.

"Why are we here, Daddy?"

John looked over at his daughter, a little taken aback that a six-year-old would be concerned with such a big question.

"You know, Deb," he said, "I really don't know why we are here. Life is a mystery." He paused, looked over at her, and said, "All I know is that I love you." Then, with a single motion, he stood up, lifting Debra into his arms. "C'mon. Let's get you to bed."

In her bed a few moments after her father's goodnight kiss, Debra nodded off. Her sleepy, full heart was eclipsed in darkness when, like clockwork, she heard a familiar sound coming from the living room bar: the ding of an ice cube hitting the bottom of a glass, the slow pour of John's Hill and Hill bourbon, the fizzy bubbling of a splash of soda. She sat up, now alert, and looked over at her baby sister, Diane, asleep in the crib next to her; Debra hoped to God that she would sleep through the night. Slipping out from under her covers, she quietly tiptoed past Diane to the bedroom door, then peered out—terrified of what monsters might await her after her father had had a few drinks.

By the time Diane had come into the world, John's depression, and his alcoholism, had started to deepen. No one could predict how a night would end once he got started. Debra sometimes spent evenings standing guard with a frying pan in front of her mother's closet, to protect Bicki from John's unwanted sexual advances. Other nights Debra would wake up at 3 a.m. to John's screaming—bloodcurdling screams—and she'd find him in bed shaking and sweating, following some horrible nightmare about his time overseas in the navy. Once he told her about an incident when several men in his platoon, seeking revenge for the killing of one of their friends, had tied a Korean soldier's two legs to two separate cars, and then slowly drove in opposite directions. Debra had sat on the edge of her father's bed, trying to comfort him but feeling confused and scared.

If the chaos of the night belonged to her father, it was the daytime when Debra's mother's demons reigned. It was unclear to Debra whether Bicki even liked her children—or any kids, for that matter. She loved John very much, but she had no life outside of being a housewife, and the role made her miserable.

Bicki made it through her days popping Dexedrine, a form of speed prescribed to her and many other housewives to help them lose their pregnancy weight. It gave Bicki the extra energy she needed to vacuum the house and do the laundry before John returned from work.

Bicki was so hopped up on pills, bourbon, and cigarettes that she would occasionally forget to feed Debra and her little sister. Debra would stare idly out the window as she waited for the sound of the Helms Bakery truck approaching with glazed doughnuts, often her main source of comfort. Bicki's most famous attempt at a "normal" family dinner landed her in the hospital with third-degree burns after she dropped a precious acrylic nail into a pot of boiling stew, and then tried to fish it out with her bare hands, accidentally spilling the contents all over herself.

What is the point of it all? Debra would ask herself. *What is the reason for all this horrible suffering in every direction? And why did God put me in this family and not with a family more like the Andersons?*

At first Debra went looking for God at Sunday school, begging her reluctant father, an agnostic who was skeptical of organized religion, to drive her down the hill to the Church of the Good Shepherd. When that only led to more confusion, she looked for God in days-long solo excursions into the wild canyons outside her front door. She'd take all her clothes off, tie two washcloths around her waist, and pretend she was Tarzan, swinging from the vines with a knife in her mouth that she'd borrowed from the kitchen drawer, getting lost, sometimes for hours, coming face-to-face with mountain lions and rattlesnakes. She never felt fear when she was alone in nature, or when she got lost.

When it rained or poured in the fall, she would happily stay outside for hours, getting drenched as she sailed small acorns downstream and felt happy and close to God. Then it would grow dark, and she'd have to head home, feeling her anxiety return with the uncertainty of what she would find when she opened her front door.

Debra got older, and the canyons no longer provided lasting peace, so she looked in other places. In her early teens, she sought God in her first romance with another girl two years older—a secret she swore no one would ever know—but that only led to shame and heartbreak when her father walked in on her kissing this new girlfriend and made it clear that he was horrified, as were most people at that time, by homosexuality.

By the early 1960s, she turned to Eastern philosophy, which was spreading rapidly across the United States, along with new music, new drugs, and a new counterculture. Debra took to all of it with enthusiasm, but especially one practice that had just come across the Pacific from Japan. She found Nichiren Shoshu Buddhism, or Soka Gakkai, as it later became known, one afternoon in 1964 in Santa Monica. In a room filled with two dozen mostly Japanese men and women, all sitting on their knees and rustling prayer beads in their hands, she joined in as they chanted toward a large scroll in the center of the room, repeating the same words in unison, over and over again: *"Namu myoho renge kyo. Namu myoho renge kyo. Namu myoho renge kyo."*

The leader of the group, and the man responsible for bringing this tradition over to the U.S., went by the name Mr. Sadanaga. He took Debra under his wing, and introduced her to all kinds of new ideas that held her captive, particularly the concept—along with cause and effect, karma, and reincarnation—that she could chant to get anything she wanted in life. It occurred to Debra then, at age fifteen, that perhaps the utter disconnect she felt from her mother and the horrible pain she felt in her heart when she watched her father drink himself into a stupor were not just random, senseless acts of bad luck; perhaps the family she was born into was her karma. Perhaps, she thought, her soul was meant to learn some great lesson. If she devoted herself to chanting these sacred words toward this magic scroll at the front of the room, perhaps she could work through this karma and finally be able to sustain the joy and happiness that were so fleeting.

Debra spent the next seven years of her life rising early in the morning to chant and gathering young people on the sidewalk on Sunset Boulevard to invite them to their first chanting meeting. She would eventually travel around the country and to Japan to proselytize alongside Mr. Sadanaga. Following his orders, she dressed in the conservative 1950s Sears catalog attire he preferred his followers to wear, even as all the teens around Debra had adopted long hippie gowns and beads. She stayed celibate, chanting to remove her negative karma of being attracted to women, as Mr. Sadanaga had instructed her to do.

John worried that his daughter had joined a cult, and he begged her to drop the round-the-clock proselytizing and go to college instead. Debra felt torn. She wanted, more than anything, to make her father proud, but these chanting meetings had given her a safe place to go when home life became too much for her, and the people at the meetings had become a new family that wasn't hers but, she felt, loved and supported her. The study and practice had also given her, for a time, hope and solace.

In Debra's late teens, when her father's finances crumbled, her home life grew even worse. As prestigious as his position as a judge was, John earned significantly less than when he'd been a lawyer in the private sector, and he was given to overspending, wanting to buy his wife and daughters all the material possessions he'd grown up with, even when he no longer had the money for them. The lights were often shut off at Bowmont Drive, and Debra's precious childhood home was repossessed by the bank. John reacted by drinking more, while Bicki hid in her closet like a scared mouse. Debra once found Diane, now thirteen, sitting in her bedroom shooting heroin with her girlfriend Joy. How two thirteen-year-old girls in Beverly Hills had gotten addicted to heroin was a mystery to Debra that would never be solved. Debra stared at Diane, nodded out with a needle in her arm, and realized, in horror, that while she had been gone on a monthslong trip to Japan with Mr. Sadanaga, chanting for material and spiritual "benefits," what was left of her family had almost completely fallen apart.

Debra did everything she could to pull her family "into the light." She begged her father to put Diane in rehab—which he did, for a few days, but then he made the biggest mistake of his life and let Diane talk him into letting her come home early. Debra begged Diane and her parents to come with her to a chanting meeting. But all the chanting in the world was not going to save the house, or cure her parents of their alcoholism or Diane of her heroin habit. Debra began spending less time at her meetings and more at home. She found odd jobs modeling and working as a housekeeper for family friends, doing what she could to help her father get their house back. She still chanted, with every fiber of her being, to fix these problems, but then she developed a crush on an androgynous Italian woman from New York who went by the name Damian, after Hermann Hesse's character of a similar name. More drawn to Damian than to any woman she had ever met, Debra suddenly felt that this idea that her feelings toward women were "negative karma" was ridiculous. To think that chanting could get you whatever you wanted, or save your father from alcoholism, was ludicrous!

She quit the Soka Gakkai, announcing to Mr. Sadanaga that she would not be leading the Parade of Happiness down Wilshire Boulevard. She cut her hair into a bob, purchased some beads, and went full 1971 hippie, bringing many of the women in the organization out with her.

"If you stop chanting, bad things will happen to you and your family," Mr. Sadanaga had told Debra when she left, a warning she ignored.

She moved out of the house that she helped her father get back, and into her first apartment with Damian. When by habit she woke to go to the Gohonzon to chant, she stopped herself. But walking away in her mind was not as easy as no longer attending the meetings, and every day she chose not to chant, Debra could not escape the uneasy feeling that she was putting her family at risk.

She applied to UCLA and called her father from a bright red pay phone the day she was accepted. She was going to follow in her grandfather's footsteps by becoming a lawyer, she told him, and then a politician. She hoped to make her father proud of her, even if she felt like she was a disappointment to him with her passion for women.

Debra started attending classes at UCLA, and she loved it. She marched with Angela Davis and became involved with the women's rights movement on campus. She majored in political science and made it on the dean's list.

One weekend, while working a random modeling job at Wilsons House of Suede, by the Peninsula hotel, Debra had a sudden desire to go home.

"I have to leave early," she told the photographer, grabbing her keys and not even waiting to be dismissed.

She drove across Wilshire toward Coldwater Canyon. When she arrived, to her great relief, she found everything and everyone in their normal state. Frank Sinatra was blasting on the record player. Her father was sitting by the pool. Bicki was in a nearby lounge chair in a bathing suit, tanning, in pigtails. John had a drink and a cigarette in his hand.

Debra gave her father a hug, stayed for a minute, then said she had to return to work. As she turned to leave, John stood up suddenly.

"Meet me at the back gate," he whispered so Bicki couldn't hear. "I want to talk to you about something."

Curious, Debra walked to her car and drove behind the house to the gate. Her father walked down some steps, then climbed into the passenger side of her car. He had tears running down his face.

"What's wrong, Dad?" Debra asked, now worried.

"Honey, I'm really, really tired," he said. "I have to leave. Please take good care of your mom and sister."

In the past, whenever John got exasperated and overwhelmed, he would joke, "Why am I even here with these three crazy women? I'm leaving for Tahiti!" It wasn't clear where the line between telling jokes and being serious met. As Debra sat in her car with her father, she assumed he was just tired. He'd been up the entire night before getting Aunt Adelle out of jail for a DUI. She hugged him, and then he reached into his pocket. John handed her a crisp hundred-dollar bill. Debra left, driving back the way she had come.

Two hours later, after Debra had returned to work, she walked into her apartment to the sound of a phone ringing. She picked up the receiver and recognized the voice of the teenager on the other end of the line. He was a neighbor on Bowmont Drive.

"Debra," he said. "Your dad drowned. He's dead."

In a haze, she jumped into her car and drove toward Bowmont. Sirens were streaming through the Canyons. Red flashing lights filled the road and lit up the trees. As she pulled into her parents' driveway, two men dressed in blue and white were carrying a body on a stretcher covered with a sheet through the yard. She ran up the steps to the backyard, where she found only her mother, standing by the side of the pool, howling like a wild lioness.

Bicki kept saying it was an accident, that John was in his terry cloth robe when she found him floating in the pool, and that somehow proved it was a mishap.

The autopsy determined that John had drowned. Debra wanted to believe it was an accident, but she spoke privately to John's old law partner, who told her that John had gone to great lengths in the weeks leading up to his death to make sure the insurance money would be paid out if anything ever happened to him; John knew that if it was suicide, Bicki, Debra, and Diane would not get the life insurance money. In her heart, she knew her father had made it look that way so his family could be taken care of after he left. He had said goodbye to Debra. She still had his hundred-dollar bill in her pocket.

"All I remember after that," my mother said to me in the bathroom that day, in tears, her body bent over the floor helplessly, "was just standing by the back door between my bedroom and Mom and Dad's, looking out at the pool, in shock. Mom was hysterical, just flabbergasted. I knew I would have to be the one who would arrange the funeral. How does a man drown himself? That was the mind fuck of it. All the what-ifs: *What if* I had not left that day but had stayed with Dad? *What if* I'd never moved out of the house and in with Damian but instead had stayed around to keep the family together? *What if* I'd never quit chanting?"

I pulled my mother into my arms as she sobbed. In the past, whenever my mother cried, which was often, I always struggled with a strange repulsion—her emotions were often too intense, and unpredictable, and overwhelming; when they got out of control, the inevitable result would be sheer destruction—she'd either start using again, or everything around us would collapse.

But now I felt nothing but love and compassion for Mom. I held her and I let her tears soak my pajamas. I felt connected to her in a way I had not remembered feeling since I was a small child, when we used to sit on our balcony, looking up at the sky together. Now I saw her not as my mother but as a woman who was just as confused and lost as I was.

I was also in a state of shock. Not that my grandfather might have committed suicide, but that my mother had kept such a formative trauma from me. How was it possible that the woman who was always revealing crazy stories about her past, often by accident and despite herself, had never once let even the tiniest detail about this memory slip?

A picture slowly began to form in my mind of my mother's life that was fuller and far more interesting than all her stories of celebrities, and politicians, and the white-picket-fence existence she had always tried to paint.

PART FIVE

THE PET STORE

Seven years after I was lying on the bathroom floor with my mother, I was sitting at a quiet Italian restaurant off Melrose Avenue with my husband, Nick, and his family—my family—nine months pregnant with our first child, who was due at any moment.

It was May 2015, and we were by the window at a giant round table. Nick's sister's two kids were nibbling on garlic bread and pizza while Nick argued, lightheartedly, about whether his five-year-old niece, Willow, should be allowed to get a hamster for her birthday.

"Absolutely not!" Leanne, my sister-in-law, shouted.

"Come on," Willow begged.

"Yeah, come on!" Nick piped in. "I vote hamster!"

A younger version of myself would have approached this restaurant and looked inside at this family like they were a different species of human. If the Ghost of Christmas Yet to Come had dragged me here, pointed inside, and said, "Chrysta, that's you in a decade, that's you enjoying a stable, happy life," I would never have believed it.

I'd met Nick by chance. After graduating from college and living in L.A. with my mother, I'd decided to take my interest in painting more seriously and applied to an obscure art school in Italy called the Florence Academy of Art, which I'd learned about through a painting teacher in Culver City.

To my great shock, I'd been accepted. I moved to Florence the next fall. I'd cross the Ponte Vecchio on my hours-long walk to school every morning, listening to hundreds of hours of audiobooks of classics I'd never read, like *Of Human Bondage* and *Les Misérables*, and then spend the next eight to ten hours drawing and painting from a nude model. Few American students attended the school; my roommate was from India, and my two best friends were from Germany and Spain. I'd never been happier. I never wanted to leave.

But across the ocean and back home in West Hollywood, the housing crisis escalated, and our fairy godfather disappeared without warning or explanation. Mom did ultimately have to sell all our furniture and Kaitlyn's piano in a yard sale before moving into a halfway house. Soon after, Kaitlyn called after having just spent a few days visiting Mom in L.A. She said that Mom's new bed was so small they both couldn't fit in it, so our mother had insisted Kaitlyn sleep in the bed while Mom just sat for the entire night on an uncomfortable wooden chair.

"No matter what happened to us in the past," Kaitlyn reflected, trying not to cry, "Mom always had a bed we could share. Now we don't even have that."

Kaitlyn was now back in New York and mentioned she was "feeling a little blue." She had considered walking in front of traffic—"not to die, necessarily, but just to land in the hospital and have someone take care of me for a few days."

I decided to put my art on hold and moved back to Los Angeles, taking the first "normal" job I was able to secure because it had a career trajectory. It involved public relations for technology companies, which was ironic, considering I had only recently been staying in Italy studying Renaissance painting as if I lived in the 1600s. I hated technology. I really did not love the job, but I hated being broke more—so I worked long hours and learned a lucrative trade. Because my heart wasn't in it, I was not averse to risk, and I eventually quit and started consulting on my own. Because the technology industry was on an upswing in 2010, and PR was a highly sought-after skill, I hustled and worked hard and I did well.

I had made the practical choice, in favor of stability, rather than the riskier choice to keep pursuing art and writing while I continued to waitress, struggling to get by. Some part of me felt that continuing to pursue my dreams—despite knowing they might never pan out—was the kind of decision my mother would make; certainly she had encouraged me to stay in school. But her words had little weight when she said them from a single bed in a halfway house.

As I began making different choices than the ones I'd been raised to make, something unexpected happened and my new job brought me the greatest gift in my life: Nick. He covered the technology industry for the *New York Times* and I'd asked him to coffee to pitch him a story about a company I was working with. Instead, we talked about art, writing, and life for four hours.

Nick was a journalist and author, and while he had experienced his own tumultuous upbringing, he was everything I'd ever said I wanted in a partner but had never actually gone for. He was kind, faithful, and smart. He lived in a small apartment and was not wealthy, but he had a job he showed up for and a dog he took good care of. He was also a great cook, which was a bonus as I could barely scramble eggs. And he was fun and lighthearted—an extrovert—which was a great complement to my more serious, often neurotic, introverted personality. I loosened up when I was around him and started to take life just slightly less seriously. We had a million interests in common. We could talk for ten hours, uninterrupted, and still have more to say.

Nick mentioned he was several years divorced, largely because he wanted children and his ex-wife had no interest. I, too, desperately wanted children. If there was a gene for the impulse to be a parent, my mother had passed it along.

"If you met someone today," I said during that initial coffee, trying to keep a casual face, as if I was not talking about myself, which of course I was, "roughly how long do you think you would want to wait to have children?"

"If I met someone today," Nick said, as if he was not talking about me either, "I guess I'd probably want to do it within a year or so?"

I looked across the table at Nick and had a strange feeling about him, like the universe was giving me a break, if I wanted to take it.

We began dating, in what Nick thought was a drama-free, sweet, and gentle courtship. Behind the scenes, I was on the phone with my therapist every other day, whispering from Nick's bathroom as I panicked because I just could not fathom that someone this uncomplicated and together would maintain an interest in me for very long.

A couple of weeks in, Nick joked that he had something to confide in me that he felt I should know before we continued dating. His family was a bit "crazy," he said. His aunt, for example, claimed to be a medium who spoke to the dead and was going to stop World War III from happening.

I laughed nervously. I was terrified because, except for James, I had never told another person the whole truth of my life. I decided to take a big chance and, to my great shock, Nick seemed to love me more, not less. We quickly moved in together, then pooled our savings to buy our first house, then rented Mom an apartment in an orange building around the corner. Now here we were, sitting around the dinner table with Nick's family, our first child due any day.

Nick stood and grabbed his niece's hand.

"C'mon, Willow," he declared, in defiance of his sister. "We are taking you to get you your hamster!"

We all piled into our respective cars and drove to the nearby Petco. As we were waiting in line to pay, Willow holding a baby hamster in a little plastic tub, Nick looked down and noticed that a man's dog was about to urinate on his leg. He quickly stepped back as the dog relieved himself on the Petco floor.

"Excuse me, sir, but I think your dog just peed," Nick said after the owner, lost in thought, hadn't appeared to notice.

It was enough of a statement that we all turned to see who Nick was talking to. There stood my father, in an old white shirt and jeans—the same jeans Mom had given him all those years ago—still with only his front teeth, his little scraggly dog Trixie by his side. It had been almost a decade since I'd seen him. In a city of four million people, made up of five hundred square miles, I had somehow managed to wind up in the exact same place as my dad at the exact moment in my life when I myself was about to become a parent. What were the odds of this chance encounter?

"Dad," I said, shaking, as our eyes caught each other's, Nick registering that this was my father.

I froze as I noticed my father's eyes move down to my very pregnant belly.

I stood in the middle of the Petco line, unable to move as I turned and looked at Nick's sister, her husband, and their daughter and son staring awkwardly, and then back at the pee spreading toward my foot.

"This is Nick," I said as casually as I could, trying to act normal. "Nick, this is my dad."

Nick, too, tried to act as if everything was perfectly normal. He shook my father's hand, then introduced him to the rest of the family.

Willow, who was holding her little hamster, looked up and glanced sideways, curious.

"Are we family?" she asked my father.

I could see that he didn't know how to answer.

"Yes, this is my dad," I told Willow.

I looked at my father, but I had no idea how to access what he was thinking.

"Do you want to see a dog trick?" he asked Willow, holding out a treat as he tried unsuccessfully to get Trixie to jump up and catch it. Willow bent down to pet Trixie, a ragged and fearful mutt, who quickly nipped at her.

We got to the front of the line as my father fumbled to pay for a few dog treats for Trixie, using one-dollar bills and spare change. I awkwardly tried to think through whether I should offer to pay, but wondered if that might insult him.

I gave my dad a hug goodbye and told him I would call him soon. Nick and I walked back to the car in silence.

The second I saw that my father was gone from sight, I burst into tears. I didn't even know my father anymore, nor did he know me. He had emailed and texted me throughout the years, to say things like "Happy birthday, Chrysta," and "Merry Christmas," often including a photo of him smiling with one of his dogs, which I'd warmly responded to. But he had not been at Nick's and my tiny wedding at the Beverly Hills Courthouse because I hadn't invited him. He was not a part of my life anymore, and he'd just seen firsthand so many people who *were*. "Together" people. "Normal." I wondered if he'd noticed the difference.

I sat in the passenger seat of our car in the Petco parking lot, hyperventilating because I was crying so intensely, while Nick rubbed my back and tried to be supportive. I realized I hadn't spent a lot of time thinking about my father over the past several years. It had been easier to just pretend he didn't exist, to compartmentalize my feelings for him and believe in some imaginary world wherein he was, indeed, just a sperm donor, rather than to face the truth of his being my real dad.

"I'm a terrible human being, aren't I?" I said to Nick through tears.

"No, Chrysta," he said, reaching over to hold my hand. "He chose this life. You are not responsible for where he ended up."

Nick had a smile on his face that I found quite odd, even annoying. He was happy we had just bumped into my father, that it had led to my brief outburst of tears. He had a long-expressed theory that my father represented some big Pandora's box of emotion I had never dealt with.

Nick looked over skeptically while I wiped away my tears and resumed my position of being completely fine. "I am a thousand percent sure this is just hormones from being pregnant."

"That must be it," he said, again with that annoying smirk. He seemed to feel it wasn't a good long-term strategy to deal with my feelings about my father by suppressing them, and the run-in was the universe's way of opening Pandora's box so I could sort through it.

We pulled up to our home in the hills of Los Feliz, which I'd spent months decorating with the zeal of an eight-year-old who decides to rearrange the furniture in her bedroom every evening. It drove Nick crazy the way I moved objects around. He'd walk into a room to sit down with a coffee and a book, only to discover that a chair that had been there hours earlier had since vanished. He was more of a put-things-in-one-place-and-leave-them-there kind of person. But he also understood that having a home of my own, one not at risk of being taken away at any second, meant more to me than it did to most people.

When we walked inside, I couldn't help but compare my life now to the life my father lived. I looked around at the living room, at several overpriced linen pillows I had just purchased, then thought about my father living in a broken-down motor home. I felt ashamed. I tried to mentally grasp how I might set aside enough money to help him financially. Nick and I were already stretched thin, supporting my mother and with a new mortgage and a baby on the way.

I decided that for now, I would start slow and attempt to rebuild a relationship with him as an adult, without having my mother involved. It occurred to me that she had always been there when I was with him, hovering over us, controlling him and the conversation, and I really didn't know my father.

It was difficult talking to Dad on the phone, and for our first two telephone conversations after the pet store, I just let him rant for almost an hour about wild conspiracy theories.

"The new world order is marching toward total enslavement," he'd say. "We have two years max before they drop neutron bombs!"

I realized the only way to have a productive conversation with him was to loudly interrupt and steer the conversation toward concrete topics of real life.

"Dad, can I ask you a question that's been on my mind?" I said one day.

"Sure."

"When you used to come visit me and Kaitlyn, as kids, what was that like for you?"

I was fishing. I wanted to learn the answer to the question I had been trying to get answered my whole life: if my father loved me.

"You know, your mother used to pay me to come over to visit you and Kaitlyn," he said casually.

I sat up in shock as I cradled my now giant belly and felt a painful kick.

"What do you mean she paid you?"

"Oh, you know. I'd come over, maybe massage her feet for a bit, then play with you and Kaitlyn, and she'd give me a little donation. Maybe twenty or a hundred dollars, depending on how she was doing."

My father kept talking, with no idea that what he'd just said was hurtful. I felt angry and confused, but I didn't know who to be angry with: my mother for coming up with this plan, or my father for going along with it and then telling me about it. Did all those birthday parties mean anything to him, or had they just been a job to him?

Mom came over later that afternoon, and we talked in my bedroom. She was incensed by the suggestion that she'd paid Jeffrey to pretend to be my father.

"I didn't pay him!" she insisted. Then she paused, perhaps wanting to cover her tracks. "Well, not for *every* visit. Sometimes he came without being paid!"

"That's great, Mom. Just great."

There seemed to be no end to the lies.

"Chrysta, your father did love you, as much as he was able to love."

I sat there, quiet, trying not to tear up as I thought again about him picking through loose change to pay for dog food.

"How does he get by, Mom?" I asked. "How does he even feed himself?"

"Your father is very complicated, Chrysta." She came and put her arm around me on the bed, her face concerned.

She told me about a time, years earlier, when she'd gone alone to

Venice to see how he was doing. He'd walked out of his car covered in open blisters. He had MRSA, he'd explained nonchalantly, as he pulled up his pants to show her that both of his legs were covered in scabs. Then he casually asked if she could drive him to the health food store to get some tea tree oil.

"Tea tree oil! Jeffrey, get in the car right now!" she'd demanded, and then rushed him to the hospital. She knew how dangerous MRSA was, that it could be fatal. As she later stared at him in the hospital bed being shot up with antibiotics, she wondered if he could have died. She had gently suggested he apply for government aid. She'd read that he could get an SSI benefit check every month, for $730, if they deemed him mentally ill, which would at least be enough money to buy food.

"They are not going to give me money," he'd said to her. "I don't have a mental illness. What will I even say when I go in there?"

"Just go in exactly as you are now," she'd said, staring at his bloody legs, and the rat's nest in his hair, and the dirt on his hands and face. "Tell them that story you just told me about the arsonist on the hunt for you, and that you are the coming of Christ. They will give you a check—trust me."

My mother laughed now, shaking her head at the memory, then turning back to me and growing visibly sad. I could see she didn't enjoy sharing these kinds of reflections about my father. "Soon after, he started to get the checks," she said. "In his mind, he thinks he conned the government into thinking he was mentally ill."

"What was he diagnosed with?" I asked. This was somehow my first time registering that my father might struggle with mental illness—that perhaps drugs and meditation had simply been his attempt to self-medicate a suffering he could not otherwise break free from.

"I don't know," my mother told me. "He always grew very vague whenever I asked him about it. Honestly, I was just amazed he even figured out how to get through the paperwork."

"What if we get him a proper psychologist?" I asked.

"Chrysta," Mom said, now stern. "I have spent thirty years trying to help Jeffrey. Trust me when I tell you there is nothing you can do. You're having a baby any minute. Do not take this on right now."

A few days later, my father began sending me angry messages in the middle of the night. He said my mother had always promised him that in return for acting as our father, his children would take care of him when he was older. This really hurt me because it once again brought into question his motivations for being in my life. And the irony was that if I trusted that his motivations were honorable, I would likely have done everything I could to help him.

I was so overwhelmed by the barrage of messages that I could focus on little else. I couldn't answer work emails or pack for the hospital. I was comatose. I realized the problem with opening this Pandora's box was that I was incapable of not crawling inside it.

My mother was right. I was not in the appropriate place, at this moment, to take this on. I gave her some money to purchase a new motor home for him to live in, mostly to ease my guilt, and then I stopped responding to his messages—even to a very sweet note he sent me after I gave birth to my son Somerset.

A TUBE OF SALIVA

It was 9 a.m. on a beautiful March morning in 2017. I was sitting in a rocking chair with Emerson, my and Nick's second child, who was less than one month old. As I held Emerson's tiny toes in my hands, I felt both profoundly in love and also grateful he was passed out so I could have a moment's rest.

I heard my mother arrive downstairs, then listened with a combination of amusement and irritation as she attempted to tiptoe her way upstairs to Emerson's bedroom, dropping her purse loudly on the way up, then realizing she had left her dog outside. She called out "Gracie!" at the top of her lungs, proceeding to swear at herself loudly for having also forgotten her phone.

"Be quiet!" I hissed as Emerson began to stir.

My mother entered the room with a sneaky look on her face as she fumbled through her purse, furiously looking for something.

"What are you up to?" I whispered, suspicious.

"I need you to spit into this tube," she said. She pulled out a plastic vial and held it to my face.

"Why?"

"I'm convinced your great-grandmother was Jewish, and I want to verify it with your DNA."

I raised an eyebrow and made the face I usually made when she assumed I would just pay for some little whim of hers.

"How much does it cost?"

"Just spit!" she demanded, holding the tube up to my lips. "It costs nothing. Consider it an early birthday present."

Running on very few hours of sleep and wanting her to leave me alone so I could nod off, I spit.

Ever since I'd married Nick, who happened to be of Jewish descent but barely celebrated Hanukkah, my mother had become obsessed with the idea that we also had Jewish roots. She explained that she had always felt "a deep connection to the Jews" and "to their plight." She now pressured us to celebrate every Jewish holiday and arrived at the house almost daily with new Jewish-themed children's books for the kids.

My mother used that vial of clear liquid and signed me up for Ancestry.com, hoping to find out more about her maternal line, and perhaps a bit more about Jeffrey's, too. What she did not realize, in all her adorable technical incompetence, was that by creating this account, she was consenting to share my results with a vast social network of people who had my same hereditary material.

To my mother's great dismay, Ancestry.com notified her that we were not even .001 percent Jewish. But she was quickly distracted from that disappointment by another Ancestry.com feature, which allowed her to fill in our family tree. In between visits to our house to fawn over her grandchildren, she now spent her days happily immersed in research, looking up names and dates and photographs of parents and great-grandparents and uncles and great-uncles on both sides, with no idea that all this information was being made public.

I was feeling more lighthearted toward Mom these days, perhaps because becoming a parent had given me more empathy for her. As much as I loved being a mother, I now lived with a constant, intense pressure to do everything "right" that was sometimes overwhelming. I could not imagine how my mother had done it alone—how any single parent raises a child by themselves—nor could I fathom how scary it must have been to do it so differently than everyone around her.

A few weeks later, the universe came knocking as my mother sat in the living room of her quaint "Tibetan Orange" apartment in West Hollywood. She had just gotten off the phone with a distant cousin of Jeffrey's who she'd bonded with in recent months because the woman was as interested in ancestry as she was, and was now helping my mother fill in holes in Jeffrey's family tree on my Ancestry.com account.

Mom logged in, excited to add a new great-uncle to the tree, still believing that everything she was doing was private. Then she noticed a little bubble at the top of her screen notifying her that she had several new messages in her inbox—or shall I say *my* inbox, which she was in control of.

She clicked on the first message.

"Hi, how are we related?" the most recent note read. It was from a woman named Jennifer.

My mother sat up in her chair, stunned, unsure what to do. She picked up her phone and dialed me.

"Chrysta, I think you might have a new sister," she said.

"Have what?" I asked.

"She just reached out to me on my Ancestry.com account. I don't think she has figured it out yet."

"Mom, that is *my* account," I said, flabbergasted at the boundary I only just realized even existed and that had long since been crossed. "That is not *your* account!"

I demanded the login and password, hoping to unravel what she had done, at which point I saw that a new message from Jennifer had just landed in the inbox.

"I feel terrible sharing this with you," it read, "but I think my uncle Bob had an affair with your mother and whoever your dad is isn't actually your biological father."

I couldn't help but laugh. Clearly this poor girl had no idea it was the other way around: she was the one who had her father wrong. I wondered how long it would take her to figure this out, if she'd already realized it as I read this.

It had been almost ten years since I'd learned about the siblings, and I had not given them a great deal of thought since. At some point, my mother had shared that a documentary had been released about my father meeting the first few biological children he had discovered, but I'd never watched the film, not even the trailer. Nor had I ever read any of the dozens of articles about him. None of the siblings had reached out since that first interaction with Rachelle on Facebook. I had been so clear in my communications with her that I did not want anything to do with the siblings that apparently she had passed along the message, and everyone had respected my wishes and left me alone.

But Jennifer had found me before she found the Facebook group.

I pulled up Instagram and stared at pictures of a blue-eyed woman in her mid-twenties who looked exactly like Kaitlyn. She had the same dimple over her left cheek, the same full lower lip, and the exact same shade of thick brown hair. I had always looked more like my mother, but Kaitlyn took after our father, and she and Jennifer were *identical*. The algorithms on my iPhone would have had a difficult time recognizing them as two separate people.

I scrolled through Jennifer's photos and saw pictures of the exact same gardening books I had literally *just* purchased—not only popular gardening titles, but obscure ones. Some of the same esoteric philosophy and art books that sat piled on her nightstand sat on mine. She also dressed exactly like me: in loose-fitting muted earth tones, usually with a scarf around her neck.

A few seconds into her feed, I scrolled past a photograph that made my stomach drop. It was an image of Jennifer with her hair pulled back and standing in a tiny painting studio. I recognized the easel and the black cloth hanging in the background. She was standing in the exact same painting studio, across the world, in Florence, Italy, on Via delle Casine, that I myself had stood in more times than I could count. She was sketching from the exact same nude model I myself had sketched. My old roommate Tanvi, from India, was standing in the background.

Jennifer had grown up across the country in upstate New York, raised by what I assumed were two stable, ordinary parents. I was sure her life had been nothing like mine, yet somehow she had wound up in the exact same place. Jennifer was more like me than Kaitlyn was. Judging by her Instagram feed, she was more identical to me in spirit than anyone I had ever met.

Just then I realized Nick was standing in front of me. I hadn't even noticed him entering the room.

"What's going on?" he asked, curious.

"I just found out about a new sister," I said, as if this was a perfectly normal event to occur on a Tuesday afternoon.

"You did what?" he asked. Then, realizing he'd heard me correctly, he gave me a concerned look and added, "Wow, how does that make you feel?"

I sat there for a moment trying to figure out how I felt. I stared at the photograph of Jennifer smiling in the painting studio, and to my great surprise I felt a light cloud of curiosity, and even amusement, at how this little whim of my mother's, as always, had several wild repercussions she had not thought through.

I looked up at Nick.

"Calm," I told him. "I feel strangely calm."

A THIRD SISTER

I've heard people describe out-of-body experiences where they see themselves from across the room, and feel strangely separated from their own bodies, as if they are watching someone else. When I met Jennifer in person, a year after our first email exchange, it was kind of like that, except it was not myself I was looking at; it was my sister.

Jennifer walked up to the front of my house, and I awkwardly and nervously opened the front door. All I could do was stare in shock at this adult woman who was a combination of me and Kaitlyn and my father, all tangled into one.

Somerset, who was almost three, walked up to the door to say hello and gave me a confused look as I introduced him to "Aunt Jennifer," who had seemingly appeared out of nowhere, as if we'd picked her up at the store and brought her home with us. (Little did he know how many aunts and uncles there really were.)

I ushered Jennifer inside and we hugged with a strange familiarity. I wasn't sure if this feeling was genetic or psychological—if being blood relations made us feel instantly familiar, or if knowing that created the feeling.

I showed Jennifer to the garage we'd converted into a guesthouse, and we made small talk as she unpacked. We had spent months emailing back and forth and speaking on the phone, so in some ways, I felt I knew her already, but being here in person with her now, staring at her face, and seeing my own in it, was much more intense.

I sat on the edge of the guest bed and watched as Jennifer unpacked several obscure objects she'd brought along with her "to make the trip comfortable"; they included her own small travel blender, a bag of organic chia seeds (for the smoothie she had, without fail, every single morning), and a sound machine and a cot with spikes on it, which she told me was called a bed of nails, to help her fall asleep. While the items I would have brought on my own trip would have been different—a custom understuffed down pillow, for example—it was clear that we shared very sensitive bodies.

Jennifer and I spent the afternoon in the backyard, bonding over our shared sleep issues, as well as all the different diets we'd tried throughout the years in order to feel less tired and lethargic, swaying between extremes of being vegan and eating mostly red meat, always trying to find the right combination of foods that would keep our heads screwed on tight and our feet planted firmly on the ground. We both suspected we had severe ADD, and neither of us wanted to take medication for it.

Jennifer was married to a Brit seven years older than her. Nick was British and seven years older than me. Unlike me, though, she was struggling in her relationship, and not sure she and her husband were a good match long-term, which was bringing her a lot of pain and confusion, as she still really loved him.

Jennifer was endearingly messy, a fact I noticed on the first day of her visit, when after only a few hours her bedroom appeared to have been hit by a tornado. She explained that her mother had always cleaned up after her and she'd therefore grown up with the somewhat problematic belief that rooms "cleaned themselves." I was, meanwhile, incredibly tidy, perhaps because of having been raised in a home that was always a tornado.

The day went on like this, with me taking note of how far nature had taken the two of us, and where nurture took over. Of all the differences between us, the one I found most interesting was how differently Jennifer felt about this large biological family.

Standing in our kitchen, Jennifer told me that finding out she had a sperm donor and all these siblings had been the single most exciting event in what she described as an otherwise "boring" life. She was an only child and had always wanted siblings. She was elated to learn that she had dozens, possibly even more, of them. She had joined the Facebook group and reached out to develop relationships with every sibling who had been discovered up until now. Of the ones she had not yet spoken to, she knew and could recite every minute detail of their lives, like she was a private detective who had spent years tracking down and investigating every member of our family. Jennifer had also discovered, in her extensive research, that we were not in fact related to Oliver Wendell Holmes Jr.—a detail that made me laugh, given Holmes is my middle name. (I decided not to share this news with my mother for now, since I knew it would throw her into a depression.)

Nick entered the kitchen with the kids, handing me Emerson to breastfeed. Nick and Somerset plopped on the floor.

"How many are there now?" I asked, teetering on the edge of being interested in hearing about the other siblings.

"Twenty-six—that we know of," Jennifer said. "Almost all girls."

"Why all girls?"

Jennifer had several theories going to explain this, the most plausible of which was that Jeffrey predominantly produced female sperm.

"And how many do you think there are out there, in total?" I asked her.

"There's clearly hundreds," she said, to which both Nick and I just stared blankly in her direction.

"Just think about the number of people who have gotten DNA tests. It's such a tiny percentage of the population. And yet we've already found almost two dozen through that. Imagine if everyone did a DNA test. I bet we would find out about a lot more."

"Do you think there could be thousands?" Nick asked, laughing.

Jennifer laughed, too.

"I don't think that's very funny, Nick," I said.

"Do you want to join the Facebook group?" Jennifer asked.

"No, thanks," I told her. For right now, I only felt comfortable connecting with Jennifer, but I was more than happy to learn about the other siblings for the first time through her.

Jennifer told me about Maddie, an actress in New York who was currently performing on Broadway in *Harry Potter and the Cursed Child*. Then there was Kathryn, who was in the army and had just graduated at the top of her class at West Point. JoEllen lived in Pittsburgh and worked in harm reduction, drug policy, and public safety, while Ryann, a software engineer, was here in Los Angeles. There was also Rachelle, who competed in national salsa dance competitions, and Kate, who was getting her master's in sociolinguistics at Georgetown. Jennifer told me they all had cats, most of them more than one, and they all seemed to share a love of nature; many played the guitar and loved music. Our siblings had grown up in seemingly every type of family, every imaginable economic circumstance, and all over the country, from small towns to wealthy coastal cities.

I sat listening as Jennifer shared details about each sibling and showed me their social media pages. She told me about, among the few boys in the group, a local council member in Duluth, Minnesota, and another who installed Wi-Fi in Denver, Colorado. Last but not least, there was one who had gone to live with my father in Venice after finding out he was donor-conceived. They had rented a motel together for several months, Jennifer told me as my mouth dropped open. Then the brother got into hard drugs, started living on the streets in Venice, and was eventually hospitalized and diagnosed with schizophrenia.

Surely Jennifer's and my obscure interest in classical painting wasn't the only trait that flowed through our blood. I wondered if whatever my father had was genetic, and if that was something I should be worried about. Then again, we also had many siblings who seemed to be leading happy, functional lives.

Kaitlyn showed up later that evening for dinner, as did Jennifer's husband, Ben.

I had called Kaitlyn in the weeks leading up to Jennifer's visit, telling her all about how lovely Jennifer was, and encouraging her to get to know her. She had agreed to come over for dinner but upon entering my house, she made it clear she had other plans later in the evening, and didn't have a lot of time to spend with us. I was a bit surprised she'd even shown up.

Kaitlyn and I were struggling to stay close in those days. She'd graduated from Barnard in New York and moved back to Los Angeles— right up the street—where she was now supporting herself in real estate in order to have the freedom to make music. She had recently signed a record deal. She'd also managed to track down two of our childhood cats, Oliver and Tonga, who had been separated. Now ages nineteen and fifteen, they'd only ever gotten along with each other, and had not been thriving in the homes our mother had found for them: Tonga had been in a basement studio apartment for four years with no sunlight, while Oliver had been living in a house with five other cats who he didn't get along with. After reuniting, they'd never been happier, nor had Kaitlyn. She was now the proud mother of two senior Bengal cats, who she often walked on harnesses in her pajamas and bathrobe.

Kaitlyn was thriving in many areas of her life, but she still had a propensity for toxic boyfriends. Having mothered her for so many years, I had a difficult time not trying to influence this side of her life, often sharing my unsolicited opinions, which was a battle within myself I continued to lose. Meanwhile, Kaitlyn, who could feel my judgment, worry, and attempts to control, had pulled back, creating an unprecedented distance between us, even more than when we were separated by thousands of miles.

My mother came over shortly after Kaitlyn left. She had been her own seesaw of emotional volatility leading up to Jennifer's visit. "Don't start inviting these people into our lives," she'd kept saying, often in dramatic tears. "We made a deal years ago. Jennifer is okay, but don't even think about the others. It will hurt me deeply."

When she arrived at the house, she just stared in quiet shock for a good several seconds, marveling at how much Jennifer looked like young Jeffrey.

"She is just so beautiful," my mother said, tearing up. "Just like he was."

Later that night, Jennifer and I sat on the floor of my family room, poring over all the photos I had of my father and me from when I was little. She asked me a million questions, some of which I was apprehensive about answering. Even if I spoke about how my father had struggled with addiction to hard drugs, like crystal meth, or discussed his ongoing homelessness, or the potential that he might be bipolar, or schizophrenic, or some combination of the two, Jennifer didn't appear overwhelmed or disappointed. She did not seem to judge my father's alternative lifestyle, and told me she found it "poetic." It was endearing to her that, even if he did struggle with some serious mental illness, it had manifested in a simple life in which he took care of animals. Jennifer had found all the articles and newsclips about him, which I myself had never dared to read or watch.

"I saw one video of him smoking a bong from a water bottle as he prayed to some guru," she said. "I just thought it was hysterical. I was such a stoner in college. No one in my family ever dabbled in drugs. No one was artistic, or spiritual."

When Jennifer and I were alone in my living room at one point, I turned to her impulsively and said, "Okay, invite me."

Before I could rethink this decision, Jennifer excitedly pulled up her phone and clicked "Invite new friend." An alert landed in my inbox with an invitation to join the Donor 150 Facebook group. I pulled up my own phone and there it was: the exact same group Rachelle had invited me to join a decade earlier, with the same cover photo of the seven original siblings on the swing set. The group had grown to twenty-six people. I looked through a few of their profile pages as Jennifer wrote an introductory message on the group bulletin board.

Over the next ten minutes, I received ten individual welcome messages, like I had just joined an incredibly enthusiastic middle school club. It felt like I was learning the secret all over again.

The next morning, I looked out my kitchen window and saw Jennifer sitting outside, taking in the California sun with her eyes closed. I clicked through three more welcome messages that had come in. Then I heard a scream and rushed outside, where I found Jennifer staring at her phone with a look of shock and delight on her face.

"What is it?" I asked.

"We have a new sister!"

Jennifer passed me her phone, and sure enough, there was an Ancestry.com message from a woman named Grace.

"How are you my first cousin?" it read. "Do you live in Indiana?"

"Oh my God," I said, shaking my head and putting my hands over my eyes. On Ancestry.com, half siblings and first cousins look the same because the site determines relations based on percentage of shared DNA. Half siblings share around 25 percent of their DNA, while first cousins share around 12.5 percent. Why Ancestry.com doesn't break them into two categories is anyone's guess—perhaps it's to soften the shock of moments like this.

Later that afternoon, I walked Jennifer to the door to leave. Her Uber was waiting for her, and I was surprised to realize I felt sad—not that Jennifer was leaving, though I'd had a lovely time with her this past weekend, but because the experience had reminded me just how far apart Kaitlyn and I had drifted. Jennifer and I were so similar; it felt like Kaitlyn and I had nothing in common anymore except genetics. Perhaps it is also true that new relationships are always easier than ones filled with long and complex histories.

"We should get all the siblings together one day," Jennifer said, half joking.

"Yeah, why not?" I laughed. "Like a family reunion."

THE FAMILY REUNION

There was a knock on the front door.

Maddie, the actress from New York, was the first to arrive. Wearing a sundress with no bra, an old Levi's jean jacket, and Converse sneakers, she was striking, like Jennifer and Kaitlyn, but more outgoing. She was also a bit shorter, and more petite, than the others—"like my mother," she explained.

Even though Maddie was almost six years younger than me, I felt a bit self-conscious as she sat down on my couch; I wondered how she felt about this whole thing, not wanting to be overly enthusiastic if she wasn't feeling that way. Maddie and I spoke for an hour before anyone else arrived. She told me about her upbringing—how she'd been raised by a stable, Jewish single mother who worked at a nonprofit. Unlike many of the other siblings, Maddie had never been interested in learning much about Jeffrey. Even when Maddie was a child, her mother had been prepared to answer any questions about her donor honestly, but for whatever reason, Maddie never asked them.

"Perhaps it was a bit of a protection mechanism," Maddie reflected, "to protect my mother."

Maddie told me her mom had found out about Jeffrey accidentally, after the mother of one of her soccer teammates recalled Maddie's donor number and phoned to say that the donor was on the cover of the *New York Times*. Maddie's mother had never planned to look up her donor, but she read the article, and, upon learning that he was living in a parking lot in a van with all these dogs, she felt devastated, mostly because she worried this information would disappoint Maddie.

Maddie's mother had hosted a reunion years earlier, like the get-together I was hosting, but with far fewer siblings, since not many were known back then. Maddie had largely lost contact with most of them. Now over a dozen siblings were flying in from all over the country—from New York, Indiana, Pennsylvania, Colorado, and Boston.

I could only imagine what it must have felt like to be sitting on an airplane, flying to Los Angeles, about to meet several siblings you hadn't even known existed just a few weeks earlier. I'd had more than a decade to process this moment.

Over the course of the afternoon, other siblings arrived. Each time, I would smile, invite them in, ask if they wanted anything to drink—tea or coffee or some wine—and then sit down and try to get to know them individually, as best I could, hoping to make them feel comfortable and at ease. It felt like speed dating. With each new person who entered the house, I felt an intense wave of energy. After each conversation, I had to excuse myself to my bedroom upstairs to take a moment to process the conversation I'd just had. But there was no time to recuperate or reflect between them. The second I went upstairs and sat down, the doorbell would ring, and another sibling would show up. I'd come downstairs, we'd talk for thirty minutes, then it would happen all over again. Eventually, there were too many people to have these one-on-one chats, and it became a group affair.

What on earth was I thinking by inviting them all here? I thought as they all stood and arranged their toes in a lineup for a photo. I stuck out my own toes, nails painted red, and we all laughed that same laugh, as Nick stared at us, shaking his head in astonishment.

"Yes, I will confirm they are all identical," he said, examining our toes closely, on his knees, as if trying to pick out the one that looked different in a police lineup.

Kaitlyn showed up a few hours in, in time for some very sweet, if silly, icebreakers she had little interest in engaging in. I didn't judge. Had I not connected with Jennifer, I likely still would not be interested in connecting with these siblings. But I was disappointed, as I'd been hopeful that Kaitlyn and I could process the experience together.

As the party began, Nick was standing in the kitchen, offering people coffee as they walked in, not realizing he would spend the next two hours as a barista as people came back for seconds and thirds.

Kaitlyn leaned against the kitchen counter next to Nick at the coffee machine and then whispered, only half joking, "I do not have time for fourteen new best friends in my life." She stayed for another thirty minutes, then left. For the rest of the weekend, she drifted in and out, never staying for long.

At dinner out that first evening, almost every order was complicated; every single person had a very specific diet, and most were vegetarians. When we left the restaurant, the waiter who had been serving us ran out, holding four—yes, four!—cell phones, two sets of keys, and three bags, all of which we had collectively left behind. The waiter found this to be equally amazing, since we'd told him the fourteen of us at dinner were all siblings. He'd even asked to take our picture after hearing the story and feeling this was the most bizarre and memorable table he had ever served.

The following afternoon, everyone gathered in the backyard, and Nick suggested we do an experiment: he would make statements to the group, and whoever agreed should put up their hand.

He started with simple statements he knew most of us would respond to, such as "Put your hand up if your phone battery is always at a single-digit percent!"

Ten hands went up.

"Put your hand up if you have a cat."

Every hand except mine went up because Nick and I were currently in a battle over whether I could get one, as he was not fond of them.

As wild as it was that they all had cats, in the back of my mind, I did wonder how many people in our age bracket in the United States had cats, or forgot to charge their cell phones, and if we were so hungry for commonalities that we were disregarding our differences. I also felt a little ridiculous playing this game; it felt like summer camp.

"Raise your hand if you are on some kind of medication for depression or anxiety," Nick said.

Apart from three siblings, every hand went up. One of my new siblings who had not raised her hand later admitted to me in private that she had been diagnosed, in her teens, with schizoaffective disorder but had been able to recover from it. Another believed she could benefit from medication, but was first trying natural remedies for her intense anxiety. I myself was now on Lexapro, as was Kaitlyn, and it had helped both of us. And my father, I knew, had several diagnoses—though I still wondered what those were.

My mother had arrived for the first time yesterday, shortly after Kaitlyn, entering the house in tears, then pulling me aside and privately tossing around threats that the weekend would break up our family. Then, upon meeting all the siblings who were there, one by one, she seemed relieved to realize that they—mostly women—were all lovely people: kind and compassionate, and seemingly all "normal."

"I have an announcement to make," she said loudly upon her arrival the second day, after several silent minutes spent observing the room.

I turned, wondering what on earth she was talking about.

"I have spent the last few weeks collecting all the family memorabilia I had carefully archived from Jeffrey's side of the family," she said. "All the birth certificates, and photos of Jeffrey and his brother when they were little, and pictures of your grandmothers and great-grandmothers, and all the historic books on the family. Whoever is interested can meet me in the guesthouse in the back in ten minutes for a presentation."

"Mom, no one wants to see a presentation," I said. I just assumed no one would take an interest in it. I couldn't have been more wrong. Everyone followed my mother out to the guesthouse like she was the Pied Piper.

They stood around as she carefully laid out hundreds of artifacts on the desk: a photo of my father, age four, sitting at a large dinner table with a linen napkin tucked into his shirt as a servant in uniform placed a silver tray in front of him, another of his mother as a young woman, smiling into the camera with rain boots on and a garden hoe in her hand.

I watched as everyone passed the photos back and forth. One of my new sisters took out her phone and snapped a picture of my father as a young man, holding his guitar and smiling at the camera, with such a spark in his eyes. Another sister handed me a photo of him in his early thirties, holding me on top of Ziggy's back, at three years old. He had so much love and presence in his eyes. I tried my best to suppress the tears rising in my chest. All of a sudden, I stared down at the desk, populated with hundreds of photos of me and my dad and Kaitlyn over the years—all the photos Mom kept in her memory boxes—and I was overwhelmed. Memories I had blocked out came bubbling up to the surface of my consciousness. I did remember him being there. I did remember a love and a connection between us. And somewhere along the line, I felt I'd lost him—and that was really sad.

When I caught someone looking at me, I quickly smiled and wiped a tear from my eyes.

My mother took out a letter she'd received in the mail from Jeffrey's mother. She had just passed away at ninety years old in her sleep, and had written this letter a few months earlier, instructing her caregiver to send it to everyone in the family after she died. My mother handed me the letter, and I read it out loud to the room, as everyone's eyes filled with tears, mine included. She didn't speak of Jeffrey or of any specific loved ones in her letter; it was mostly a beautifully written homage to the sunrises and rainbows and all the nature she had enjoyed in her decades of living on Maui.

I looked at my mom standing there proudly as she glanced around the room, clearly feeling like the matriarch of this big, sweet, unconventional family. I realized that without her, none of these people would be alive, at least in the iteration in which they currently existed. I could sense that the heavy burden of my father's troubles and mental challenges was lifting from her, as it was from me.

At breakfast on the last day of our gathering, after everyone had checked out of the Airbnb, Jennifer told me she and a few others were planning to go see Jeffrey.

"Do you want to come with us?" she asked.

"No, thanks," I told her. I had tried, in the months leading up to this reunion, to reengage with my father, but he'd made it clear he didn't want to see me. He was hurt, perhaps rightfully so, that I'd dropped out of his life.

I listened as the group talked amongst themselves about what it had been like when some of them had met Jeffrey years earlier, shortly after the *New York Times* article came out. A few had hoped they could have a normal father-child relationship with him, but had soon been disappointed by his inability to connect. Others had no interest in ever meeting him; for them, connecting with the siblings was enough.

I sat there quietly listening to Jennifer make plans, and I wondered if she would end up in the same place as the others—hoping to have a relationship with our father, but quickly disappointed by his limited capacity to connect. I also wondered if she would succeed where I had failed, and form a deep father-daughter connection with him. I was a bit envious that however the next few hours went, she could at any time just decide to walk away from our father. For me, it was so much more complicated. For better or worse, he was my dad.

INDIA

For as long as I can remember, my father talked about how he was only staying in Los Angeles for a brief stint, because he was on his way to India, to the mountains, where he felt he belonged.

Now he insisted that he was leaving in a few days, and he told Kaitlyn and me that he would like to say goodbye. His inheritance from his mother's passing had come in, he explained, so he had purchased a plane ticket and was preparing to leave.

I wondered about the likelihood that he would leave. Kaitlyn and I decided to go see him and say goodbye, just in case. We assumed he would not follow through with the trip, but in his mind, he believed he was leaving, and that was enough for us.

We got in the car and drove toward Culver City. We parked in the lot outside the Coffee Bean and sat at a small café table.

It had been several months since the reunion, and during that time I had decided to try, again, to mend my relationship with my father. If I didn't at least try, I would regret that I had never shown him how much he had meant to me—even if the feeling was not returned.

As Kaitlyn and I sat waiting for him to arrive, I thought about the siblings. Five new siblings had popped up on Ancestry.com since the reunion. It seemed like we had a new one every two or three months now as DNA testing kits were becoming more popular.

There was Evan, our first Republican, an investment banker who caused quite a stir when he joined the Facebook group. He was a Trump supporter, while most of the other siblings were in the Bernie Sanders camp. Then came Lindsay, a scientist at Harvard studying Jupiter. Then Hector, our first Latino brother, a male model with an alpaca farm. There was also Christie Rose, who was from Hawaii and self-employed as a holistic nutritionist and "wild woman guide." Finally, there was Markie, a costume designer who was married to a marine biologist and living on Cape Cod and in the process of choosing donor sperm for herself. Finding her siblings had made her take her own donor search more seriously. Whereas before she had looked mainly at physical attributes, wanting someone tall because her father had been six-four, Markie and her wife now spent more time poring over what the donors had written about themselves. She was in a shared message board with five families who'd had babies by the same donor she'd just selected. She was going to have a second generation of sperm children. Her child would have a grand-sperm!

As time went on, I'd started to lose track of how many siblings we had, and forgot some of their names, and which stories belonged to whom. My capacity for retaining information about each individual sibling seemed to have a cap in the mid-thirties range, and I found myself checking the massive group thread, which had moved to WhatsApp, less often over time. There were too many birthdays and cat names and engagements to keep track of now, and I sometimes found myself having to dig for hours to remember what I was supposed to be congratulating someone about. But there was something strangely wonderful, too, about having a place I could go at any time if I felt lonely, or a little bored, a place where I would always find at least five people excited to connect and get into a discussion—about health, or philosophy, or politics.

I pulled out my phone to text the group.

"Not surprisingly," I wrote, "he's almost two hours late."

"Do you think he's going to show up?!" Jennifer wrote back.

"I'm really not sure," I wrote.

A few minutes later, Kaitlyn nudged me, and I saw my father approaching with Trixie. He looked better than the last time I had seen him. He had showered, and had clean, new clothes on. The color had returned to his face. His mother's inheritance was having a good effect on him.

Once he was at our table, he sat down and whispered a warning I had heard several times in the past few months, but which Kaitlyn was hearing for the first time: he made us put away our phones, in case the government "was listening." Then he leaned forward in his chair to whisper that there was a black flag attack coming to the United States, that the government planned to set off three nukes across the country, at which time the aliens would be coming to harvest our eggs.

Kaitlyn looked at me, and I gave her thigh a comforting squeeze under the table.

"Come with me to India," he said to us. "It's not too late. I will buy you each a ticket."

"We're not going to India, Dad," I told him. "But that is a really kind offer."

It frustrated my father that we did not believe him. He explained that he had converted his $200,000 inheritance into gold bars, and had purchased a wig as a disguise to evade the CIA and FBI. He was bringing all his animals with him, and he had paid an Indian family to join him on the journey because only Indian citizens could travel with dogs and cats.

"Can we see the wig?" Kaitlyn asked.

Kaitlyn and I stood up and our father walked us to his car—a nice car that he had clearly purchased with some of his inheritance. He opened the door, reached inside, pulled out a wig, and put it on over his hair. He looked utterly ridiculous. I tried not to laugh as I imagined him walking through security with this long brown wig on and $200,000 in gold bars. I didn't know whether to laugh or cry.

With a serious look on his face, he gave me a tight, stiff hug. I realized he genuinely believed it would be the last time he would ever see me and Kaitlyn—that we would both be killed in the coming days by nuclear bombs.

"Are you sure you don't want to come with me?" he said.

"We're sure, Dad."

"Okay, then I want to teach you a technique for disconnecting from feelings," he told me. "For when they come."

"Dad, you already taught me TM a long time ago. I'm okay, but thank you."

I watched him close his tear-filled eyes tight as he silently meditated, and I felt he'd inadvertently told me what I needed to hear. That he did care. That he had loved Kaitlyn and me, as much as he was capable of loving us. Kaitlyn would later tell me that she'd felt it, too.

"Oh, I forgot!" he said, opening his eyes. He spent a few moments rifling through the contents of the back seat of his car, and then pulled out several flowery dresses with tags from a nearby thrift store. "I got you guys these. I don't know if they will fit, or if you will like them, but here—"

"Thank you, Dad," we said, smiling, as we took the dresses from him. We headed to our car, got inside, and started driving back toward my house.

"How did we survive?" Kaitlyn asked after a few beats of silence.

"I really don't know," I said, shaking my head.

"Well, at least we're not boring!" she added.

I realized then that I could have gone to see my father with Jennifer, or Grace, or Evan, or any of the others. But this moment would not have held the weight it did now unless I was there with Kaitlyn. She glanced at me with a tenderness I hadn't seen her look at me with in years, and we smiled at each other.

"Kait, you know you are my only sister, in the most profound sense of that word, right?"

Her eyes welled up, and she turned away. Kaitlyn was not great with vulnerability.

It now occurred to me why that weekend with the siblings had been so heavy for her, and why it had annoyed her so much when I called them my brothers and sisters.

"No one will ever replace you for me," I said. "It's me and you forever, okay?"

"Okay," she whispered, slowly turning back and looking me in the eye in an open way I almost never witnessed in my sister.

"And then of course it's also Nick now, too, and the kids," I reflected. "Poor Nick. I don't think he knew what he was signing up for when he married into this family."

"How will I ever find a husband?" Kaitlyn said at the thought of convincing someone to marry into our family. She sank down in her seat and folded her arms across her chest.

"You just have to trust in the universe," I replied as I turned to give her a wink. "And also, you might want to wait until you are a few months in to introduce him to Dad. Make sure he's really hooked first."

WHY WE'RE HERE

After we saw our dad, Kaitlyn came home with me. We took turns giving the kids a bath and reading them stories.

"Get in here right now!" I suddenly heard Mom calling from Somerset's room. We all ran in to see her pointing out the window at a bright, full moon, light spilling out, illuminating the tops of the hundred-year-old camphor trees that lined our block.

"Let's go out onto the balcony so we can really see it," Mom said as she ushered the boys, dressed in their pajamas and socks, out of their beds and onto the balcony. I reminded my mother that it was bedtime. "It's the full moon, Chrysta!" she snapped as she brushed me away with a scowl and a flick of her hand and began teaching Somerset and Emerson how to do oms to the moon. The boys, naturally, thought this was fabulous, and Nick, Kaitlyn, and I looked on as the three of them tilted their heads back, howling toward the glittering night sky like a pack of wolves.

Nick put Somerset to bed and Mom went across the hall with Emerson. Before I made my way downstairs, I peeked in the doorway of Somerset's room. The room was dark except for a small lion night-light emanating a soft, warm glow. I watched for a moment as Nick lay with Somerset, rubbing his back, the room filled with the dreamy quiet that takes over as a child drifts off to sleep.

I crept down the hall to Emmy's room, and listened with amusement as my mother, who he called Mimi—the family nickname for her own grandmother—read him her favorite book. Emmy always plucked the book from the bookshelf and handed it to her. It was *Siddhartha,* Hermann Hesse's tale of the spiritual journey of a prince named Siddhartha.

"You know he has no idea what you are reading to him, right?" I said, laughing. Emerson was only two.

"He does understand it!" my mother insisted. "Children understand much more than we think they do."

To my incredible disbelief, my father had left for India. After two decades of threats, he drove to the airport with Trixie, two cats, an Indian family of five, and a couple hundred thousand dollars in gold bars in his suitcase, and he boarded the airplane. He was now on his way to the Arunachala mountain in South India, a "sacred Hindu mountain," with a temple to Lord Shiva at its foot. He'd been granted a humanitarian visa to rescue street dogs there.

As I walked downstairs and sat down on my living room couch, waiting for the others to join me, I let my mind wander for a minute to what might happen to my father's gold once he got to India. He had never been good with money, because he was always duped into giving what he had to people he felt needed it more than he did. For a minute, I got anxious thinking about him all by himself in India, then closed my eyes and decided to let go of my worry. I could love my father, but also accept him for who he was. I just had to trust in the universe, I guess. It had gotten him this far.

A profound shift had taken place inside of me. As I had stood in that Coffee Bean parking lot with Dad before he left, I didn't care in the slightest if anyone stared at us. I would have proudly, and with a laugh, introduced them to my dad. Every drop of my shame was gone.

As I was losing myself in these thoughts, Kaitlyn walked into the room with two cups of tea, handing me one. I could feel a breeze coming from the window next to me and smiled at her as I turned on our gas fireplace and put "Have Yourself a Merry Little Christmas" on the stereo, playing it quietly so as not to wake the kids. It was August. When we were kids we *loved* Christmas. Not just in the way any child whose family celebrates Christmas does, but because Mom always managed to pull it together around the holidays. When things were really bad, Kaitlyn and I tried to usher in Christmas earlier and earlier in the year.

When she heard the song, Kaitlyn smiled back at me with a big smirk. She sat on the couch and draped a white knitted blanket across her lap.

"Remember when Mom volunteered to drive me and a bunch of other kids for a field trip at school?"

"No, tell me," I said, having forgotten the story.

"We were halfway there and Mom said the museum was stupid. So, without calling to inform anyone, she told us, 'I'm taking you guys on a way better field trip,' and drove us to the Ashram in the Santa Monica Mountains."

"Then what?" I asked with a chuckle.

"Well, obviously, the parents weren't thrilled since no one knew where their children were for almost an entire afternoon. This was before cell phones. But my friends and I loved it. They all thought Mom was so cool as she showed them a giant geodesic dome with crystals hanging down from the ceiling."

Once the kids were asleep, Nick and Mom joined Kaitlyn and me downstairs. My mother was sixty-nine now. Her blond hair was still immaculately dyed to hide her gray, her nails perfectly painted bright red to match her red lips. But her arthritis made her hands hurt and shake a little. She tripped so often I now followed her around to tell her to look where she was going. She just didn't like to be reminded she was not a kid anymore, or that her body had any limitations as it aged. But I didn't recall her ever looking more alive in all my life.

She still attended women's marches, and was still politically involved—in the lead-up to the 2020 primaries, she was somehow on a first-name basis with Kamala Harris. And while Mom was still sober, and financially stable with Nick and me supporting her, she was just as crazy as ever. Recently, we had discovered that when we thought we were paying for some unexpected doctor's bills, Mom had in fact used that money to employ an assistant to help her post photos of her grandchildren on Instagram. She'd also hustled us into unknowingly employing an actor to narrate an audiobook version of a biography she had self-published about her grandfather. And her boundaries in the family were often nonexistent: she showed up at the house unannounced six days a week; constantly called *our* pediatrician with irrational concerns about the boys' health; and after a few months on an expensive diet program that *she* had begged Nick and me to help her pay for, Kaitlyn pulled up next to Mom one day, sitting at a traffic light in her car, where she was devouring a tub of ice cream, which she subsequently threw out the window when she realized she'd been caught, then denied was hers. There was no end to the comedy of my mother's daily adventures. I'd recently run into an old friend of hers—who'd known her since she was a teenager—who told me, "Your mother is one of the great characters of the Western world."

As we talked around the fire, we got onto the subject of spirituality. Nick had recently lost his mother and was preoccupied by the existential questions of life and death in the same way my mother had been when her father passed away.

"Why do you think we're here, Deb?" he asked.

Mom sat up and leaned forward, giddy at being asked by Nick to impart some wisdom. He was usually very rational and not often open to these types of conversations with her.

She answered first with an overview of all the years she'd spent in search of answers—first with Soka Gakkai Buddhism in Los Angeles, then with Osho in Oregon, which many people now consider to have been a cult and a cult leader, respectively. Her search had taken her to Egypt, where she'd stayed for a week under the three great pyramids reading the Dead Sea Scrolls, and to India, where she'd ridden an old train to Rishikesh, to the Maharishi's Ashram, and meditated for several days in a little hut in search of the answer to Nick's great question. She'd walked the walk that Christ walked in Jerusalem and stayed in a Christian monastery, and then spent a week in a kibbutz in Israel. With every one of these experiences, she'd left unsure if she'd learned anything at all about the meaning of life. Then one night, when she was at a very private lesbian nightclub in Paris in the mid-1970s, high on champagne and women, someone told her about a supposedly enlightened mystic who had spent the past thirty years in a cave, high in the mountains of Kashmir, contemplating the answer to Nick's question.

As my mother told it, she got on a plane and flew back to India. She trekked for days through the mountains, barefoot, across streams and hills, up higher and higher, past the clouds, to this cave, nestled in a mountainside. She walked in and saw him, a very old man with gray hair and, as my mother told it, a beard that flowed to the floor, sitting deep in meditation.

He looked at her for a moment, then motioned for her to ask.

"What is our purpose in this life?" she said. "Why are we here?"

The man sat silent, his eyes closed in contemplation, for almost twenty minutes. It felt like hours to Debra. But finally he opened his eyes and looked straight at her.

She held her breath, motionless.

"No one knows," he said.

My mother sat upright and looked at Nick, Kaitlyn, and me. "No one knows," she repeated with great wisdom. All at once, we all burst into laughter.

"Well, what do you think the answer is, Mom?" I asked. "Why are we here?"

She thought for a minute, then stood and walked across the room to where Kaitlyn and I were sitting. She sat between us on the couch, by the fire, lifting my feet into her lap to massage them.

"I have no idea why we're here," she said. She pulled my big toe up to her lips and kissed it, like she did when I was little, and smiled at me. "All I know for sure is that I love you, Beanie."

ACKNOWLEDGMENTS

My deepest gratitude goes to my husband, Nick, for his unwavering faith in—and encouragement of—this book. No matter how long it took me to write a single word, you always believed I'd finish it, and that meant the world to me. Thank you for all the late-night conversations about plot and structure, for all the pep talks when I felt discouraged, and for the countless mornings and weekends you took the kids, and kept me fed, so I could write. Most of all, thanks for bringing so much joy into my life with Somerset and Emerson. I love you and our little family unit so much.

I am also deeply grateful to my editor, Vanessa Mobley, at Little, Brown, for taking a chance on me as a first-time author and for her dauntless efforts on behalf of this book; to my agent, Liz Parker, for making everything possible and for being there every step of the way, not just as an agent but as a friend; and to my UK publishing family, Jake Lingwood and Mala Sanghera-Warren, for all their keen insight along the way. To Karen Landry, Jean Garnett, Sabrina Callahan, Nell Beram, Barb Jatkola, Louisa McCullough, Gabrielle Leporati, and all the others in the Little, Brown family who worked on this book—thanks so much for your contributions.

Big thanks also to the many friends who took time out of their busy lives to read and provide feedback on early drafts: Mindy Marin, Allan Loeb, Leanne and Michael Citrone, Mollie McDowell, Nicole Blank, Eileen Foliente, Alisa Wolfson, Danielle Pagano, Madeline Weinstein,

Evan Scott, Josh Rudnick, and Liz Kerber (yes, "Little Lizzie"). This book and my life have been enriched by each one of you. Liz Biz: you are so talented, and I hope you will get up the courage to write your own book one day.

For inspiring me to say "yes" to the adventure, I owe a lot to Jennifer Keltos. To all the siblings (biological and otherwise): thank you for opening my heart to this big, beautiful extended family. And for those we have yet to discover—welcome!

Dad, thank you for saying yes to Mom all those years ago in the hair salon, for giving me the gift of life, and for always making me laugh. I have inherited so many beautiful traits from you. In equal measure, I owe so much to all the mother figures who stepped in over the years: Ann Weldon, Mommy Fay, Sable, Damian, Madeleine Rose, Joanna Staudinger, Laura S., Kathy R., D.D., L.R., Peggy Caserta, Hanne S., and my late aunt Diane.

Kaitlyn, thank you for being the bright star that always lit up the dark night for me, for always being my best friend and partner in crime, and for somehow finding something hilarious about even the direst of circumstances. You inspire me every day with your adventurous spirit and your giant, generous, sensitive heart.

Last but certainly not least: thanks, Mom, for willing Kaitlyn and me into existence, for always coloring outside the lines, for loving us so fiercely, for staying sober since rehab, for being such an incredible grandma to the boys, and, most of all, for letting me tell the story despite your many reservations and a few nervous breakdowns along the way. I love you more than all the cars and the stars in the universe.

ABOUT THE AUTHOR

CHRYSTA BILTON is an American writer who lives in Los Angeles with her husband and two children. *Normal Family* is her first book.